How to Sell Music, Collectibles, and Instruments on eBay®

Other books by Dennis L. Prince

How to Sell Anything on eBay®. . . and Make a Fortune!

Unleashing the Power of eBay®

How to Sell Antiques and Collectibles on eBay®. . . and Make a Fortune! coauthored by Lynn Dralle

Other books by William M. Meyer

AuctionWatch.com's Official Guide to Online Buying and Selling

How to Sell Music, Collectibles, and Instruments on eBay®... and Make a Fortune!

Dennis L. Prince
William M. Meyer

McGraw-Hill

New York   Chicago   San Francisco
Lisbon   London   Madrid   Mexico City   Milan
New Delhi   San Juan   Seoul   Singapore
Sydney   Toronto

The McGraw·Hill Companies

1 2 3 4 5 6 7 8 9 0   DOC/DOC   0 9 8 7 6 5 4

ISBN 0-07-144570-6

How to Sell Music, Collectibles, and Instruments on eBay®... and Make a Fortune! is
in no way authorized by, endorsed, or affiliated with eBay or its subsidiaries. All
references to eBay and other trademarked properties are used in accordance with the
Fair Use Doctrine and are not meant to imply that this book is an eBay product for
advertising or other commercial purposes.

Readers should know that online auctioning has risks. Readers who participate in
online auctions do so at their own risk. The author and publisher of this book cannot guarantee financial success and therefore disclaim any liability, loss, or risk sustained, either directly or indirectly, as a result of using the information given in this
book.

McGraw-Hill books are available at special quantity discounts to use as premiums
and sales promotions, or for use in corporate training programs. For more information, please write to the Director of Special Sales, Professional Publishing, McGraw-
Hill, Two Penn Plaza, New York, NY 10121-2298. Or contact your local bookstore.

Library of Congress Cataloging-in-Publication Data

Prince, Dennis L.
    How to sell music, collectibles, and instruments on eBay . . . and make a fortune! /
Dennis L. Prince and William Meyer.
        p. cm.
    Includes index.
    ISBN 0-07-144570-6 (alk. paper)
    1. Internet auctions.   2. Electronic commerce—Management.   3. Music trade.
I. Meyer, William (William M.)   II. Title.
    HF5478.P7533   2004
780'.68'8—dc22   2004020078

From William
*For my wonderful wife, Tricia,
and loving parents, John and Lorna.*

*"Car, vois-tu, chaque jour je t'aime davantage,
Aujourd'hui plus qu'hier et bien moins que demain."
Rosemond Gérard*

From Dennis
*For my brother, Dave.
You were the first "music appreciation" teacher
in my life and I'm forever thankful for that.*

Contents

Acknowledgments

From William

I'd like to express my sincere gratitude to my friend and co-author on this rewarding project, Dennis L. Prince. Without his clear vision, determination, and kind guidance, this book would never have come to fruition. Also, many, many thanks to my ever-patient and thoughtful editor Donya Dickerson at McGraw-Hill, who was a joy to work with—always insightful and professional, and never inflexible.

A very special thanks also goes out to the many wonderful music professionals I spoke with during this project. Not only were they smart, open, and engaging, their enthusiasm and entrepreneurial spirit was inspiring. I, as well as this book, was greatly enriched by their contribution.

And, love and thanks to my generous family, whose precious confidence and support has always helped me stay in key.

From Dennis

Though only my name is credited on the cover of this book, the truth is that any good book one person writes is made better by the team with which he works. Certainly, my case is no exception and it's my duty—no, it's my pleasure—to extend my sincerest thanks to those with whom I've worked to bring this book to completion.

Of course, I begin with my co-author and musical compatriot, William M. Meyer. It's been my privilege to have had the opportunity to work and write with him since 1999 and it's truly been a blast working together on this book. William, you rock!

Next, at McGraw-Hill, I give my deepest thanks and ask Donya Dickerson, Project Editor, to take a well-deserved bow. She has the innate vision, enthusiasm, and terrific timing to bring a new title like this to publication without ever missing a note. Donya, you're the best and I'm always happy to play along in your "band." Rounding out the McGraw-Hill players are the

xii   Acknowledgments

indispensable Mary Glenn, Anthony Sarchiapone, Brian Boucher, and the
entire Sales and Marketing team. Thanks to all of you for playing along here.
We certainly make beautiful music together.

Next, my thanks to Deborah Masi at Westchester Book Group, production editor par excellence, for giving this book the rest of the polish and
perfecting touches.

And, last but not least, thanks to everyone at eBay, both those who operate the site as well as those buyers and sellers who truly make it work. It's a
symphony of beautiful business and classic collecting and I'm pleased to have
met, worked, and played with each and every one of you.

Introduction

When was the last time you met someone who didn't like music? Probably never. You obviously like it or you wouldn't have picked up this book. It's a rare bird that doesn't like some configuration of those seven tones of the gods (sans sharps and flats) that we mix and match around the world. We might not all know a cadenza from a concerto, a minuet from a musette, an octave from an octet, but we all know (well, most of us, anyway) how to put our hands together, tap our toes, and shuffle our feet to the beat. A lot of us can't get enough of those white hot karaoke lights. (Have you seen the numbers? According to the International Music Products Association, sales of home karaoke machines increased more than 70 percent in 2001.) Then there are those of us who actually play instruments. The National Association of Music Merchants' (NAMM) 2003 Gallup survey reports that 54 percent of U.S. households have at least one musical instrument player.

What am I getting at here? If you want to make some money on eBay, selling music-related merchandise and paraphernalia is a great idea. Not only does the stuff sell, but if you're like most folks, you probably know a thing or two about music—or at least enough to master one of the many music niches without too much trouble. That's the whole point behind this book: helping you make real money—a living, in fact, or at least a rewarding part-time income—from something you love. In your case, that's not vintage cars, it's not Lionel Trains, it's not McCoy pottery, or dusty old books: it's music, the language of the world (well, I guess there's love, too)—from boogie-woogie rock-n-roll to classical opera to breezy cocktail jazz to trucker road songs. Now there's an eBay book just for you, the musical entrepreneur—a guide that gets beyond the basics and delves into the specifics, enabling you to pinpoint the trends and growth opportunities in your world.

YOU CAN DO IT

Why will you succeed on eBay? Well, first of all, eBay has worked for millions of other individuals and more than 150,000 true businesses, by eBay's count.

eBay's success is a reflection of the success of its sellers. If people weren't making money (finding qualified buyers, completing sales, and generating repeat business), they wouldn't keep listing their products on eBay and eBay wouldn't be the billion-dollar business it is today (its annual net revenues exceeded $2 billion in 2003).

eBay does have competitors for your dollars (you can read about them in its public annual report), but no immediate challenger. Though it continues to raise its fees, it's earning points with its users by reaching out to them more than it did in the past and including them in key decisions that determine of the future of the site. Its eBay Voices effort, eBay Live conference, and eBay Developers Program for business sellers all exemplify this spirit of collaboration.

eBay TIP: Most days, you'll find around 650,000 to 700,000 music-related items listed in eBay's Music, Musical Instruments, and Music Memorabilia categories. Multiply that by an average insertion fee of $0.60 and you get $390,000, the amount of gross revenue eBay might earn in a day from music listing fees alone. Never mind the fee-based listing upgrades, PayPal charges, Store subscriptions, and final value fees. As underground music PowerSeller Stephen Benbrook of Zion's Gate Records notes, "eBay's making money every second." Not bad for a day's work.

The point is that eBay is a global and cultural phenomenon that people and businesses not only enjoy but *need*, and that makes all the difference. It attracts a critical mass of buyers (in the millions every day), something eBay arguably values above all else. If you have access to product (an issue we'll cover extensively), a good business plan and marketing strategy (Chapter 5), expert knowledge of your industry (Chapters 10–13), and a true appreciation for hard work, you'll come out ahead on eBay. The odds aren't stacked against you on eBay, because eBay businesses are "scalable"; that is, the platform enables entrepreneurs and business owners like yourself to *manage your risk* and quickly and easily adjust your business activity appropriately. An eBay business lets you dip your toe in the water instead of gulping down a deep breath and leaping in head first into potentially uncharted waters. Instead of accepting a pricey lease on a commercial property, based on some rosy assumptions in a business plan, you can experiment first on eBay and validate that there actually is a market for your products and services. As appropriate, you can slowly increase your exposure to risk and open that store or invest in warehouse space and increase your listing volume. Even when fees start to add up (the "cost of doing business" we must all manage), at least you're making an investment in a form of advertising that's been proven to work.

If the idea doesn't pan out for some reason, you can easily tweak your approach here and there or even try something entirely different without the usual (and sometimes financially debilitating) costs of a traditional business. You'll be wiser than before but not dangerously in debt. After all, it's a lot easier to close an eBay Store, just $9.99 a month, than to end a year lease on a 1,500-square-foot retail showroom that rents for $2 per square foot.

If you're a dealer or professional already in the music game, then this book is also an opportunity to expand your horizons, either on eBay, if you've never sold there, or in an eBay category you might not have considered breaking into yet. We cover three major music industry categories—recorded music, music products and musical instruments, and music memorabilia—providing experienced music sellers the knowledge and confidence to cross-sell in other related categories. Of course, there's a right way to do this as well as wrong way, and we'll cover mistakes others have made so that you don't go out on a limb and fall out of the tree.

Whether you're new to music as a business, new to selling your music products on eBay, or just new to some of its music categories, this book gives you the tools and insights to successfully establish your new music business or take an existing one to higher heights. The best news is that we've done the leg work for you: based on our combined professional experience in the online auction industry and in the music industry, and along with the thoughts, musings, and successes of numerous other eBay music PowerSellers, we join you in tapping the potential of the three key areas of focus.

Please note that this book is just one in McGraw-Hill's *How to Sell Anything on eBay . . . and Make a Fortune* series, which also includes books dedicated to antiques, collectibles, and many other topics. Dennis Prince's comprehensive start to the series—*How to Sell Anything on eBay . . . and Make a Fortune!*—provides the bedrock for your eBay business, answering essential questions new sellers and buyers have. *How to Sell Music, Collectibles, and Instruments on eBay . . . and Make a Fortune!* and other books in the *Make a Fortune* series talk specifics, giving readers an eBay perspective on their chosen industry, showing them just how eBay has impacted their field and what to do about it. After all, eBay can't be painted with one brush. It's a marketplace of categories and a world of niches, each with individual characteristics and rules. Successful eBay sellers get this. They strive to understand the new opportunity created by the intersection of their industry and eBay.

WHAT'S UNIQUE ABOUT THIS BOOK

There's no other book like this one on the market, covering all three of eBay's core music categories. In short, this is the only eBay business book for music professionals. It provides an expert look at how to exploit opportunities in the music industry on eBay, not just a simple understanding of the mechanics of the world's largest online consumer marketplace. Readers will not only learn how to sell on eBay, but will also gain an understanding for the organization and characteristics of several major components of the music industry: the multibillion-dollar recorded music and musical instruments industries and the music memorabilia market.

This book is unique also because it's aimed not just at novices, but also at existing eBay entrepreneurs and music dealers. Today's eBay and Internet users don't need another general eBay guide aimed at beginners. Many eBay users (perhaps you) have years of experience under their belts. While there's still more for them to know and try, they are experts in their own right and ready to learn how to make their fortune by specializing in a category they love. These experts need specific seller opinions and eBay insights related to their industry so that they can generate new best practices for eBay or just validate and refine their existing ones. They need to know what their peers are doing, what works, and what doesn't. Featuring expert insight from top music PowerSellers, as well as our own professional and practical perspectives, this book allows seasoned entrepreneurs to do just that. And that means something. After all, successful entrepreneurs don't stop honing their skills and knowledge. In a dynamic marketplace, of which eBay is certainly one, complacency spells disaster, not to mention lost dollars.

This book is laid out in three parts, providing a basic, intermediate, and advanced course in selling music merchandise of eBay:

- Welcome to the World of Music Selling (Chapters 1 through 4)
- Selling Music Merchandise with Success (Chapters 5 through 9)
- Becoming a Music Specialist (Chapters 10 through 13)

By the time you're done reading this guide, you'll have the skills and tools to not only develop your eBay Music strategy, concerning market segmentation and supply, but also execute sales and marketing tactics that effectively target and motivate music fans and aficionados and generate reliable sales and repeat customers. Here's what to expect:

- What industry eBay and off-eBay trends are affecting the business of selling music merchandise? What special challenges exist? What are the financial realities and common misconceptions?
- What are the best brands, manufacturers, and distributors of goods in our three core areas? (Chapter 3, Chapters 10 through 12)
- Where's the market in recorded music, musical instruments and music products, and music memorabilia? How do I track prices in my niche? (Chapters 10 through 12)
- What suppliers and sources should I tap for reliable inventory? What are my responsibilities as a reseller? (Chapter 6)

- How do I create a viable plan for my eBay music business? (Chapter 5)
- How do I avoid fakes, frauds, and misrepresentations when sourcing product? (Chapters 3, 4, and 6, Chapters 10 through 12)
- How do I become a true insider in my chosen niche? (Chapter 4, Chapters 10 through 13)
- How do I effectively use eBay to target customers? What eBay tools and services are worth using and investing in? Should I advertise *off* eBay to drive sales on the site? (Chapter 7, Chapters 10 through 12)
- How do I best merchandise my products and position my brand to turn customer leads into sales? What customer incentives work? (Chapters 7 and 8, Chapters 10 through 12)
- What are the right ways to manage fulfillment and packing and shipping in our three core areas? (Chapter 9, Chapters 10 through 12)

INTRODUCING YOUR AUTHORS

William M. Meyer—eBay Music Specialist

I'm a writer, musician, part-time music critic, and eBay expert in my own right. For the last five years, I've been writing nonstop about eBay and its truly inspiring buyers and sellers, many of whom are now savvy, seasoned entrepreneurs, defining eBay's transformation into a true business-to-consumer and business-to-business platform. My eBay journey started in May of 1999 as the Director of Content for the successful seller-services company AuctionWatch (now Vendio), enabling me to first meet friend and collaborator Dennis Prince. Prior to that I was a senior editor for the information and technology arbiter CNET for several years.

These days, I work directly with eBay as a consultant and contractor, interviewing and profiling scores of eBay buyers and sellers about their businesses, triumphs and disappointments, and best practices. Of course, I've also bought and sold stuff on eBay, including music merchandise. Music is one of my other passions, which I hope will become clear by the time you finish reading this book. In fact, you might say I'm the kind of person you'll be selling to on eBay, another music addict with a weakness for old American guitars, who has spent his fair share of time combing budget record bins and playing three-chord confessionals in smoky bars, not to mention breaking my bank, much to my wife's chagrin, on a few independent CD releases. In other words, I'm not speaking from the mount. I'm down in the trenches with you, just another one of the musical masses. What else can I tell you about me? Hmm . . . well, for fun (more than income), I also dabble in music journalism, reviewing releases in the New Acoustic and Americana genres for the likes of *Acoustic Guitar Magazine, Acoustic Guitar World, All Music Guide, Dirty Linen,* and *Harp Magazine.*

Dennis Prince—eBay Expert

I, Dennis Prince, was bitten by the nostalgia bug and developed a fast eBay fever after finding a much-cherished board game (Does anyone remember "Poppin' Hoppies"?) from my youthful days available on the fledgling auction site back in December 1995. Driven to acquire more such long-lost treasures of my past, I realized that many of my own items could be put up for auction and essentially offset the cost of the items I was winning day by day, week by week. Two weeks after finding eBay, I launched my first auction (a promotional set of California Raisin figures) and was $80 richer within seven short days. I've since bought and sold roughly $100,000 dollars' worth of collectible goods and show no signs of slowing.

YOUR SUCCESS WAITS!

Enough about us. We're here to talk about the future, *your* future as music reseller on eBay. While you're reading, feel free to e-mail either of us: Bill at *liveoak@wmmeyer.com* or Dennis at *dlprince@bigfoot.com*. Ask questions, make comments, or share successes. We're eager to hear from you, to better understand how we can continue to help you while keeping an active pulse on your experiences and the evolution of the music market on eBay. As with music, there's always more to know, more to explore, more to experience. So *let's rock!*

PART 1

WELCOME TO THE WORLD OF MUSIC SELLING

1

Why Specialize in Music Selling?

Most people would have a hard time living without music. We all need a personal soundtrack to uplift, inspire, and just plain pull us through the day—regardless if it's one by Blink-182, Kitty Wells, Brother Ray, Tchaikovsky, or a choir of chanting Benedictine monks (see Figure 1-1). No wonder, then, so many businesses and entrepreneurs specialize in music-related merchandise. After all, if you're going to start your own business and invest real time and money in its success, then why not sell a class of inventory that has been successfully commodified, one you know people really want and one they won't consider completely discretionary when times get tight? Well, music in its many shapes and forms certainly fits the bill. Few consumer categories elicit more interest and passion than music, and that puts real dollars in music businesses' pockets. We also don't have to worry that the world's love affair with music is a passing trend. Music is a fundamental form of human and cultural expression, and that means people will be performing it, loving it, and buying it into the next millennium and beyond. Styles and means of delivery will certainly change and evolve, but people's basic need for music will exist as long as people walk the earth upright. Before we go off on a tangent, though, what does this all mean for your local record shop, guitar store, or online music collectibles business? It means you've picked a stable product category with real staying power and sales potential. Good thinking.

BROAD IS GOOD: PRODUCT AND CUSTOMER DIVERSITY

Music also is a fantastic bet because it is such a broad opportunity, encompassing several billion-dollar categories in the United States' $3 trillion retail

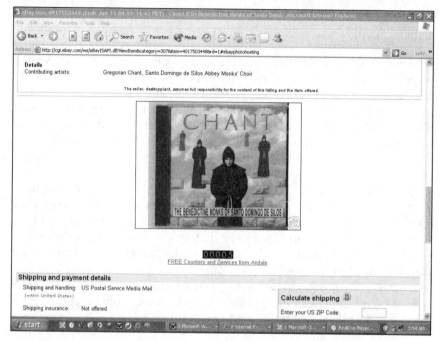

Figure 1-1 And you thought we were kidding. Everybody loves a good Gregorian chant once in a while.

trade.[1] For starters, there's recorded music and music merchandise (posters, T-shirts, pins, and the like). Music manufacturers sold more than 745 million audio CDs in 2003, earning net receipts of $11 billion (unfortunately, down from $14 billion in 2000), reports the Recording Industry Association of America (RIAA). The related category of concert ticket sales also is thriving (though somewhat dependent on the dinosaurs of popular music). According to concert-tracking publication *Pollstar*, the concert industry sold more than 35 million tickets in 2002 and grossed $2.2 billion, an increase of 20 percent over 2001. Another huge vertical in the music category is "music products" (musical instruments, performance gear, pro audio, and the like). Manufacturer shipments in this industry totaled $6.9 billion in 2002, according to the International Music Products Association (IMPA), formerly the National Association of Music Merchandisers. That number doesn't include the vintage market, either, which is probably even bigger, according to IMPA spokesman Scott Robertson, as it aggregates products from the last 75 years

---

1. U.S. Census Bureau; 2002 Economic Census *Advance Report;* Retail Trade.

and more. Then there's the music memorabilia industry, which covers both new and vintage merchandise. It's harder to track total revenues in this highly fragmented industry, but this industry is also a robust niche, particularly when you figure in collectible records and new concert memorabilia. Several other heavyweight categories (which we won't have time to cover in this book) also are part of the mix, most importantly home and car audio. In short, this monstrous category appeals to millions of customers and generates tens of billions of dollars in sales every year. Better yet, there's a piece of that pie waiting for you, if you push the right buttons and play the right notes.

eBay TIP: Why is broad good? Well, it gives sellers options and the flexibility to change their product and customer acquisition strategy when changes in the market dictate this. Put another way, the music category affords entrepreneurs the flexibility to be just who they want to be and develop just the kind of business they want to run. Since there's so much to sell and so many different customers to serve, entrepreneurs can set their own rules, develop their own markets, and live their own version of the American dream. Isn't that why most people decide to go it alone and start their own businesses?

MARKET CHOICES 101

Without getting too specific, here are some general thoughts on how music sellers might leverage music's large base (no pun intended). In the most general terms, music sellers have the option of building a profitable business by specializing or by staying general and mass market. Music merchants can work to become true experts in a narrow market (e.g., '70s arena-rock memorabilia or antique banjos) in the hopes of developing a passionate repeat customer base, which sticks with them year after year (see Figure 1-2), or they can do the polar opposite, developing a broad, low-touch business, with a focus in technology and logistics, which relies on impulse, volume sales of new products, and creating new customers on a continual basis across a range of loosely related categories. Here, per-unit margins go down, but so do customer support and the cost of doing business. Either scenario can have the same desired result: high customer satisfaction and more profit for you.

Depending on a seller's strengths and interests, he or she also might try to become an authorized dealer of front-line music merchandise (guitars, value-priced drum sets, recording gear, etc.). If auctioned by an authorized dealer, hot, new releases can sometimes best a manufacturer's suggested retail price (MSRP). If a seller would rather avoid the commitments of a running a dealership, the seller also can specialize in a diversified portfolio of surplus,

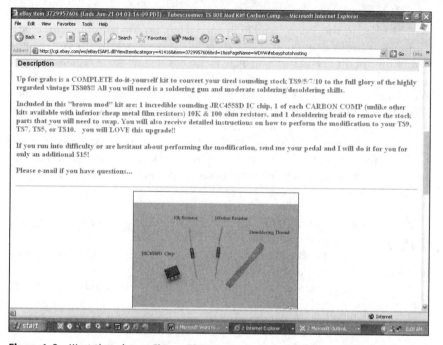

Figure 1-2 Want that vintage Ibanez TS-808 sound without the vintage price? A number of eBay sellers (aramat_effects, *1guitartech*) specialize in mod kits for new effects pedals.

off-price items (such as floor models defects, customer returns, and slow-movers). If priced to move (listed at a steep discount or with a low-opening bid) and sold in volume, surplus products can be very viable. Tons of music products, literally, end up in liquidation every year, so there's plenty of material to go around. Additionally, there are plenty of music dealers looking for discount wholesalers, of which you can be one. If you have a strength in product merchandising, you might also become a market maker in undervalued surplus merchandise. Many eBay music dealers exploit overlooked lines of discontinued products and market them as rare, exotic, or just a steal. Remember, somebody's trash can be someone else's treasure. Another market route: premium sales of collectible material or high-grade custom items, from Elvis paraphernalia to retro guitar "stomp boxes" from boutique builders. In short, you rarely find music sellers at a loss for something to sell. If one product line isn't performing well, a replacement is usually easy to find and add, even if that requires rebranding one's business a bit. What are some other thoughts? Well, if you're already committed to a category outside music, you might consider becoming a music cross-seller. Cross-selling means making markets in categories that are outside, but related to, your core business. Here are some examples. Business and industrial sellers might dabble in pro-audio sales of used 24-track mixing boards and high-end Neumann condenser microphones. Clothing dealers might supplement their off-the-rack sales with vintage apparel from the Rockabilly '50s or hair farm '80s. Estate-sale specialists could develop a niche in oddball antique instruments, music-themed housewares, and vintage sheet music. Consumer electronics dealers might up-sell CDs and DVD audio to their home theater buyers. You get the picture: almost *all* eBay sellers can leverage eBay's music-related categories to increase their sales. Though this book won't focus on sales outside eBay's three core music channels, the preceding cross-sell examples do illustrate just how vast the music category is and what an important component of our global society it is.

> **eBay TIP:**   Here are two merchandising concepts every eBay seller should understand.
>
> Cross-sell: Merchandising goods across several related product categories to reach new customers.
>
> Up-sell: Merchandising additional products to qualified customers at the point of sale.

DO THE NUMBERS

Enough rhetoric—let's look at some of the hard facts and numbers, which demonstrate just how healthy the music market is on eBay. Currently, music-related merchandise is sold in more than 500 categories and subcategories on eBay. As mentioned before, the *Music (http://music.ebay.com)*, *Musical Instruments (http://instruments.ebay.com)*, and *Music Memorabilia (http://entertainment-memorabilia.ebay.com)* categories on eBay feature around 700,000 listings every day (see Figure 1-3). The company expects to earn revenues of $3 billion by 2005, and it's well on its way, earning more than $2 billion in net revenues in 2003. According to its 2003 year-end earnings report, eBay now has ten categories that support $1 billion or more in worldwide, annualized gross merchandise sales. The *Books/Movies/Music* category is the fourth largest, with $2 billion in gross merchandise sales, just behind eBay *Motors* ($7.5 billion), *Consumer Electronics* ($2.6 billion), and *Computers* at $2.4 billion. Sellers in eBay's *Musical Instruments* category estimate that the category's gross merchandise sales are approaching $500 million. According to NAMM's 2003 Music USA statistical report, eBay supported $350 million in music products sales in 2002, making it the second or third largest venue for music products.

With those kinds of results, it's no wonder that eBay has become fundamental to the success of thousands of music enterprises, enabling them to lower costs, boost sales, build brand awareness, and export their businesses

Figure 1-3 eBay's *All Categories* page under "Browse" is a great way to monitor listing numbers in your music categories. Just be prepared to scroll.

around the globe. Take Geff Ratcheson, owner of Dandylion Records (username: dandylion_records) in Seattle, Washington. eBay's *Music CD* category enabled Ratcheson to reestablish a music business he closed in the mid-'80s for lack of sales. While reinventing himself as a computer network specialist, he began selling off some of his vinyl on eBay. Before he knew it, he was resurrecting his old business online via eBay. "The eBay business and my sanity won," jokes Ratcheson. "I left school around February 1999 to take the business full time again."

Today, Ratcheson lists 2,000-plus CDs on eBay per month and also operates a successful Web site, enabling him to build a brand for his business without the overhead of a physical store. His angle: making markets in unique CDs other sellers don't have. In five years' time, Ratcheson has completed more than 50,000 transactions and maintained a 50 to 70 percent sell-through.

"The more varied the items we sell, the better," says Ratcheson. "When we get something I am really fond of and I show that in a lengthy, educated description, we almost always sell a lot of them."

For music memorabilia business Autograph Pros (username: www.auto graphpros.com), eBay hasn't just increased inventory turn and cash flow, it's also enabled the company to introduce its own unique line of new memorabilia: autographed art guitars, signed by major acts and airbrushed by professional artists.

"eBay has had a major impact on Autograph Pros' business," says Michael Kasmar, the company's president, "and is certainly the primary reason why we are now the largest distributor of authentic autographed guitars in the world."

Another eBay music success story: Jay and Marie Sinese of Marie's CDs and Online Auctions (username: jayandmarie). In four years, the husband-and-wife team has completed some 550,000 eBay transactions and boasts one of eBay's highest feedback ratings at 170,000-plus and growing. They sell in every imaginable recorded music category, from children's to rock to world music. Every week, according to their About Me page, they purchase 5,000 to 10,000 CDs for sale on eBay, typically from music businesses reducing excess inventory. Today, their customer base is larger than most regional music chains.

Regional guitar dealer Mark Morse is a major eBay proponent because it levels the playing field for small businesses. "The beauty of eBay is there's no big guy, little guy," says Morse. "If you can offer great customer service and bundle that with a good feedback rating, then you don't need to spend $5,000 to $10,000 a month in rent to compete with the bigger guys."

MUSIC BY eBAY

Those are some of the basics. How about a little bit more specific look at eBay's music categories to get your wheels spinning? In this section, we'll review some of the hot top-level categories and subcategories in our three primary areas of focus: music, musical instruments, and music memorabilia. By the end, you'll know where you should be selling what. Let's start with music, the granddaddy of music categories on eBay.

Music: *http://music.ebay.com*

Accessories	DVD Audio	Wholesale Lots
Cassettes	Records	Other Formats
CDs	Super Audio CDs	

Music is eBay's recorded music category, featuring both new, shrink-wrapped compact discs and collectible recordings such as records and 8-track tapes. That's important to note, because you'll be listing your collectible vinyl here as opposed to in *Music Memorabilia*. *Music*'s biggest category is CDs, with 250,000 listings per day on average, from front-line releases (sometimes directly from the manufacturer, such as the Universal Music Group) to secondhand CDs, be they out-of-print rarities, imports, or just moldy oldies you are now embarrassed to have in your collection. Also home to the *CD* category (and *DVD Audio*) are high-dollar box sets and complete works collections (e.g., Duke Ellington's complete RCA recordings). The most valuable, collectible material is in *Records* (yes, you will find those infamous Butcher covers—The Beatles LP *Yesterday and Today*, T 2553—featuring the Fab Four posing with assorted doll appendages), *Other Formats* (featuring those groovy 8-tracks and reel-to-reels, often sold in bulk), and *Cassettes* (the valuable stuff in this category being demos from now popular bands). To sift through the usually 150,000 records for sale, you can browse by genre (there are 23 of them), subgenre (13 for *Rock* alone), record speed (16, 33, 45, 78 RPM), and duration (EP, LP, single, other).

eBay TIP: eBay tracks what categories are hot, very hot, and super hot in its Hot Categories Report. In brief, the report demonstrates what Level II, Level III, and Level IV categories, in eBay nomenclature, are experiencing more demand than supply. The March 2004 report had four very hot *Music* categories in the *Entertainment* vertical.
- Accessories > **Accessories**
- CDs > **Children**
- CDs > **Folk**
- Wholesale Lots > **CDs**

The meaning of *very hot*: growth in bids per item (in the category) outpaced growth in listings by 15 to 35 percent. In other words, there's more demand than supply in the category. For more, check out *http://pages.ebay.com/sellercentral/hotitems.pdf*.

Next up: the equally impressive musical instruments category.

Musical Instruments:
http://musical-instruments.ebay.com

Brass	Harmonica	Sheet Music, Songbooks
Electronics	Keyboard, Piano	Strings
Equipment	Percussion	Woodwinds
Guitar	Pro Audio	

The heavyweights of the category by a fairly significant margin are *Guitar*, *Pro Audio*, and *Sheet Music*. The *Guitar* category regularly features 50,000 listings per day, while the latter two typically are in the 20,000-plus range. This isn't too surprising, really. Guitars are the most popular music products category on and off eBay. In fact, U.S. guitar sales topped $1 billion in 2002, according to the International Music Products Association's 2003 MusicUSA report. That's partly because we like to copy our rock heroes and rebels and more of them play guitar than anything else. (Elvis probably wouldn't have driven the ladies wild behind a drum kit.) Guitars also are probably the most portable and democratic of instruments. Even a beginner who just knows the chords G, D, and C can play thousands of songs and hold court with a cheap acoustic. From a sales perspective, guitars are produced for a wide variety of price points and skill levels, inflating their production numbers.

Before you assume keyboards are the next big opportunity on eBay, consider that there are a lot of drummers and student band musicians out there in need of instruments. Interestingly enough, Percussion, Strings, and Woodwinds frequently have more listings than the *Keyboard, Piano* category. One last note: all eBay *Musical Instruments* categories are ripe for up-selling, that is, offering additional related products, such as accessories, with one's core items at the point of sale.

 eBay TIP: eBay's March 2004 Hot Categories Report had five super hot Level IV *Musical Instruments* categories.

- Amplifiers > **Kustom**
- Computer Recording > **Sound Cards**
- Sheet Music > **Rag**
- Violin > **1/4 Size**
- Saxophone > **Baritone, Bass**

The meaning of *super hot*: growth in bids per item (in the category) outpaced growth in listings by 35 percent. In other words, there's more demand than supply in the category. For more, check out *http://pages.ebay.com/seller central/hotitems.pdf*.

Last but not least, here's a breakdown for *Music Memorabilia* in the *Entertainment Memorabilia* category.

Entertainment Memorabilia:
http://entertainment-memorabilia.ebay.com

MUSIC MEMORABILIA

Big Band, Swing	Pop	Other
Blues	Punk	
Classical	R&B, Soul	**Autographs**
Country	Rap, Hip-Hop	Music
Jazz	Reggae	Other
Opera	Rock-n-Roll	

True music memorabilia (as opposed to collectibles with a music motif) is concentrated in eBay's *Entertainment Memorabilia* category within the *Music Memorabilia* subcategory. Interestingly enough, listings in *Music Memorabilia* often outnumber those in *Entertainment's Movie Memorabilia* category. The top *Music Memorabilia* subcategory: *Rock-n-Roll*, averaging 70,000 to 80,000 listings daily. Dig deeper in main Level III categories (*Country*, *Pop*, *Rap*, *Rock*) and you'll find items organized by artist or memorabilia type. *Rock-n-Roll* has 50 artist categories, from the genre's dinosaurs (*The Grateful Dead*, *Lynard Skynard*, *The Who*) to newer, tenser acts (*System of a Down*, *Tool*), and finally those dudes in cheap sunglasses—*ZZ Top*. Big, Level III categories with more than 1000 listings (*Elvis*, *Beatles*, *KISS*, *Madonna*, etc.) are further divided into categories such as *Apparel*, *Concert Memorabilia*, *Guitar Picks*, *Handbills*, *Novelties*, *Patches*, *Photos*, *Pins*, *Posters*, *Record Awards*, and more. This isn't all vintage stuff. Some of it, particularly the concert merchandise, is brand new and inexpensive, appropriate really only for volume sales.

eBay TIP: eBay's March 2004 Hot Categories Report had four very hot Level IV *Music Memorabilia* categories.

- Blues
- Country
- Rap, Hip-Hop
- Rock-n-Roll

Why are these four categories *very hot*? In each, growth in per-item bids outpaced growth in listings by 15 to 35 percent. For more, check out *http://pages.ebay.com/sellercentral/hotitems.pdf*.

So there you have it, music on eBay in a nutshell. Don't get tired yet, though—there's plenty more to know and plenty more to learn. Chapter 2 awaits, the history of selling different types of musical merchandise. As Bob Marley famously said, "In this great future, you can't forget your past."

2

The History of Selling Music

Understanding what trends and forces have shaped your industry is essential, regardless of what type of merchandise you sell on eBay. You don't need to know every footnote—that Emile Berliner of Germany invented the gramophone in 1888 or that Hawaiian music played an intriguing role in the rise of popular commercial music in the United States, not to mention the electric guitar and amplifier, or that the Beatles arguably made the infamous Butcher cover to protest the artless repackaging of their music. You should understand the broad strokes, however, particularly how the distribution of your product has evolved over the years and what key figures and technologies have advanced your industry and the products you sell. In this chapter, we'll emphasize why that's important and then describe how the distribution and retailing of merchandise in our three core areas have evolved over the last several decades. Finally, we'll discuss the emergence of eBay and what impact it has had—a tremendous one in all cases.

HISTORY MATTERS

History isn't just something you took in high school. It's a tool that helps you make informed decisions about the niche you choose and the products you offer. It's also indispensable for businesses that deal in vintage or collectible material. After all, they're selling history. If dealers aren't part-time historians with a basis in the facts and an appreciation for what makes their items special and distinctive, then they won't be able to effectively buy, value, and merchandise their goods.

To be blunt about it, they'll probably buy the wrong stuff and maybe even misrepresent things. Those who avoid these mistakes carefully study their industry and manufacturers. They learn who founded them and why;

what individuals contributed to their successes and failures; what twists of fate conspired against them; what processes, technologies, and products made them famous; how they marked and catalogued their products; and what business decisions helped or hurt them. At the end of this process, they understand not only why certain items are valuable, but also why others are not, and that can be just as important.

Let's illustrate this. In 1965, the Columbia Broadcasting System, also known as CBS, purchased Fender Musical Instruments. During the CBS period, quality assurance declined at Fender. As a result, in the 1970s, the company produced quite a few playable yet problematic instruments. Common issues included sloppy finishes and loose neck joints. The introduction of micro-tilt, three-bolt necks also didn't sit well with some players. Today, these instruments have a stigma with true collectors and players and command fewer dollars on the secondary market. What if you weren't aware of this? You'd probably think your gear was worth more that it was. Here's another example: In 1983, Marshall introduced hybrid amps, featuring tubes and printed circuit boards, such as the JCM 800, Master Volume. While these have some cool extras (channel switching and effects loop) and are popular with Metal players (Metallica used them on their early albums), many players prefer the company's more straightforward all-tube amps from the '60s and '70s. (Some channel-switching Marshall amps utilize clipping diodes to model pre-amp power tube distortion, which many feel is less musical than natural tube distortion.) What does this all mean? Don't buy a "Master Volume" JCM 800 for resale, figuring it's hot vintage gear. It's a good amp, but it's not a classic in the true sense of the word (see Figure 2-1). A look at the Hammond B3 market is also instructive. In 1975, Hammond started to introduce printed circuit boards in its B3s. These models are turned on with a single switch. As expert B3 dealer Dennis Delzer (eBay ID: oldspeed) put it, "They're not worth hauling to the dump." Market a one-switch, printed circuit board B3 as a true vintage example and one of two things will probably happen, neither good. At best, you'll look like an amateur to educated collectors. At worst, you'll have to eat return shipping on a 450-pound instrument.

History is fun. Let's do some more. How about antique violins, from twentieth-century makers like Pistucci or Marchetti? If you didn't know the history of these makers and how they produced their instruments, you might unintentionally sell a violin that was made by one of the luthiers' assistants instead of the master himself. That's a real problem because these examples are far less significant and valuable. Along the same lines, what if you happen upon an old violin that has an Amati, Guarneri, Klotz, or Stradivarius label in it? Well, folks who know their violin history know these are generally fakes or "trade copies." Very few authentic instruments from these old-world Italian and German makers have turned up in the last 50 years. (Yes, that's right, some things actually aren't on eBay.) Consider Stradivarius. Turns out Anto-

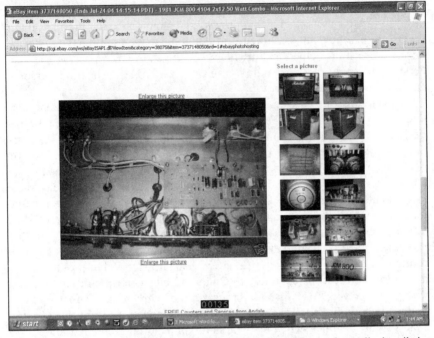

Figure 2-1 There's that printed circuit board. This '81 JCM does not have clipping diodes (for distortion) like some models. It is, as a result, a more desirable model to some.

nio built only 1,100 or so instruments in his lifetime (from 1644 to 1737) from his Cremona workshop with the help of his sons. Of those instruments, which aren't just violins, only about 650 remain (many lost during the fire-bombing of Dresden). In light of that fact, it's probably not reasonable to assume your grandma's Strad-labeled violin is real. In point of fact, 99.9999 percent were mass-produced in France and Germany in the nineteenth and twentieth centuries by small shops, who labeled them just like the master. Interestingly enough, some were handmade and are worth a few bucks—usually under $1,000, though.

It's also wise to be aware of historical shifts at the industry level. A case in point: the movement of instrument production to Asia (first Japan and Korea, now China and Indonesia) and more economical labor markets in Eastern Europe. Some instrument dealers have been following this trend for decades, and now are in a good position to evaluate which overseas manufacturers, such as AXL Musical Instruments, are producing the best budget instruments. Take violin dealer Jaap van Wesel (eBay ID: jwesel). Though he sells more antique instruments than student varieties, Wesel is tracking the globalization of the violin trade. "Traditionally, student instruments were produced in Germany, and to a certain degree in France," explains Wesel. "In the last five to ten years, a lot of that has shifted to the Far East and China and to a certain extent Eastern Europe—Romania and Bulgaria—because labor is much cheaper there." He adds, "The quality of these instruments, especially from China, has increased dramatically. Also, they are much cheaper than comparable German instruments. My guess is that the Europeans will not be able to compete in the long run."

 eBay TIP: Joining trade associations in your niche helps you learn about the larger trends shaping your industry.

Bobby Boyles, owner of BestPriceGuitar.com (eBay ID: bestpriceguitar) in Oklahoma City, Oklahoma, echoes that sentiment. "From guitars to mandolins to banjos, Chinese products are coming up very fast," he says. "We have some Chinese guitars and banjos that could give Martin and Taylor a real run for their money. To say just junk is coming out of China anymore is a real misnomer. It's not necessarily where it's made now, it's how it's made."

A sense of history is critical in the Music Memorabilia category, too. Take those popular Bill Graham Presents/Family Dog concert posters. One of the necessities of selling these '60s psychedelic lithograph posters is successfully differentiating first printings from second and third printings. Sometimes that's easy and sometimes it's not, according to expert rock memorabilia dealer Jeff Gold, owner of *Record*mecca.com (eBay ID: recordmecca). Most sellers defer to the bible of this cottage industry: Eric King's 655-page manual, the *Collector's Guide to Psychedelic Rock Concert Posters, Postcards and Handbills 1965–1973,*which pinpoints differences between printings. If you were unaware of the history of how these posters were produced and reprinted in the '70s and '80s and how minute differences can be between printings, an unscrupulous or uninformed seller could seriously take you for a ride. And don't think that doesn't happen to even skilled collectors and dealers. It does. Concert ticket, backstage pass, and program dealer Roger Pavey (eBay ID: thewyzyrd) got burned on his first buy when he made the switch from baseball cards to rock memorabilia in 1994. He was stuck with 3,000 worthless backstage passes he couldn't resell. "I started out 9 grand in the hole," says Pavey. We can't close this kind of discussion without a word about Beatles autographs. In 14 years on the job, Beatles autograph expert Frank Caiazzo has seen only ten authentic signed American Beatles albums. That's good to know since you'll find about ten on eBay every week (see Figure 2-2).

Becoming an expert in any particular object or product, especially rare, valuable ones, requires educating yourself about the finer points of their production and finding other seasoned appraisers with whom you can confer. This is fundamental. It will prevent you from wasting money on misrepre-

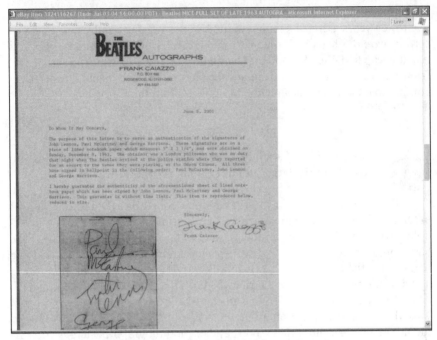

Figure 2-2   What do you know, here's a real Beatles autograph.

sented examples or unintentionally misrepresenting items yourself. Finally, history gives one an appreciation for why people seek to spend good money on old stuff, from collectible gramophone players to pre-war '40s Selmer horns to first pressings of John Coltrane's *Love Supreme*, when they could just buy something similar new. They command significant dollars not just because they sound good and are made from bygone materials or because they are dated, handmade, or even beautiful. They are coveted because they reflect what's best about the human imagination and its capacity for invention, and in appreciating these objects we commune with the spirits that created them.

    eBay TIP: If you don't have a sense of history, it's hard to see sometimes what is in fact timeless, what's temporary, and what is just junk.

THEN AND NOW

We won't try to give you an abridged guide to the last thousand years of music history. Instead, let's cover some recent developments related to our three industries during the age of eBay. We probably don't have to tell you that eBay has had an important impact on all three.

Recorded Music

The recording industry has seen better days. Review the numbers, available at the Recording Industry Association of America's website (*www.riaa.com*), and you'll see. CD sales are slumping. Those in the know offer a number of reasons for this: CD piracy, illegal downloading of music via peer-to-peer music services, and consolidation of music retailing. The rise of alternative forms of entertainment, such as video games and the Internet, is also playing a role.

The silver lining is that music sales are increasing dramatically on the Web, and that's good news for folks like you. Why? Well, the Web is leveling the playing field for small independent retailers who operate small stores and Web sites. It enables these businesses to reach customers outside their local market and compete more effectively against mass merchandisers, who now dominate new music sales, despite often carrying a smaller in-store selection of titles and offering less choice and customer service than small retailers and traditional chains, such as Tower Records. (For some insight on this topic, visit the National Association of Recorded Merchandisers' Web site.) Essentially, channel share has shifted to the Wal-Marts and BestBuys because they are logistically advanced with incredible leverage and buying power that enables them to slash their prices below competing retailers. Small retailers have disappeared or changed their businesses in order to survive. Many of these survivors are discount Internet retailers, which use online channels such as GEM and eBay, or specialty click-and-mortar shops that sell online and off and cater to niche audiences that are being ignored by the superstores, which generally stock surefire hits, not niche releases.

That these specialty music operations are finding some success on the Web is good news for music lovers. It means a wider variety of music will be produced and sold. How does eBay fit into the equation? If you are a music seller, it's one of the channels you should use to promote your business and brand in the hopes of driving sales on your own Web site. It also provides music retailers the opportunity to merchandise cutting-edge releases and recast themselves as music educators or "tastemakers" (not just traditional content aggregators). Tastemakers do have a significant competitive advantage over mass merchandisers. One eBay seller taking this to its logical extreme is Zion's Gate Records (eBay ID: zionsgate) in Seattle, Washington (see Figure 2-3). Its strategy is to not carry anything the mass merchandisers do: "This place is really dangerous because it's all cool stuff, and people are scared to even come in sometimes," laughs owner Stephen Benbrook.

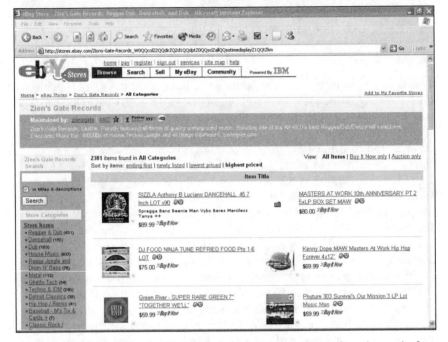

Figure 2-3   Specialty CD seller Zion's Gate Records specializes in cutting-edge music, from House and Techno to Reggae and Dub to Acid Jazz.

Musical Instruments

Small independent dealers in the modern musical instrument trade have been impacted by some of the same business trends affecting recorded music retailers. Large retailers, such as Guitar Center and Sam Ash, are the major forces in the industry and difficult to compete with for smaller regional retailers. Essentially, these "full-line" superstores, selling everything from guitars and pro audio to drums, have the ability to buy for hundreds of stores instead of just one or a few, enabling them to earn significant volume discounts on product. As a result, music instrument dealers cannot compete on price with these chain stores and have had to diversify their businesses to succeed, moving into vintage products and embracing online sales via eBay and their Web sites. The movement of authorized dealers and other music product marketers online has caused some waves in the industry.

 eBay TIP: You don't have to be an authorized dealer to sell new products on eBay. Many eBay resellers specialize in selling new overstock, still in the box, without a warranty.

Early on in this transition, online competition compelled many authorized dealers and other marketers to offer products at a variety of different price points, often far below manufacturer suggested prices. The result: manufacturers felt their products were being devalued. Additionally, authorized dealers (big and small) complained to manufacturers that Internet sellers were eroding their regional in-store prices. A backlash against the sale of new products on the Web ensued. This is starting to ease as eBay becomes a bigger and bigger channel for music product sales. (Boyle of BestPriceGuitar estimates that annual music product sales on eBay have reached half a billion.)

To prevent further online price wars (and some say placate Guitar Center and protect its online superstore Musician's Friend), many major manufacturers have instituted "minimum advertised price" policies, also known as MAPs. These stipulate that authorized dealers cannot advertise their products below a specific price. Some major names, such as Fender, Gibson, Martin, and Paul Reed Smith, also forbid dealerships from selling new products on the Internet. Industry opinions on MAPs are mixed. Some call them a form of price-fixing; others believe they are a necessary evil. Interestingly enough, consumer groups successfully challenged the use of MAPs in the recording indus-

Figure 2-4 Music retailer L&M sells its demo models and returns on eBay, but not frontline product.

try. Today, music stores can price their CDs any way they want. (When you add Wal-Mart into the equation, though, there's an obvious downside to this.)

MAPs are having some interesting results. On the one hand, the Internet-friendly policies are actually increasing the sale of warrantied instruments and equipment on the Internet. Many boutique makers of guitars, effects pedals, drums, and orchestra instruments have MAP policies but allow their dealers to sell online, recognizing the viability of the online market. Essentially, they can't afford not to sell online. Guitar maker Tacoma has an interesting policy: it's Internet-friendly and has no MAP for its value-line of Olympia instruments, made overseas. It only MAPs its higher-priced American line. On the other hand, MAPs are causing some resellers to question the benefits of being an authorized dealer, particularly if they're not allowed to sell new online. Drum and guitar dealer Indoor Storm (eBay ID: indoor_storm1), located in Raleigh, North Carolina, has turned down some major dealer relationships for this reason (see Figure 2-4). "We do 95 percent of our business on the Internet," notes Barry Knain, the company's percussion specialist. Indoor Storm now sells boutique drum kits exclusively to avoid limiting dealership agreements and differentiate itself from big-box retailers. Some guitar resellers are specializing in "B-stock" or discontinued product (often new-in-box), purchased from authorized dealers and sold without a warranty. The upside: buyers get a good product at a low price. The downside: if it breaks, the manufacturer won't fix it under warranty.

Music Memorabilia

Of all three of our industries, eBay has probably had the most profound effect on the music memorabilia and autograph industry. It not only has made this cottage industry bigger and more diverse, but also has made it global. "It was a slow, mail-driven business and it has become this instantaneous, worldwide market driven by eBay and dealers on their Web sites," explains Gold of *Record*mecca.com.

Until the late 1980s, the music memorabilia trade was still primarily focused on records. Print ads in magazines like *Goldmine* and *The Rock Marketplace* (no longer published) connected dealers and collectors. "I would say it was entirely driven by record swap meets and advertising in record collector magazines," says Gold. Only with the arrival of the Internet and then eBay did collector interest in rock posters and various kinds of ephemera really take off. In essence, cheap global communication enabled more dealers and collectors to interact and trade in a wider variety of collectibles, from posters and handbills to artist-owned objects and autographed ephemera.

eBay and the Internet search engines have also had a huge bearing on the industry, making it much easier to find once obscure material. "I regularly have people contact me and say that they found a record on my Web site that they've been searching years and years for," explains Gold. "There also are many records that I was searching for that I now see with some regularity on eBay." The bottom line? Previously rare items are now in greater supply because collectors and noncollectors alike have more awareness for what's popular and a simple way to bring them to market.

The accessibility of online payments is also expanding the record and music memorabilia business, enabling collectors to participate in a vastly greater number of transactions. "On occasion, something you put it up gets bought in 10 minutes and the money is in your PayPal account in 12 minutes," marvels Gold. "That could have never happened before."

What are other drivers of today's burgeoning rock memorabilia trade? Most of the material that is now considered valuable was once considered disposable—those tacky jerseys, glossy concert programs, back passes, and tickets. Being disposable, a lot of it did get thrown away, limiting supply today. This explains the value of mass-merchandised Beatles and KISS products, from action figures and nodders to lunchboxes, which were never designed to stand the test of time and be collectible. (One wonders what the trade will be like tomorrow since more people now collect and stash material.

Figure 2-5 Bill Graham Presents posters and handbills can be beautiful, thought provoking, and expensive.

Supply is a double-edged sword.) Many 30- and 40-somethings, who threw away or lost items, are now adults with disposable income and a desire to relive their early rock-n-roll experiences (see Figure 2-5). The temporary decline of the sports card and memorabilia market in the early 1990s and subsequent transition of dealers into records and rock also have contributed to a larger music memorabilia business.

Globalization of music memorabilia, due to the Internet and eBay, hasn't been all good. The industry now has a serious fraud and misrepresentation problem. Gold estimates that more than 99 percent of the Beatles autographs and 75 percent of the rock autographs on eBay are fake. Rock autograph dealer Larry Lindt of U.S. Trade Discount (eBay ID: axop) acknowledges that there is a serious problem with misrepresentation on the Internet. "There is much more fraudulent merchandise for sale now where there really wasn't any before," he says. For this reason, he and many other autograph dealers don't sell signed memorabilia from deceased artists. They also take a number of other precautions to reassure buyers, such as including photographic proof of the actual artist signing with each autograph.

So, what do you think? Ready to proceed? Good. We knew you had it in you. In our next chapter, we'll delve deeper into our three areas of focus, giving you a fuller appreciation for the challenges and rewards that lie ahead for eBay music resellers. Get ready, get set, GO!

3

Getting Better Acquainted with Music Selling

Understanding the rules of the game—how your industry works and how your business fits in it—that's square one for any aspiring reseller. Sounds rudimentary, but you'd be surprised how many eBay businesses aren't really prepared for the challenges that lie ahead before they make their first move. Many assume too much and grasp too little about the basic facts, from who supplies their goods at the best prices to how much warehouse space they'll need to how to provide timely customer support. This is especially true in the age of eBay, which has lowered barriers to entry and removed some of the hurdles that once stopped businesses dead in their tracks. If anything, eBay has inspired entrepreneurs to dream bigger and believe even more passionately that they can beat the odds.

However, before you sail off into La-La Land, give yourself a little reality check. Dig in and get a handle on the real requirements and rigors of doing business in your chosen music niche. Sure, you played bass in your buddy's prog-rock band (and you had great hair), but does that qualify you for immediate success in the competitive musical instruments trade, dominated on eBay by the likes of Infinity Music Instruments (username: wwwinfinitymusicinstruments), National Music Supply (username: nationalmusicsupply), or Gold Standard Guitars (username: goldstandardguitars), all PowerSellers in their respective markets? You made a bundle selling your sister's collection of Sean Cassidy 45s. That was neat. But does that prepare you to compete against, say, BoogieBob's Records (eBay username: boogiebobrecords), which has completed more than 15,000 vintage vinyl transactions on eBay? These sellers have something in common. They understand how their industry operates and what their business partners and customers expect. The point:

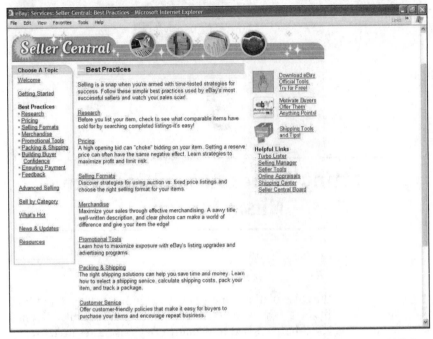

Figure 3-1 Spend some time with Dennis's *How to Sell Anything on eBay . . . And Make a Fortune!* before you start your eBay business. Also, study eBay's Seller Central section.

don't plug in before you have an idea of how to play (see Figure 3-1). You'll waste time and money. (Word to the wise: eBay is getting expensive. Some high-volume businesses incur more than $100,000 in fees annually.) You might also jeopardize relationships with important suppliers and customers you're going to need down the road.

That said, let's review how our three music industries are structured and go over some of the rules of the road for small to medium-sized businesses in the recorded music, musical instruments/music products, and music memorabilia trades.

BROAD STROKES: BUSINESS CHARACTERISTICS

There are some strong parallels and some dramatic differences among our three industries. Right now, let's highlight what makes each unique and distinct to give you a better foundation for your future eBay business. Ready? It's time to roll up your sleeves.

Recorded Music

The recorded music industry is a highly hierarchical one, which has undergone a tremendous amount of consolidation in the last 20 years. Today, five global music companies (soon to be four), dubbed the "Big Five," control the industry: Universal Music Group, Sony Music, Warner Music Group, EMI, and BMG. These companies own the majority of major record labels and their catalogs (many of which you probably know and love) and account for about 85 percent of all record sales. They also are subsidiary themselves to even larger multinational conglomerates, such as General Electric's NBC and Bertelsmann (BMG). (Wikepedia.com has an excellent history of the Big Five.) What does this mean for the ma-and-pa operations and regional independents that sell on eBay? The industry's top-down structure creates both opportunities and challenges for music resellers. On the one hand, it means that the industry has resources and never lacks product or promotion for its releases, providing merchants, whatever their size, plenty of product to sell and built-in-awareness and demand for these products. On the other hand, this structure tends to favor the big players, the major distributors and mass-market retailers with the greatest leverage. Small players, as a result, must develop attractive niches and innovative sourcing strategies to survive and thrive.

Fortunately, eBay helps businesses do just that. Some might bemoan the efficiency of the eBay marketplace, which can depress regional prices and also prevent dealers from exploiting limited local supply, but at the end of the day the positives outweigh the negatives. This is particularly true in the age of the supercenter. In its report *Looking Back, Looking Forward* (Crupnick & Josephson), the NPD Group verifies what we basically already know: channel share in recorded music retailing has fundamentally shifted from CD and record shops to electronics chains, discounters, and mass merchandisers.

eBay TIP: In 1990, mass merchandiser channel share was less than 9 percent, according to the Recording Industry Association of America. By 2002, it had jumped to 50.5 percent, with record store share declining to 37 percent.

Fortunately, online sales are also poised for growth in 2004, says the NPD Group's report. The long and the short: eBay is changing businesses, but it's also keeping them in business in the face of relentless cost-cutting by mass merchandisers. If Tower Records and Sam Goody can't retain market share against the likes of Wal-Mart and Target, what makes you think you can—that is, without the Internet and eBay helping to give you a national and international customer base?

The recorded music industry has an established supply chain, one you need to understand and work within. The Big Five as well as the industry's many independent labels generally sell their product to large national distribution companies which are essentially extensions of the record companies, aggregating, promoting, and distributing new music. Some examples: Allegro Corporation, BMG Distribution, Caroline Distribution, EMI North America, Koch Entertainment Distribution, Navarre Corporation, Ryko Distribution, Sound Choice, and still others, some affiliated with the Big Five. (Check out Chapter 10 for a more complete list.) That means, in general terms, if you want to sell hot products on the charts, you won't be buying first-run merchandise direct, but from national distributors (via the Internet, for example) or what are called *one-stops*, independent regional distributors or wholesalers (see Figure 3-2). If you specialize in specific types of musical genres, there might be specific distributors you need to know. Most releases have a 90-day forecast, in which most of the units will sell. According to the National Association of Recording Merchandisers (NARM), the average annual inventory turn for music is 4.4 times. In other words, each title sells an average of four times. If your store were 2,500 square feet and could hold 20,000 titles, you'd hypothetically sell 88,000 titles every fiscal year.

Before you pick up the phone and contact a supplier, here are some basics you need to know.

- Wholesalers will require you to have a state resale license for the purposes of reporting sales to the state and remitting sales tax.
- Some distributors require buyers to have a physical storefront and business license. They also might want to see a business plan to evaluate if you are a good risk.
- Distributors generally require minimum "initial orders" (I.O.) or "buy ins," based on how much they expect their releases to sell. These weed out the amateurs.
- Some distributors expect stores to have computer-based inventory management systems, which can record point-of-sale (POS) data, used to grade your store's performance.
- Order discounts are generally granted as order sizes increase. In other words, low prices are reserved for big orders.
- Distributors generally allow music retailers to send back unsold inventory for a refund, called a return. The refund will vary depending on several factors, including the timing of the return. According to NARM 2002 data, the industry return average is 19.5 percent.

Some small distributors (which need business) are more flexible and will sell to small, Internet-only dealers. If you don't mind selling more niche material from small labels (High Street Records, Putamoyo, Welk Music Group),

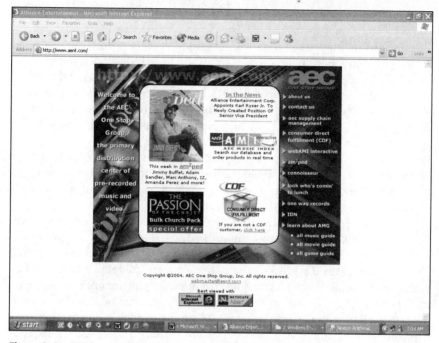

Figure 3-2 AEC is one of the largest one-stops in the recording industry.

you can often buy directly from them. There are limits to this, though. In the hopes of getting their material in high-profile retail settings, they reserve product and low prices for distributors. Another option: buy music direct from independent or unsigned artists, who need distribution. Independent music distributor Orchard.com bases its business on this idea. So does Miles-ofmusic.com in the Americana genre.

If you don't have to buy new and you plan to compete on price, then purchasing liquidation stock is another option. To do this, though, you have to be ready to make inventory investments on the fly. When you sell surplus, your supply points are more diverse, typically regional stores going out of business or reducing overstock to recoup costs; distributors with unsold merchandise; or true liquidators, tasked to sell distressed, end-of-life merchandise. If you plan to sell collectible material, such as out-of-print CDs, 8-tracks, and reel-to-reels, you'll often fish in the same pond as off-price CD vendors, buying in bulk from regional chains and other secondary markets. True vintage material, such as collectible vinyl, is truly supply restricted and must be sourced through specialized dealers, collectors, estate sales, and shows, just like any antique.

Music Products

The musical instruments/music products trade is unique from the recording industry in that it is still fairly dealer focused. Though this trade, too, is dominated by some big names (Fender, Gibson, Roland, Yamaha) and features some middlemen (wholesale distributors, independent "repping" companies), its new products are generally distributed directly from the manufacturers to dealerships. This is a function, in large part, of the products themselves. Unlike CDs, which can be sold everywhere from 7-Eleven to Tower Records to Pottery Barn, music products require real dealer service and support. This is particularly true of more complex electronic instruments and expensive Pro Audio equipment. As a result, third-party dealers, authorized or not, have always been part of the sales process and equation.

Authorized dealers essentially buy directly from their manufacturers via a regional or national sales representative or an independent rep from a partner company of the manufacturer. Small specialty shops, modest regional chains, Internet-only resellers, and major instrument retailers like Guitar Center and Sam Ash can all obtain dealerships, helping manufacturers penetrate both large and small, isolated markets. The upside of this distribution model for eBay sellers is that it doesn't discriminate against small businesses, if the manufacturer allows Internet sales and the sellers meet specific requirements. That is, even small businesses can gain reliable access to brand name merchandise from top companies, serving the various price points.

Dealers have to meet the same general requirements as recorded music resellers before they can do business with music product manufacturers or independent reps. Usually, dealers must secure appropriate state and city licensing, open a physical storefront (some companies' reps will visit), and have enough cash or strong enough credit to fill minimum orders (they'll do a credit check). Other fundamentals:

- Candidates will have to sign a dealer agreement, which in all likelihood will require them to comply with a minimum advertised price policy. The agreement might even prohibit Internet sales of the manufacturer's products or only allow "B-stock" sales of their merchandise online, material that has been used in the store, returned, or just over-purchased.

eBay TIP: Most musical instrument manufacturers have minimum advertised price policies in their dealer agreements. These prohibit dealers from advertising a product below a predetermined price. Study your dealer agreements before signing them.

- New authorized dealers are often asked to carry a manufacturer's entire line or more of it than they might care to. Remember, dealer outlets are vital for advertising new products.
- Authorized dealers are expected to support the manufacturer's in-store merchandising programs, hence the need for a physical space.
- Manufacturers look for dealers whose brand image reflects theirs. They also don't want to overserve any one market. Before approaching a manufacturer or rep, do your homework. See if there is another store close by selling the supplier's products.

Another interesting development in authorized sales, applicable to eBay, is the buying of value instruments directly from overseas manufacturers, particularly those in Asia (China, Korea, and Indonesia). Guitar and percussion dealers are particularly active in this arena, selling value brands such as Jay Turser and Titan. eBay PowerSeller MusicLandCentral (username: musicland central) is one of the United States' biggest dealers in Turser guitars.

The instrument and music products industry also has a vibrant vintage trade, of course, which touches almost every category, from guitars and amps to drum sets and keyboards to analog recording equipment. The household names from the '50s and '60s will sell well on eBay. A lot of the sought-after material was produced at the dawn of mass-production, and it was built to last. As a result, even though the market is dependent on the recycling of old gear, a fair amount of the most popular items were produced in significant amounts, so that product continues to surface and turn over. The exception is prewar material, which is bought by true collectors and often sold on a per-piece basis for $5,000 and up.

Because the musical instrument trade has such a long, storied history (the NAMM show has been around for more than a hundred years), vintage dealers have several approaches they can take. They can deal in established names with fairly set prices, or they can try to make new markets in more esoteric material from boutique makers or bygone manufacturers, or they can do a little of both like stringed-instrument guru George Gruhn (*www.gruhn guitars.com*). Vintage dealers also can supplement their secondary-market inventory with new, boutique products, designed to approximate the great instruments, amps, and accessories of the '50s and '60s.

Music Memorabilia

The business of music memorabilia has some parallels with the vintage instrument trade, but depending on your niche, it's not just about bygone pieces of Fab Four memorabilia and Elvis Sun singles. It also features newer items, from pop-star 8×10 photos to Rage Against the Machine concert T-shirts to

Jerry Garcia ties. Obviously, vintage memorabilia with provenance has the most value and margin. Novelty merchandise for new acts has to be sold in volume, but the upside is that it is more readily available, as the concert industry is also thriving. As for sourcing bona fide music history, that requires putting on your antique dealer hat. Expect to develop networks of dealers and estate reps in important music cities, such as Los Angeles, Nashville, New York, and Memphis, who buy and sell major collections. Attend important sales at minor and major auction houses, from JulienEntertainment.com and Mastronet to Christie's. Don't be afraid to do some digging at the open-air markets, either, such as the Pasadena Flea Market. You never know where the next original Hendrix promo or Robert Johnson 78 will surface. One of the benefits of this segment is that it allows sellers to be as formal or informal as they want, especially if they just intend to resell on eBay. Sourcing inventory from dealers and estate representatives doesn't require any special credentials. When you sell memorabilia, just be prepared to pay a capital gain.

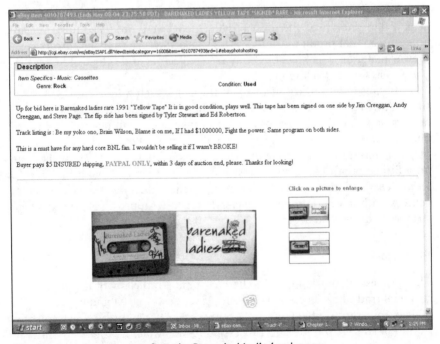

Figure 3-3   A demo cassette from the Barenaked Ladies' early years.

MARKET SPECIFICS AND MARKET OPPORTUNITIES ON eBAY

Don't make the mistake of choosing your niche before you've really studied the entire music opportunity. You might just find you are better suited to sell pop-diva CDs than out-of-print jazz records or keyboard workstations instead of baby grand pianos. Additionally, there's a chance you might miss opportunities to cross-sell merchandise because you didn't see natural synergies among different categories. That in mind, let's now take a closer look at some of the action in our main categories on eBay. The goal: to help you better identify your focus and some of your future customers.

Recorded Music

If it rocks, if it rolls, if it hips or it hops, it's here.

> **Cassettes:** Believe it or not, this Level II category still has some sales humph. It consists almost exclusively of secondhand material (see Figure 3-3). The money-making listings are either bulk lots ("Lot of 85 Metal Emo Hardcore Punk Cassette Tapes!"), live bootlegs ("40 live Grateful Dead Tapes and Skeleton Key Book"), and rarities—either original demos for now popular rock and alternative bands ("BARE-NAKED LADIES YELLOW TAPE *SIGNED* RARE!") or autographed tapes ("Oingo Boingo—Farewell—Cassette Set—Signed").
> *Customers:* Serious deal hunters (if not cheapskates) and obsessed fans. Demo cassettes are popular with enthusiasts.
> *Price Range:* Demo tapes, under $100; autographed tapes, $25–$50; bulk collections, $100–$300, depending on content and number.
> **Compact Discs:** By far, this is the largest recorded music category on eBay, with 200,000-plus listings per day, featuring a variety of CD formats and album types. For audiophiles, there are limited edition 24-Karat Gold CDs ("MFSL—Tommy—The Who—Ultra Disc—MINT!"), which were pressed in limited quantity (usually 5,000 to 10,000). Buyers also can sort by regular 16-bit full-length CDs, which go up in value if signed or out of print ("Blue Mitchell THE THING TO DO Blue Note OOP"). Box set artist/label retrospectives also are popular in the category. These take a variety of forms, including mini-LP import box sets ("LED ZEPPELIN-JAPAN LP SLEEVE BOX SET RARE"). Related to box sets are complete works collections ("MOZART—COMPLETE WORKS—170 CD SET—NEW!!"), which can have a 100 or more CDs and retail for hundreds of dollars if new. Less numerous but often more valuable than regular CDs are the category's CD singles and EPs (extended play). Some

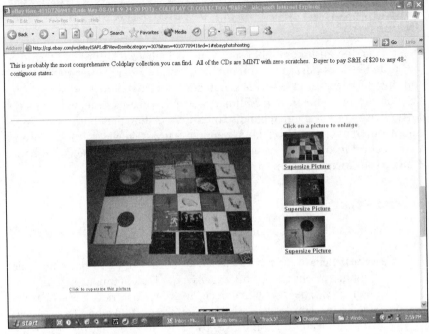

Figure 3-4   A pretty enticing collection for Coldplay fans.

dealers and individuals also sell their own collections, featuring both CDs and vinyl ("COLDPLAY CD COLLECTION *RARE*"). (See Figure 3-4). Finally band promo-CD collections are hot.

Customers: General CD buyers; serious enthusiasts or artist-specific collectors, interested in out-of-print material, hard-to-find imports (w/unreleased material), Japanese box sets (w/OBI—Original Band Intact), and complete works.

Price Range: Factors dictating value include the CD or collection's rarity (out-of-print/import), pressing number, and if autographed. Gold CDs, $25–$50; new full-length CDs, $10–$20; new box sets, $100–$250; individual out-of-print/import CDs, $15–$30; rare promo EPs/singles, $50–$500; import mini-sleeve LP box sets, $200–$500; complete works, $600 plus.

DVD Audio: This category is still in its infancy on eBay, rarely having more than 1,000 listings, but it's interesting. Essentially, the category features sets of DVDs for high-fidelity DVD/CD home theater systems. Expect massive complete-works collections ("Time Life—*DOO WOP GOLD*—6 dvd set WOW"), concert movies ("MARILYN MANSON DVD'S!!! BOX SET OF FOUR LIVE SHOWS!"), video collections, artist documentaries ("Bruce Springsteen This is Your Life 8 DVD SET"), and more.

Customer: Home-theater enthusiasts, who love their music; teens with hot-rod computers.

Price Range: For all of the above, $25–$60

Records: The second largest category in eBay Music, featuring its most collectible material. Records have varying sizes, speeds (RPM or revolutions per minute), and durations (LP, EP, single). They also have been made from two different materials: vinyl (introduced in the 1950s) and shellac (1950 and earlier). All the different record sizes (7-inch, 10-inch, 12-inch), record speeds (16, 33, 45, 78 RPM), and durations are represented on eBay. There's a lot of crossover between speeds, sizes, and durations as well. For example, there are 7-inch singles that play at 45 RPM and 33 RPM. Also, 12-inches can be LPs that play at 33 RPM or singles that play at 45 RPM. Generally, the most valuable records are first pressings of LPs for the big acts ("Beatles Help SWISS Pressing 1965 SMO 984008 Mint Yellow"); 7-inch, 45 RPM singles from the pioneering labels of the '50s and '60s ("Elvis— Rare Original UNPLAYED Sun 45"); and early shellac 78s. Rare, out-of-print jazz LPs from the '50s, '60s, and '70s generate strong interest, too (see Figure 3-5). Modern colored vinyl ("Rolling Stones Some Girls Orange Colored Vinyl") is also popular and worth seeking out. LPs pressed on 180 gram virgin vinyl are hot with collectors, audiophiles, and DJs. These records have no recycled plastic, higher sound quality, and lower pressing numbers than standard 125 gram records.

Customer: Serious record collectors; budget music lovers looking for cheap music; audiophiles and DJs seeking high-quality vinyl.

Price Range: Collectible LPs, $250–$1,500; collectible 7-inch singles, $250–$1,000; rare jazz LPs, $50–$500; colored vinyl, $15–$50; 180 gram vinyl, $15–$45.

Other Formats: Here's where niche gets really niche, but there's still money to be made in this small category, which includes 8-track tapes, reel-to-reel tapes, Super Audio CDs, and assorted other oddities. The most valuable listings are reel-to-reel tape masters from recording sessions ("ALLMAN BROTHERS 1991 Network Radio Show MASTER TAPES!"). The Super Audio CD format has yet to gain strong support, so it's still small on eBay. However, *Super Audio CD* will be a major category in the years to come. As for vintage material, sell it if you find it, but don't expect to make a business out of it. Reel-to-reels in original boxes with little cover wear earn the best returns. What is the attraction of these bygone formats? Enthusiasts will tell you these formats have fuller sound than CDs. Also, some reel-to-reels and 8-tracks were not transferred to CD, making them

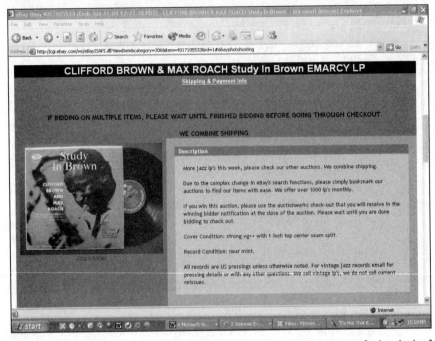

Figure 3-5 Original first pressings of Jazz LPs from the '50s and '60s can go for hundreds of dollars.

unavailable elsewhere. Most sellers list them in bundles of five to ten tapes.

Customer: Throwbacks infatuated with the groovy '60s and '70s or collectors of rare music formats.

Price Range: Individual reels, $20–$30, bundles, under $100; 8-tracks, under $30.

Musical Instruments

This is the most specialized of eBay's music categories, featuring more than 300 subcategories.

Brass, String, Woodwind: We've grouped these three separate eBay categories together because they have common customers. The first major market: student musicians playing in high school marching bands, high school and university orchestras, student jazz groups, and more. These buyers are looking for entry- to intermediate-level instruments at affordable prices ("SELMER BUNDY II ALTO SAX SAXO-

PHONE STUDENT GUARANTEE"). Businesses serving this crowd should be prepared to sell in volume. The second more lucrative customer base consists of part-time professional musicians, who purchase premium instruments ("Violin—Jan Lorenz Professional Handmade 4/4 Size"), both new and vintage, for their side pursuits or careers, be that as a fiddler or mandolin player in a bluegrass band, horn player in a jazz quartet, or serious violinist in a regional orchestra. All three eBay categories support a wide range of customers and price points. Saxophones, flutes, and clarinets in *Woodwind*, trumpets and trombones in *Brass*, and banjos, mandolins, and violins in *String* tend to command the most interest and highest prices. One word to the wise: budget deficits and cuts in school music programs do have a real bearing on the success of businesses selling student instruments in these categories. Interestingly, as awareness for eBay's *Musical Instruments* category increases, more students are buying new online, rather than renting their instruments.

Customer: Students and professional musicians in bluegrass, classical music, and jazz, looking for both budget and premium instruments.

Price Range: Student instruments, $250–$750; performance grade, $1,000–$5,000; collector grade, $5,000–$50,000 plus.

Guitars: Guitars are the biggest musical instrument category in the music products industry, and also the biggest category in *Musical Instruments* on eBay. Guitars come in two types, acoustic and electric, with electrics typically being twice as numerous. Players and collectors purchase both new and vintage guitars in both categories. In both acoustics and electrics, there are three core markets: beginners looking for value instruments ("Jay Turser Serpent Les Paul Electric Guitar FREE S&H"), dubbed starter guitars by eBay, usually produced in Mexico or overseas in Japan, China, Korea, and Indonesia; serious players or performers, looking for either new or vintage American instruments ("G&L ASAT S/H VINTAGE SUNBURST BRAND NEW!!!") from the brand names such as Fender, Gibson, Martin, or more boutique manufacturers such as Paul Reed Smith, G&L, Goodall, and Santa Cruz; and collectors, who buy very specific models and years, paying particular attention to condition and originality ("Martin 1930 OM 28 Brazilian Rosewood Herringbone OM28"). You'll find all three markets on eBay (see Figure 3-6). This category also features bass guitars, amplifiers, guitar effects, guitar parts, and luthier kits, all significant categories in themselves, capable of supporting a specialized business.

Customer: Students, amateur or weekend performers, music professionals, and collectors.

Figure 3-6 New guitars autographed by major rock-n-rollers are becoming a hot commodity in eBay's *Musical Instruments* and *Music Memorabilia* categories.

Price Range: Starters, under $500; performance grade, $500–$2,500; collector grade $2,500–$50,000.

Keyboard, Piano: Core to this category are new digital keyboards or synthesizers (from the likes of Casio, Korg, Kurzweil, Roland, and Yamaha), which provide beginners and professionals amplification and portability. More expensive, advanced models ("Korg Trinity Pro 76-Key Music Workstation—MINT!") also are popular with professional performers and recording engineers, because they can be used as workstation/samplers, simulating other instruments or adding sound loops to recordings or performances. Second to electronic keyboards in eBay's Keyboard category are pianos, which can be a serious investment if built by one of the top high-end makers, such as Baldwin, Bluthner, or Steinway ("STEINWAY Grand Piano Model B Louis XV Style IMMACULATE"). Options include *Uprights*, the smallest of eBay's piano subcategories, *Baby Grands*, and *Grands*. The upright side of the business on eBay features new pianos, antique examples, and also digital keyboards in traditional cases. Organs are the other core niche in *Keyboards*, particularly vintage analog units, from the likes of Hammond, Yamaha, and Korg, for musicians looking for that vintage Jimmy Smith-sound ("1958 Hammond B3 Organ with 145 leslie!"). Finally, eBay has become a popular venue for piano roll enthusiasts and businesses that operate piano rolls.

Customer: Students, performers, music professionals, and recording engineers.

Price Range: Fine pianos, $25,000–$100,000; Family uprights, $2,500–$10,000; electronic keyboards, pro, $1,000–$4,000; vintage organs, $1,000–$10,000.

Percussion: The *Percussion* category and market are similar in structure to *Guitars,* just smaller. Few parents are willing to listen to their kids bang on their skins and give up the space necessary for a kit, reducing the starter market for this instrument. (Remember, guitars and amps fit neatly back in the case in the closet after a particularly grievous jam session.) Plus, five- and eight-piece entry-level kits, made from a blend of inexpensive woods, from the likes of Hammer and Slingerland ("DRUMS *20 LUG* DRUM SET—HAMMER SETS, SPECIAL HEADS!") are generally more expensive than starter guitars, when you add in shipping ($100). Some sellers do import them and sell them in volume from $300 to $500. There is a legitimate market for midlevel and professional-grade drum sets and pieces on eBay. More serious buyers on eBay are looking for maple kits from the major makers, such as Gretsch, Hart, Pearl, Tama, and Yamaha, as well as custom sets from smaller manufacturers, such as Drummers Workshop (see Figure 3-7). Experienced players also hunt eBay for individual pieces and parts, particularly snares, drum heads, cymbals, and floor toms, with which they can upgrade a nicer budget kit from the likes of Hammer Percussion. Many players supplement new sets with costly vintage snares from other manufacturers, as different players prefer different snare tones. Other market opportunities include electronic drums and natural, nonmaple kits made from birch and mahogany by trusted manufacturers.

Customer: Students, amateur bands and performers, and professionals.

Price Range: Starter kits, $300–$500; midrange kits, $1,000–$2,000; custom kits for pros, $3,000–$5,000; vintage snares and cymbals, $500–$1,500; cymbal packages (hi-hat, crash, ride, splash), $200–$1,000.

Pro Audio: Thanks to the power of the PC, pro audio has truly entered the home in the last ten years. Now everyone with a good computer, a few high-quality microphones, and a guitar and keyboard can record their own music and do it quite well, thanks to computer recording interfaces (for instruments, mics, etc.), high-end soundcards, and

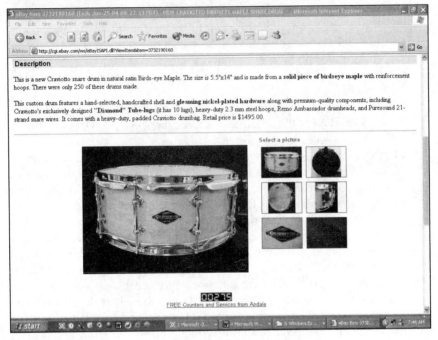

Figure 3-7   You'll find drums for beginners and professionals on eBay.

recording software. The result: pro audio is bigger business than it has ever been on and off eBay. In fact, it's now eBay's second largest category in the *Musical Instruments* vertical. *Pro Audio* is only second to guitars in Level III and Level IV categories, including not just computer recording equipment but also DJ equipment, microphones, mixing consoles, analog and digital multitrack recorders, and studio rack gear for processing sound (from effects processors and equalizers to compressors and signal gates, not to mention studio monitors and other speaker equipment). In short, *Pro Audio* features a number of segments, each of which could sustain a full-time business, though most stay broad and sell in several areas. It's also worth noting that most subcategories in *Pro Audio* have merchandise for the enthusiast, hobbyist, and professional, meaning there's a range of price points to sell.

Customer: Home recording enthusiast; performing songwriter, musician, and band; professional recording engineer.

Price Range: From a few hundred dollars to tens of thousands of dollars for professional-grade microphones, signal processors, recording units, and mixing consoles.

Sheet Music, Song Books: Even the best of the best need to refer to their charts sometimes. That means everybody, from beginners to seasoned pros, buys music reference material. Hence, not surprisingly, sheet music, songbooks for popular new artists and bands, and instructional videotapes and DVDs are big business on eBay.
Customer: Students, teachers, and professionals.
Price Range: $15–$100.

Entertainment Memorabilia

The next best thing to taking them home with you: music memorabilia.

Music Memorabilia: It's interesting to note that *Music Memorabilia* is often the biggest category in *Entertainment Memorabilia*. The *Rock-n-Roll* category steals the show in *Music Memorabilia*, with some 50 categories and an average of 75,000 to 100,000 listings per day. Featuring categories for the Beatles, Elvis, and U2, Music Memorabilia also has the priciest items. By far, these three famous acts realize the biggest returns. In regard to authentic memorabilia, the towering figures, or just notorious ones, of rock, pop, country, and blues (Jimi Hendrix, Madonna, Nirvana, The Rolling Stones, KISS, and B.B. King) earn top prices. Generally, memorabilia for prefab stars like Britney doesn't have lasting value. These "tween" stars don't appeal to collectors, who are generally a bit older. Hot new rock acts, such as Dave Matthews or Tool, on the other hand, can be lucrative, particularly if a dealer is selling their memorabilia when they are touring or hitting it big. As for types of material to sell, original concert posters, handbills, T-shirts, ticket stubs, record awards, and concert props and costumes generate the most interest (see Figure 3-8). (Heads up: the '80s are now retro. Yeah, you're that old.) You can also take a volume approach in *Music Memorabilia* by selling mass-produced pins, stickers, patches, T-shirts, lighters, and other inexpensive music paraphernalia. Avoid trying to sell both new and vintage memorabilia, however. You'll lose credibility with collectors.
Customer: Serious collector, casual and die-hard fan.
Price Range: Novelty material and photo reprints, $5–$20; original concert paraphernalia (ticket stubs, tour guides, T-shirts, "crew" shirts), $25–$100; record awards or album art, $100–$500; rare, original '40s, '50s, '60s boxing-style posters and handbills and Bill Graham Presents handbills or posters, from several hundred to several thousand dollars.

Autographs: The *Autographs, Music* category isn't huge, but it does attract premium property. Here you'll find a wide variety of auto-

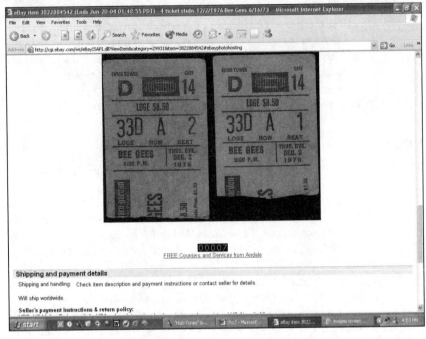

Figure 3-8　Some hardcore fans buy it all—even used tickets.

graphed music memorabilia, from various kinds of vintage ephemera, some with interesting provenance, to signed vintage records ("John Lennon signed & dated 1975 LP photo mtd/frd *w/LOA") to autographed guitars—the new rage—to promo photos, some matted and framed to add additional value and margin ("SIGNED—FRED DURST FRAMED/MATTED 8×10 PHOTO W/COA"). Autographed memorabilia generally earns more if it is sold with a signed letter of authentication (LOA) from an appraiser on letterhead or with a photo of the musician signing the object at an event ("Freddie Mercury QUEEN SIGNED PIC *IN PERSON*"). Some autograph dealers only sell items signed by living artists so that they can always provide customers visual proof of signing. Another way to markup your autographs: have them signed to an object with an established value, such as a guitar. Joining dealer associations also increases credibility and sales, as fraud is a problem in this industry. The volume approach: selling signed photo reprints for $10 to $20. The *Autographs* category is rife with these items.

Customer: Serious collector, casual and die-hard fan.

Price Range: Depending on the item (who signed it, when, and on what), autographed memorabilia can command several hundred to several thousand dollars, but rarely above $10,000.

*   *   *

Well, that's just a taste. There's plenty more to come, particularly in our industry-specific chapters (10 through 12), each of which focuses on one of our three areas. Next up: how to become an expert in recorded music, musical instruments, or music memorabilia. The truth is out there!

4

Becoming an Expert in Music Sales

Regardless of what category you specialize in, you have to be an expert. There's no way around it. Why? Well, the fact of the matter is that your competitors are bona fide experts.

It is essential to have insider's appreciation of your market if you hope to gain a true competitive advantage over other dealers in your niche. After all, most true enthusiasts aren't just looking to stockpile obscurities and curios; they're looking to develop a partnership with their dealers and resellers and join a vibrant community of other passionate collectors and users. We live in a world of diverse lifestyles. Dealers who make those lifestyles more compelling and satisfying win in the end. In other words, if you're just peddling products and not offering an experience, beware. It's likely that casual window shoppers won't become loyal customers and pick you when looking for advice on how to invest their dollars.

Keep this in mind, too: only true experts can effectively protect themselves from the vagaries and ups and downs of the market. If you can't identify what's authentic, what's legitimately innovative, and what's not, you just might get burned right out of the business by unscrupulous suppliers or secondary-market dealers, who convince you to invest in merchandise you can't sell or, worse, you end up unintentionally misrepresenting.

In addition, if you don't have an intimate understanding of your products and customers, enabling you to determine which products will sell at a premium and which will just sell fast at an acceptable margin (providing you steady cash flow), your enterprise might wither on the vine. Finally, if you haven't bothered to do your homework so that you can become a leader in your field, forget about making markets in items that other dealers have forgotten, ignored, or just not discovered. Knowing something other dealers don't and tapping underappreciated markets before others flock to them generates real revenue.

eBay TIP: Don't get caught pretending you are an expert when you're not. That's the kiss of death for any business. To avoid this fate, select a music niche that you are genuinely passionate about, even if you are selling a commodity product. Sellers who are passionate about their property go the extra mile for their customers without even knowing it. Their descriptions go beyond the spec sheets because they are connoisseurs themselves, their auction photos are artful out of respect for their discipline, and their customer support is first rate because they use the devices they sell and know the potential frustrations of trouble-shooting them.

There are other ways to generate a competitive advantage, of course, such as lower prices, authorized dealer relationships, great shipping rates (just consider Amazon), and more, but these logistical advantages are the most easy to duplicate. A true expertise has to be formed the hard way, through study, experience, and the inevitable mistakes.

WHAT DOES IT TAKE TO BE A MUSIC EXPERT?

So, how do you become an expert and get better acquainted with your niche, even if you are an established dealer or reseller? Well, first off, don't start selling anything in the music category until you've had some experience buying and using it yourself—online and off. If you haven't purchased some of the material you are about to sell, then you won't have the right mindset, an appreciation for what motivates and satisfies your customers. And if you don't know that, you won't be able to forecast demand in your new niche as reliably as you might otherwise, reducing your sales.

What do we mean, exactly? A buyer should know, for example, the excitement of stumbling on a rare Bob Wills 78 and the disappointment of having it sniped away by another bidder in the final seconds. Understand, from experience, the limitations of the manuals that are included with most computer recording soundcards and interfaces. Know that some budget, low-wattage tube amps from the '60s (Champs, Maestros, Silvertones, Supros) make great rock *studio* amps because they provide natural distortion at low volumes. They're also increasing in value, as a result. (Getting a classic crunchy tone out of a Fender Bassman or Marshall JCM 45 can be hard on the ears. Legend has it that many early Led Zeppelin tracks were recorded with a Telecaster and cheap Supro, not a Les Paul and Marshall.)

Recognize that uncut, blue-line poster proofs are sometimes cooler than original posters.

After you've gotten your feet wet, don't stop studying your market and refining your understanding of what market factors drive the trends. That means leveraging both traditional and unconventional sources of information. If you're new to your market, talk to local experts at shops and shows and ask them as many questions as you can before they tell you to buzz off. While you're at it, identify the most authoritative reference bibles in your niche, from rock-n-roll encyclopedias to music-manufacturer histories to leading identification and pricing guides. Then, read them religiously to establish a foundation on which to build. Don't gloss over histories, either. These are valuable tools that can provide you with an understanding of how your industry evolved and what major figures made it the way it is. You'll be surprised how valuable this can be and how much it will affect your ability to gain and retain customers. With some historical perspective, you'll gain an appreciation for the forces that shaped your industry and understand why certain products actually do have greater value than others (see Chapter 2). In short, you'll start to see that there's actually a logic to your industry. And when you see history repeating itself (as it often does), you'll be ready to take advantage of it. In the long run, you'll be able to give customers the guidance and confidence they need to invest in your high-dollar items on a regular basis.

Quality references also are a must for learning how to identify and authenticate resale items. These references illustrate manufacturer marks and labels; codes, dates stamps, and serial numbers; and other product characteristics so that you can date and authenticate historically significant property. With experience, you'll learn what to check to determine if an item is real or if it is being misrepresented (sometimes unintentionally) or forged. Here's an example: Silverface Fender amps are generally less valuable than earlier Blackface amps, the black and silver referring to the color of the amp's control panel (not its grill). However, many first-year Silverfaces, with metal trim around the grill, feature the same circuit (the AA764) as Blackfaces, which are now highly desirable and can fetch $1,500 and up. If you didn't know how to distinguish between various silver faces, you could sell an example for less than what it was worth. If you're selling a desirable Vox AC30 amplifier from the '60s, you need to know Dick Denny equipped them with EL84 power tubes, which only produce 30 watts of power in "Class A" mode; top-mounted, rear-facing controls; multiple input channels (normal, vibrato, and bright); and two 12-inch Celestion G12 Bulldog speakers. Continue to buy important books, particularly those with large photos, and build a reference library. Just like markets, good references change and evolve.

What else should you know? Music sellers, regardless of their focus, should learn as much as possible from print price guides, Internet sheets, and, of course, eBay's Completed Items feature (more on that later). They also should consider joining regional, national, and international trade groups, collector societies, and user groups, from the National Association of Recording Merchandisers (NARM) and International Music Products Association (IMPA) to the Rock Record Collectors' Association (RRCA) and Automatic Musical Instrument Collectors' Association. Besides increasing your standing and credibility with eBay buyers, these organizations often are excellent sources of market information and data. Many feature valuable reference libraries, if not research staffs that produce regular reports and briefings that highlight important trends and provide important statistical analysis. Most important, these associations usually operate trade shows, symposiums, and member events, where you can evaluate new products before release, network with other professionals, and develop supply relationships.

It's also wise to subscribe to important industry trade magazines, such as *Music Trades* in the instrument trade, *Billboard* in recorded music, and *Goldmine* for commentary on new markets in music memorabilia. Find out what releases are on the horizon and how products have been reviewed and received. Don't be a traditionalist. Embrace new online sources beyond eBay, such as Internet bulletin boards and chat rooms, populated by true users and insiders. For example, see Harmony Central in the instrument and accessories category.

PRIMARY SOURCES

To help you hit the ground running, here are a wealth of sources you should investigate before starting your eBay business.

Trade References

RECORDED MUSIC

- *Collectible Compact Disc Price Guide 2*, by Gregory Cooper (Collector Books)
- *Goldmine British Invasion Record Price Guide*, by Tim Neely (Krause Publications)
- *Goldmine Country Western Record & CD Price Guide*, by Tim Neely (Krause Publications)
- *Goldmine 45 RPM Picture Sleeve Price Guide*, by Charles Szabla (Krause Publications)
- *Goldmine Heavy Metal Record Price Guide*, by Martin Popoff (Krause Publications)
- *Goldmine's Price Guide to Collectible Jazz Albums*, by Neal Umphred (Krause Publications)

- *Goldmine's Price Guide to Collectible Record Albums*, by Neal Umphred (Krause Publications)
- *Goldmine Price Guide to 45 RPM Records*, by Tim Neely (Krause Publications)
- *Goldmine Promo Record & Compact Disc Price Guide*, by Tim Neely (Krause Publications)
- *Goldmine Record Album Price Guide*, by Tim Neely (Krause Publications)
- *Goldmine Standard Catalog of American Records 1940–1975*, by T. Neely (Krause Publications)
- *Goldmine Standard Catalog of American Records 1976–2000*, by T. Neely (Krause Publications)
- *Goldmine Standard Catalog of Rhythm & Blues Records*, by Tim Neely (Krause Publications)
- *A Music Lover's Guide to Record Collecting*, by Dave Thompson (Backbeat Books)
- *Official Price Guide to Records*, by Jerry Osborne (House of Collectibles)
- *Rockin' Records*, by Jerry Osborne (Osborne Enterprises)
- *Vinyl Junkies: Adventures in Record Collecting*, by Brett Milano (St. Martin's Griffin)
- *Warman's American Records, 1950–2000*, by Chuck Miller (Krause Publications)

MUSICAL INSTRUMENTS/MUSIC PRODUCTS
- *Acoustic Guitars and Other Fretted Instruments*, by George Gruhn (Backbeat Books)
- *Acoustic Guitars: The Illustrated Encyclopedia*, by Tony Bacon (Thunder Bay Press)
- *Analog Days*, by Frank Trocco (Harvard University Press)
- *Blue Book of Acoustic Guitars*, by Zachary R. Fjestad and S. P. Fjestad (Blue Book Publications)
- *Blue Book of Electric Guitars*, by S. P. Fjestad and Gurney Brown (Blue Book Publications)
- *C.F. Martin and His Guitars, 1796–1873*, by Philip F. Gura (University of North Carolina Press)
- *The Drum Book*, by Geoff Nicholls (Backbeat Books)
- *Electric Guitars: The Illustrated Encyclopedia*, by Tony Bacon (Thunder Bay Press)
- *Electronic Music Pioneers*, by Ben Kettlewell (ArtistPro)
- *The Fender Book: A Complete History*, by Tony Bacon (Backbeat Press)

- *Fender Telecaster: The Detailed Story*, by A.R. Duchossoir (Hal Leonard)
- *Fender: The Sound Heard 'Round the World*, by Richard R. Smith (Amsco Publications)
- *Gibson Electrics: The Classic Years*, by A.R. Duchossoir (Hal Leonard)
- *Gibson Guitars: 100 Years of an American Icon*, by Walter Carter (Gibson Publishing)
- *Gibson's Fabulous Flat-Top Guitars*, by Eldon Whitford (Miller Freeman Books)
- *The Great American Drums*, by Harry Cangany (Hal Leonard)
- *Gruhn's Guide to Vintage Guitars*, by George Gruhn and Walter Carter (Miller Freeman Books)
- *Guide to Vintage Drums*, by John Aldridge (Centerstream Publications)
- *Guitar Identification: A Reference Guide*, by A.R. Duchossoir (Hal Leonard)
- *The Guitars of the Fred Gretsch Company*, by Jay Scott (Hal Leonard)
- *The Hammond Organ—Beauty in the B*, by Mark Vail (Hal Leonard)
- *Martin Guitars: An Illustrated Celebration*, by Jim Washburn (Reader's Digest)
- *Official Vintage Guitar Magazine Price Guide*, by Alan Greenwood and Gil Hembree (Vintage Guitar)
- *The PRS Guitar Book*, by Dave Burrluck and Tom Wheeler (Backbeat Books)
- *The Stratocaster Chronicles*, by Tom Wheeler (Hal Leonard)
- *Vintage Synthesizers*, by Mark Vail (Backbeat Books)

Music Memorabilia
- *The Beatles, A Reference & Value Guide*, by Barbara Crawford (Collector Books)
- *The Beatles Records on Vee-Jay*, by Bruce Spitzer (full series recommended) (498 Productions)
- *Complete Book of Doo Wop*, by Anthony J. Gribin (Krause Publications)
- *Elvis Presley Memorabilia: Unauthorized Collector's Guide*, by S. O'Neal (Schiffer Publishing)
- *Goldmine Kiss Collectibles Price Guide*, by Tom Shannon (Krause Publications)
- *Goldmine Price Guide to Rock 'N' Roll Memorabilia*, by M. Allen Baker (Krause Publications)

- *The Monkees Collectibles Price Guide*, by Marty Eck (Krause Publications)
- *Official Price Guide to Beatles Records & Memorabilia*, by Perry Cox (House of Collectibles)
- *Official Price Guide to Elvis Presley Records and Memorabilia*, by J. Osborne (H.O.C.)
- *Presleyana V*, by Jerry Osborne (Osborne Enterprises)
- *A Price Guide to Rock & Roll Collectibles*, by Greg Moore (Rock & Roll Collectibles)
- *Rock and Roll Magazines, Posters and Memorabilia*, by David Henkel (House of Collectibles)
- *Rock & Roll Memorabilia: A History of Rock Mementos*, by Hilary Kay (Simon & Schuster)
- *Rock-N-Roll Treasures*, by Joe Hilton and Greg Moore (Collector Books)
- *The Sanders Price Guide to Autographs*, by Richard Saffro (Alexander Books)
- *The Sheet Music Reference & Price Guide*, by Anna Marie Guiheen (Collector Books)

Major Magazines

RECORDED MUSIC

Trade
- Billboard *www.billboard.com*
- Hits *www.hitsdailydouble.com*
- Music Connection *www.musicconnection.com*
- Pollstar *www.pollstar.com*
- Radio and Records Charts *www.radioandrecords.com*
- Twice *www.twice.com*
- Variety *www.variety.com*

Consumer/Collector
- Discoveries *www.collect.com*
- Downbeat *www.downbeat.com*
- Goldmine *www.collect.com*
- Gramophone *www.gramophone.co.uk*
- Harp *www.harpmagazine.com*
- Jazz Times *www.jazztimes.com*
- Maximum Rocknroll *www.maximumrocknroll.com*
- Mojo *www.mojo4music.com*
- No Depression *www.nodepression.com*
- Pulse *www.towerrecords.com*

- Q Magazine *www.q4music.com*
- Record Collector *www.recordcollectormag.com*
- Rolling Stone *www.rollingstone.com*
- Source *www.thesource.com*
- Spin *www.spin.com*
- Vibe Magazine *www.vibe.com*

MUSICAL INSTRUMENTS/MUSIC PRODUCTS
Trade
- MIX Magazine *www.mixonline.com*
- Music and Sound Retailer *www.msretailer.com*
- The Music Trades *www.musictrades.com*
- Music USA *www.namm.com/musicusa/*
- Musical Merchandise Review *www.mmrmagazine.com*
- PlayBack *www.namm.com/playback*
- Pro Audio Review *www.proaudioreview.com*
- Remix *www.remixmagazine.com*
- Vintage Guitar Magazine *www.vintageguitar.com*

Consumer/Collector
- Acoustic Guitar *www.acousticguitar.com*
- Bass Player *www.bassplayer.com*
- Electronic Musician *www.electronicmusician.com*
- Guitar Digest *www.guitardigest.com*
- Guitar Player *www.guitarplayer.com*
- Guitar World *www.guitarworld.com*
- Guitarist *www.futurenet.com/guitarist/*
- Keyboard Magazine *www.keyboardmag.com*
- Latin Percussion *www.latinpercussion.com*
- Modern Drummer *www.moderndrummer.com*
- Performing Songwriter *www.performingsongwriter.com*
- Strings *www.stringsmagazine.com*
- 20th Century Guitar *www.tcguitar.com*
- Windplayer *www.windplayer.com*

MUSIC MEMORABILIA
Primary
- Autograph Collector *www.autographcollector.com*
- Discoveries *www.collect.com*
- Goldmine *www.collect.com*
- Planet Collector *www.planetcollector.com*
- Record Collector *www.recordcollectormag.com*

Trade Associations, Organizations and Societies

RECORDED MUSIC
- Association for Recorded Sound Collections *www.arsc-audio.org*
- International Records Media Association *www.recordingmedia.org*
- National Academy of Recording Arts & Sciences *www.grammy.com*
- National Association of Recording Merchandisers *www.narm.com*
- Record Collectors Guild *www.recordcollectorsguild.org*
- Recording Industry Association of America *www.riaa.org*
- Rock Record Collectors Association *rrca.diskery.com*
- Wolverine Antique Music Society *www.shellac.org/wams*

MUSICAL INSTRUMENTS
- American Musical Instrument Society *www.amis.org*
- Association of String Instrument Artisans *www.guitarmaker.org*
- International Clarinet Association *www.clarinet.org*
- International Foundation for Music Research *www.music-research.org*
- International Music Products Association *www.namm.com*
- International Trombone Association *www.ita-web.org*
- International Trumpet Guild *www.trumpetguild.org*
- Music Industries Association of Canada *www.miac.net*
- National Association for Music Education *www.menc.org*
- National Association of Young Music Merchants *www.namm.com/naymm*
- Percussion Marketing Council (PMC) *www.playdrums.com*
- Violin Society of America *www.vsa.to*

MUSIC MEMORABILIA
- Association of Music Memorabilia Professionals *www.recordmecca.com*
- Association for Recorded Sound Collections *www.arsc-audio.org*
- Automatic Musical Instrument Collectors Association *www.amica.org*
- Internet Autograph Dealers Association *www.iada.net*
- The Old Crank *www.oldcrank.com*
- Professional Autograph Dealers Association *www.padaweb.org*
- Universal Autograph Collectors Club *www.uacc.org*

Industry Shows, Conventions, and Events

RECORDED MUSIC
New Products
- Consumer Electronics Show *www.cesweb.org*
- Digital Content Delivery Expo *www.dcdexpo.com*
- GRAMMY Awards *www.grammys.com*

- Home Entertainment Show *www.homeentertainment-expo.com*
- NARM InSights & Sounds *www.narm.com*
- NARM Music Retailing Summit *www.narm.com*
- Recording Media Forum *www.recordingmedia.org*

Collectible Records

- Aron's Records (Los Angeles, CA) *www.aronsrecords.com*
- Austin Record Convention (Austin, TX) *www.austinrecords.com*
- BRC Record & CD Show (Birmingham, AL) *www.birminghamrecord.com*
- Cincinnati Record & CD Music Mania Expo (OH) *www.pmshows.com*
- Des Moines Music Collectors Show (IA) *www.zzzrecords.com/recshow*
- Down Home Music 78rpm Swap (El Cerrito, CA) *www.downhomemusic.com*
- Downtown Oakland Record Show (Oakland, CA) *www.21grand.org/recordsale.html*
- Eugene Record Convention (Eugene, OR) *www.chromeoxide.com*
- Greater Orange County Monthly Record Show (Buena Park, CA) *www.asavinyl.com/record_show.htm*
- KFJC Record Swap (Los Altos, CA) *www.kfjc.org*
- KSPC CD & Record Expo (Claremont, CA) *www.kspc.org/events.html*
- KUSF Rock'N'Swap! (San Francisco, CA) *kusf.org/rocknswap.shtml*
- Nashville Record & CD Music Mania Expo (TN) *www.chromeoxide.com*
- Northwest Record & CD Collectors Convention (Seattle, WA) *www.nannyagentmusic.com*
- Pasadena City College Flea Market and Swap Meet (CA) *www.chromeoxide.com*
- Pennsylvania Music Expo (Lancaster, PA) *www.recordcollectors.org*
- Pittsburgh Record & CD Music Mania Expo (PA) *www.pmshows.com*
- PM Productions *www.pmshows.com*
- Progressive Rock Record and CD Convention (Buena Park, CA) *www.chromeoxide.com*
- Record Bonanza Record Collectors Show (Canby, OR) *www.chromeoxide.com*
- Record & CD Show (AK, TN, TX) *www.chromeoxide.com*
- Record Show (Minneapolis, MN) *www.chromeoxide.com*
- Rhino Records Parking Lot Sale (Westwood, CA) *www.rhinowestwood.com*
- River City Record Club Show (IA) *www.chromeoxide.com*

- Rockin N' Rollin Record Collectors Convention (Newark, CA) *www .chromeoxide.com*
- San Diego Record Show (CA) *www.sandiegorecordshow.com*
- S.F. Bay Area Music Collectors Expo (San Mateo, CA) *www.chrome oxide.com*
- Show Logic Productions *www.showlogic.net*
- Tacoma Music Show (Tacoma, WA) *www.tacomamusicexpo.com*
- Universal Record Show (Universal City, CA) *www.chromeoxide.com*
- Vinyl Only Record Expo (Edison, NJ) *www.chromeoxide.com*
- VRCA Record & CD Show (Vancouver, BC) *www.neptoon.com*
- WMSE 91.7fm Music Meltdown (Milwaukee, WI) *www.wmse.org/ rummage/index.php*
- Wolverines Antique Music Society *www.shellac.org*

MUSICAL INSTRUMENTS/MUSIC PRODUCTS

- Brookdale Guitar Show *www.brookdaleguitarshow.com*
- Buffalo Niagara Vintage Guitar Show (Buffalo, NY) *www.vintage guitar.com/events*
- Canada's Annual Vintage Guitar Show (Ontario) *www.vintageguitar show.com*
- Capitol Region Guitar Show (Saratoga Springs, NY) *www.saratoga guitar.com*
- Carolina Guitar Show (Charlotte, NC) *www.bee3vintage.com*
- City of Roses Guitar Show (Clackamas, OR) *www.vintageguitar .com/events*
- Classic American Guitar Show (Long Island, NY) *www.tcguitar.com*
- Dallas Guitar Show *www.guitarshow.com*
- Great American Guitar Show *www.bee3vintage.com*
- Great Midwest Guitar Show (St. Louis, MO) *www.sheldonconcert hall.org*
- Guitar Shows *www.guitarshows.com*
- Guitar Show Calendar.com *www.guitarshowcalendar.com*
- Indiana Guitar Show & Swap Meet (Indianapolis, IN) *www.road worthyguitars.com*
- Michigan's Annual Guitar Show (Dearborn, MI) *www.gordysmusic .com*
- Music & Sound Expo *www.musicandsoundexpo.com*
- Music City Guitar Show (Nashville, TN) *www.vintageguitar.com/ events*
- Music Industries Association of Canada *www.miac.net/tradeshow .htm*
- NAMM *www.namm.com/tradehow*
- Ohio Guitar Shows (Toledo, OH) *www.ohioguitarshows.com*

- Orlando International Guitar and Music Expo (FL) *www.guitar expo.net*
- Southern Illinois Guitar Show (Ina, IL) *www.vintageguitar.com/ events*
- Southern Ohio Guitar Show (Chillicothe, OH) *www.southernohio guitarshow.com*
- Texas Guitar Shows *www.texasguitarshows.com*
- USAMusician.com *www.usamusician.com/news/Guitar%20Shows/*

MUSIC MEMORABILIA
- Atlantique City Antiques Show (Atlantic City, NJ) *www.atlantique city.com*
- Austin Record Convention (Austin, TX) *www.austinrecords.com*
- Des Moines Music Collectors Show (IA) *www.zzzrecords.com/ recshow*
- Fest For Beatles Fans (Chicago, IL) *www.thefestforbeatlesfans.com*
- KISS Expos (national) *www.kissonline.com*
- S.F. Bay Area Music Collectors Expo (San Mateo, CA) *www.chrome oxide.com*
- Tacoma Music Show (Tacoma, WA) *www.tacomamusicexpo.com*

TRADE TALK

Now, that we've covered why you should become an expert and where to start your journey, let's get into some of the more technical aspects of being a music seller in our three markets. For starters, sellers need to master the language, or ontology, of their trade so that they can communicate efficiently and effectively with other sellers (from whom they'll source material) and their buyers. Here's a rundown of key terms and abbreviations, which appear frequently in eBay descriptions, so that you don't scratch your head the next time you pull up a listing. You'll find many of the following terms are used by sellers in their listing titles and descriptions to effectively merchandise their items to buyers. (In fact, quite a few of these words are search terms that you'll want to include, when appropriate, in your listing titles so that your buyer can easily find them.) Keep in mind that this is not a complete list. At the end of each section is an Internet resource featuring complete glossaries.

After reading these sections, you'll have a very solid understanding of what rival dealers are presenting and marketing in their listings—and that matters. After our trade terminology primer, we'll look at grading in our three industries.

Recorded Music

There's lots of jargon in the recorded music category, particularly for vintage records.

7 Inch: Vinyl record format introduced in the early '50s for 45 RPM singles.

10 Inch: Vinyl record format, which today is less common.

12 Inch: Vinyl record format typically for EPs and LPs and sometimes DJ singles.

180+ Gram Pure Vinyl: Higher weight vinyl with no recycled vinyl for audiophile releases.

33⅓ RPM: Record speed in revolutions per minute for long play (LP) vinyl records, typically.

45 RPM: Record speed in revolutions per minute for vintage 7-inch vinyl singles, typically.

24-Karat Gold CD: Limited edition, 24-karat-gold-plated audiophile CDs, taken from original master recordings. Many "OMR" and "Ultradisc" Gold CDs from Mobile Fidelity Sound Lab are highly collectible.

Acetate: A metal plate covered in a layer of acetone, used in the production of a finished vinyl record. Produced in small quantities and distributed to industry professionals to evaluate a record's sound before it's cut.

Album: Another name for records, CDs, and cassettes. Dates back to the use of book or photo-like albums, which housed several 78s.

Audiophile: High-quality pressing of a record, typically on 180-Gram vinyl or Gold CD.

B/W: Backed with (A side "backed with" the B side).

Back Catalogue: A labels catalog of previously released music.

Bootleg: An illegal recording of material that is not commercially available.

Catalogue Number: Identifying number assigned to an album release by a record label.

CD: Compact disc format, featuring 16-bit red-book audio or 24-bit super audio.

CD-R: CD-recordable compact disc format, allowing recording on compact disc.

CD-RW: CD-rewritable compact disc format, allowing rerecording on compact disc.

COA: Certificate of Authenticity, guaranteeing the authenticity of an item.

Cutouts: Albums that have been physically marked (punched, drilled, sawed) to indicate that they are unsold surplus. Cutouts: cutout hole (label), cut corner, punch, and sawmark (sleeve).

Dead Wax: The silent or "run-off" groove at the end of a record before the label.

Deep Groove: Blue Note label term, referring to concentric grooves on '50s releases.

Double: Album with two records, CDs, or cassettes. Often notated as Dbl.

Edge Wear: Wear to the edge of a record sleeve or jacket, which diminishes condition.

EP: Extended play; 12-inch (45-RPM) records or CDs with more songs than a single, but fewer than an LP. An alternative to singles and LPs in the '50s and '60s. Revived by indie bands in the '90s.

Export: Record manufactured in one country for sale in another. Example: Beatles Export LPs.

First Pressing: The first run or pressing of a record by a record company.

Gatefold: Record sleeve or jacket with a spine that opens like a book. Also notated as g/f, g/fold.

Gold Disc: Special designation by the British Phonographic Industry for U.K. albums or singles that have sold 100,000 or 400,000 times, respectively.

Goldmine Standard: Goldmine magazine's grading system or standard.

Import: Second cover inside a record. Most are plain paper; some from the '70s are printed.

Inner Sleeve: The protective plain paper or printed sleeve inside a record cover sleeve.

Inserts: The printed material in a commercial CD jewel case.

Jacket: Another name for a record sleeve or cover.

Jewel Case: The plastic receptacle that holds a CD.

Label: The record company that produces a record as well as the round label in the center of a record.

Master (Original): Metal negative from which vinyl records are pressed. Original master tape or CD from which other recordings are duplicated.

Matrix Numbers: Identifying numbers cut into vinyl masters, which appear on records in their dead wax or run-off groove.

MFSL: Mobile Fidelity Sound Labs, manufacturer of gold CDs.

Mini-LP: Like a 12-inch EP, featuring fewer tracks than a normal LP, but more than a single or EP. Most play at 33⅓ RPM.

Misspressing: A pressing that features different material than what is stated on the label. A real misspressing isn't just a record with a label on the wrong side.

Mono: Short for monophonic; primary sound format until the introduction of stereo recordings in the '60s, featuring a single channel of audio signal.

NOC: No Original Centre; refers to U.K. 7-inch singles with push-out centers.

Numbered: The number of an individual copy in an original release.

OBI: Original Band Intact; refers to the paper sash wrapped around many Japanese imports.

O/O/P, OOP: Out of print.

Original Issue: Copies of a record, which has now been rereleased, from the original pressing.

Picture Disc: A vinyl record with a picture on it.

Picture Sleeve: A sleeve that has a picture on it. Single examples from the '60s are highly collectible. Often notated as Pic Slv.

Promo: Short for promotional; prerelease promo records and CDs sent to radio stations and the press to generate airplay and publicity. They often feature unique radio promo sleeves.

Punch: A hole made in a cover sleeve or label by a distributor to indicate that it is unsold surplus.

Record: A grooved disc made from shellac or vinyl that holds music information. Records come in a variety of sizes (7-, 10-, 12-inch) and play at a variety of speeds (33⅓, 45, 78 RPM).

RIAA Award: Record or CD award from the Recording Industry Association of America.

Ring Wear: Circular damage to a record sleeve, caused by the rim of the record inside.

RVG: Rudy Van Gelder, prominent jazz engineer and producer.

Scuff: Abrasions or grazing on the sleeve of a record, diminishing condition and value.

Sealed: An unopened album or CD, often still shrink-wrapped.

Seam Split: Separation along the edge or seam of an LP record sleeve diminishing condition and value. Often notated as sp.

Shellac: Fragile, brittle material used for 78 records before the introduction of vinyl in the '50s.

Single: A record release featuring one to four tracks. Many valuable singles are 7-inch 45s from the '50s and '60s.

Skip: Physical defect, affecting the sound of second-hand albums and CDs.

Sleeve: A record's cover or jacket.

Sleeve Splitting: The separation of a record sleeve or jacket along any edge.

Spindle Mark: Wear to a record's center hole caused by contact with a turntable's metal spindle.

Spine Damage: Damage to the spine or gatefold record jacket or sleeve.

Stereo: Short for stereophonic; sound format, widely introduced in the '60s, with two different channels of audio signal. Allows a different signal to be run through each of two speakers.

Sticker Damage: Damage to a record sleeve or label caused by a record label promotional sticker. Removed stickers can damage the design of a sleeve.

Stock Copy: Commercially available copy.

Surface Noise: Background noise on vinyl or shellac records when the needle is in the run-in or run-off groove.

Tape Peel: Tape placed on a sleeve seam split that is peeling off slightly.

Tri-Centre: Push-out center with a triangle in it. Useful for dating U.K. records.

Unplayed: A record that has not been played, usually sealed or shrink-wrapped.

Unreleased: Recordings that were produced but never put on a commercial album.

Vinyl: Hard, durable material used for the manufacture of records since the '50s.

White Label Promo: Promo records featuring a plain white label.

e B a y   T I P :   Places to go for further reading:
- A History of Vinyl *www.bbc.co.uk/music/features/vinyl/*
- Collectors Help *www.collectorshelp.com*
- Good Rockin' Tonight *www.goodrockintonight.com*
- Mobile Fidelity Sound Lab *www.mfsl.com*
- Record Collecting Resources *www.helsinki.fi/~tuschano/records/*

Musical Instruments and Music Products

Learn these instrument and equipment terms and you'll be better prepared to identify your niche in eBay's incredibly diverse Musical Instruments category.

BRASS AND WOODWINDS

Alto: High-pitch saxophones, lower in pitch than a soprano, but higher in pitch than a tenor.

Baritone, Bari: The largest-sized and lowest-pitched saxophone.

Bb: B-flat, one of the two keys for clarinets.

Bell: The flared open end of brass and woodwind instruments.

Body: The main section of a brass or woodwind instrument, not including the detachable crook.

Bore: The internal body shape of a brass or woodwind instrument. A saxophone has a conical bore, wider at one end than the other.

Bow: The U-shaped portion of a saxophone body. Implement used to play a violin.

Brass: A family of valve-based wind instruments, including the cornet, French horn, flugelhorn, trombone, trumpet, and tuba.

Con: Popular saxophone company.

Concert: A violin-sizing term.

Cork: Sheets of cork at the ends of the crook, connecting the crook to the mouthpiece and body.

Corks, Felts: Pieces of cork positioned near woodwind keys restricting their opening.

Crook, Neck: The curved tube or neck of a woodwind instrument, connecting the detachable mouthpiece to the body. Stringed instruments (cellos, guitars, violins) have necks, too.

Eb: E-flat, one of the two keys for clarinets.

Ebonite: Body material for value clarinets.

Gold Plated: Yamaha flutes offer a choice of 9k or 14k gold.

Grenadilla Wood: Dense African hardwood used in the construction of many woodwinds.

Keys: Components on a woodwind instrument that are pressed to play different notes.

King: Popular saxophone company.

Lacquer (Clear, Gold, and Black): Type of finish used on woodwind and brass instruments.

Lightweight Slide: A type of lighter slide on trombones for easier playing.

Lip: The curved edge of a woodwind or horn bell.

Mouthpiece, MO: Detachable woodwind part that holds the reed.

Nickel, Silver, and Gold Plated: Both brass and woodwind instruments feature different types of plating, which affect both sound and price.

R13, R-13: Popular model of clarinet from manufacturer Buffet Crampon.

Screwbell: A detachable bell on a brass or woodwind instrument.

Selmer Mark VI, MK 6: Popular model of saxophone from France's Selmer Company.

Shepherd's Crook: An extra crook in smaller-sized cornets.

Soprano: The smallest-sized and highest-pitched saxophone.

Springs: A component of woodwind keys, allowing keys to close and spring open again.

Tenor: Midrange brass or woodwind instrument.

Tone Hole: The holes in the body of a woodwind.

Woodwind: A family of reed instruments including the bassoon, clarinet, flute, oboe, and saxophone. Name refers to wind blown through wood reeds.

GUITAR, KEYBOARD, STRINGS, AND PRO AUDIO

1/4, 1/2, 3/4, 4/4: Refers to the four main sizes of violin.

4-, 5-String: Banjos come in both a four- and five-string configuration.

Amplifier: An electronic device that increases the level of an audio signal from an electric guitar, electronic keyboard, or other instrument. Many amps are housed with speakers.

Archtop: Acoustic guitars and hollow-body electrics that feature curved tops and F-holes.

Binding: Thin strips of wood or plastic, which connect or bind a guitar's back, top, and sides.

Bridge: Key component of acoustic guitars, violins, and other stringed instruments, positioned on the body below the sound hole, anchoring the instrument's saddle. It also determines string height above the finger or fret board. Most bridges are adjustable for altering the string height.

Controller: Any device, such as a keyboard or effects processor, programmed to change the operation and sound of another device.

Cutaway: Attractive and practical feature on some concert-sized acoustic guitars and hollow-body electrics. The body's bottom front is "cut away" for greater access to notes above the twelfth fret.

DAT: Digital Audio Tape; cassette-based digital recording format, often used for final recording mixes.

Dreadnought: Generic term, introduced by Martin Guitars, for large flat-top acoustic guitars, such as Martin's D-28. Gibson uses the term Jumbo—Gibson J-45.

Effects: Devices that perform analog and digital signal processing. Effects include chorus, delay, distortion, flanger, overdrive, reverb, and more.

Equalizer: Audio processor for adjusting the level or gain of individual frequencies in a signal.

ES: Electro Spanish, as in the Gibson ES 125 or 335.

F, F-5: Popular line of Gibson mandolins.

F-holes: Pairs of F-shaped sound holes on a guitar or other stringed instruments, such as violins.

Flat-top: An acoustic guitar whose soundboard or top is flat.

Footswitch: A unit with a foot-triggered switch that activates an effect, such as amp reverb.

Fretboard: The wood top, often rosewood, on a guitar neck, featuring metal markers or frets.

Frets: Metal markers fixed to a guitar's fingerboard, marking changes in key or pitch.

Hammond: Popular electric organ invented by Laurens Hammond in the 1930s.

Head: An amplifier unit that is separate from its speaker.

Headroom: Refers usually to guitar amplifiers. The amount of signal that can be pushed through an amplifier or amp head before clipping distortion occurs.

Headstock: The component at the end of a stringed instrument neck that features its tuning pegs.

Horn: The component of a public address (PA) speaker that projects high frequencies.

Humbucker: A type of guitar pickup with two coils wired out of phase and two magnets oriented with opposite polarities. Gibson Les Paul guitars have humbuckers.

Jack: A connection plug.

KHz: KiloHertz (thousands of Hertz).

Leslie: A cabinet with a rotating speaker that produces a whirring sound.

Limiter: A type of compressor, which prevents any level from exceeding a set limit.

Loop: A short segment of audio set to repeat and enhance another piece of audio or music.

MIDI: Musical Instrument Digital Interface.

Mixer: A piece of recording equipment used to manipulate multiple audio signals.

Mod Chip, Mod Kit: Modification kits or components for modifying overdrive guitar pedals.

Monitor: A type of speaker system, used in recording situations or on-stage as part of a PA system, allowing engineers and performers, respectively, to monitor sound.

Multitrack: A recorder capable of recording and playing several independent audio signals simultaneously. Examples: 4-tracks, 8-tracks, 16-tracks, 24-tracks.

NC: No case.

Neck: One of the three central components of a stringed instrument, connecting the body to the headstock. The neck also features the fret or fingerboard.

Noise Gate: Processor that automatically shuts off a channel when no desired signal is present.

Nut: Plastic or bone component on stringed instruments that holds or channels strings at the end of the fret or fingerboard before the headstock.

Ohm: Unit used to measure electrical resistance or impedance.

OSC: Original soft case.

PA: Public address; system of mics, mixers, amps, and speakers used for public performance.

Pegbox: The headstock of a violin, viola, or cello, featuring its tuning pegs and scroll.

Pickups, PU: Electromagnetic devices that register the vibration of guitar strings and convert them into an electric signal for amplification.

Piezo: A type of nonmagnetic pickup used to amplify acoustic guitars and basses.

Power Amp: An amplifier designed to drive one or more speakers. Combo guitar amplifiers have preamps, power amps, and speakers in the same unit.

Preamp: An amplifier circuit that conditions a signal for further amplification. Preamps may also include equalizers, compressors, and other effects.

Rack Mount: A piece of recording or performance gear designed for a standard 19-inch rack.

Reverb: An audio effect, similar to delay, which gives a signal spatial ambience.

Saddle: A guitar component that directs strings over the bridge. Acoustic guitars have one saddle, while most electric guitars have individual saddles for each string.

Sample: A segment of audio.

SC: Soft case.

Sequencer: A device or computer program that can record, generate, edit, modify, and play back MIDI information.

Single Coil: A common type of electric guitar pickup, featuring a single coil of wire wrapped around a transducer magnet. Fender Stratocasters have single-coil pickups.

Solidbody: A guitar with a body made from a solid piece of wood, such as a Telecaster constructed from ash. Most electrics are solidbodies.

Speaker Cabinet: An enclosure for a speaker.

Stack: Two or more speaker cabinets stacked on top of one another.

Subwoofer: A speaker cabinet designed to handle very low frequencies.

Synthesizer: An electronic instrument that can be programmed to simulate different sounds.

Tailpiece: A guitar component that anchors strings at the end of a guitar body.

Teardrop, A-Style: Mandolins with a teardrop, lute-like shape.

Transistor: Semiconductor device used in "solid-state" amplification systems.

Tremolo: An amp effect that oscillates the amplitude of a signal.

Truss Rod: A rod inside guitar necks, which prevents them from bowing due to string tension.

TS-9/TS808: Tubescreamers; highly sought-after analog, overdrive guitar pedals from Ibanez.

Tube Amps: Amps that use sealed glass vacuum tubes or valves to conduct electricity, boost preamp signal, and power speakers. Tube amps often have a warmer, rounder tone than solid-state transistor amps.

Tweeter: A small speaker component designed to project high frequencies.

Vibrato: An amp effect that oscillates the pitch or frequency of a signal.

Wattage: The output power of an amplifier.

Woofer: A large driver designed to project low frequencies.

Workstation: A synthesizer or sampler used for electronic music production.

eBay TIP: Places to go for further reading:
- MusicPlayer's Back Stage Lounge *www.musicplayer.com/lounge*
- Gruhn Guitars *www.gruhnguitars.com*
- The International Saxophone Home Page *www.saxophone.org*
- International Trumpet Guild *www.trumpetguild.org*

Music Memorabilia

1st Edition: Copy in the initial release or printing of a work.

2nd Edition: Copy in the second release or printing of a work.

8×10 Original: An 8-by-10-inch photo.

AP Poster: Advance proof or black or blue line used to proof work before printing.

Autographed: Memorabilia or photo signed by a significant artist or performer.

BPI Award: British Phonographic Industry award.

COA: Certificate of Authenticity.

Concert Poster, Tour Poster: Poster designed to promote or venerate popular music performances.

Concert Program: Collectible pamphlet sold or handed out at popular music performances.

Corner Holes: Corner holes in promo posters from pins or staples. Decrease poster value.

Derek Hess: Popular alternative, modern-rock poster artist.

Edition Number: The number of a given copy in an edition.

Family Dog: A series of Avalon Ballroom posters, designed by Victor Moscoso.

Frank Kozik: Popular alternative, modern-rock poster artist.

Handbill: Concert promotion, designed to be handed out before and during concerts.

Hatch Show: Popular three-color poster style, originally developed for country music performances, which is now frequently copied.

Licensed Dealer: Dealer who is authorized to sell merchandise by a manufacturer or is licensed or regulated by a collector organization or society.

Limited Edition: Any work produced in limited quantity, not likely to be released again.

Lithograph: Popular printing technique used to produce many valuable '60s rock posters.

LOA: Letter of Authenticity.

Numbered: A piece of memorabilia, such as an original poster, with an edition number.

Original First Printing: Copy in the first printing of a work.

Original Poster: Copy from the first printing or edition of a poster.

Photo Reprint: Reproduction of a photograph, sometimes with a copy of an autograph.

Press Kit: A publicity kit distributed to music industry professionals (journalists, radio stations) promoting new releases. A press kit often features publicity photos, bios, and press briefings or releases.

Print: Printed form of artwork. Many valuable music memorabilia prints are lithographs and silk screens.

Promo Card: Postcard-sized (6-by-8-inch) photo card produced by record labels to promote their artists and new releases.

Proof Sheet: Preproduction black or blue line used to proof a work before printing.

RIAA Award: Recording Industry Association of America record sales award.

Rick Griffin: Popular '60s-rock poster artist.

Signed in Person: Autograph signed in front of a seller, documented with photo.

Stanley Mouse: Popular '60s-rock poster artist.

Tape-Pulls: Posters that have marks from the removal of tape used in their posting.

Ticket Stub: Remaining portion of a pulled ticket from concerts for popular artists or acts.

Uncut Proof: An uncut black or blue line used to proof several works before printing.

Uncut Sheet: Sheet of posters, tickets, handbills, or proofs that has not been cut into singles.

Victor Moscoso: Popular '60s-rock poster artist.

 eBay TIP:　Places to go for further reading;
- Collectorshelp *www.collectorshelp.com*
- Good Rockin' Tonight *www.goodrockintonight.com*
- *Record*mecca.com *www.recordmecca.com*
- Wolfgang's Vault *www.wolfgangsvault.com*

MAKING THE GRADE: GRADING MUSIC MERCHANDISE

Buyers and sellers in our three core categories all speak the same general language in terms of grading. Understanding condition grades is critical for all buyers and sellers of collectible material in our three industries. Here's a brief explanation of the general grading terms used in each.

Recorded Music

Valuable pieces of recorded material are often given multiple grades. This is particularly true of vinyl records. Often the vinyl itself, the cover, and the label are given individual grades. Fortunately, they use the same basic grading terms for all three. Cover grades are generally more lenient than vinyl grades. Recorded music dealers also often add plus and minus signs to their grades, implying that the item is at the high or low end of the grade. Many eBay dealers use qualifying abbreviations, such as FL for faded label, SK for skip, or WOC for writing on cover. The following vinyl grades generally can be applied to collectible CDs, 8-tracks, and reel-to-reels.

M = Mint: Vinyl, cover, or label have no significant imperfections. Vinyl has full gloss. Label has bright original color.

NM = Near Mint: Very minor vinyl and label imperfections. Original gloss isn't perfect, but full. Record has no surface noise when played. Cover looks new at a glance. Colors somewhat subdued.

EX = Excellent: Vinyl has trivial imperfections and most of its original gloss. Label has some wear and fading. Some record surface noise. Cover has modest wear, including slight flaking. Corners relatively sharp. Some browning of whites on cover. Sometimes notated as VG++.

VG = Very Good: Noticeable but not major imperfections to vinyl. Some vinyl gloss. Label has noticeable wear. Record has slight surface noise. Cover has obvious blemishes. Portions of cover artwork may be flaking. Cover may feature writing, small tears, and stains. Corners slightly rounded.

G = Good: Vinyl has scratches. Label well worn; faded with lost letters or graphics. Record plays but may skip. Cover has heavy wear, such as ring wear, scratches, tears, seam splits. Corners rounded.

F = Fair: Vinyl and label have serious defects. Portions of label flaking or peeling. Record barely plays. Cover is considerably damaged, faded, scratched, torn, split at seams.

Musical Instruments

Dealers in vintage amplifiers and guitars (acoustic and electric), collectible drum equipment (snares and cymbals), jazz and band instruments (saxophones, trumpets, violins), and other stringed items (antique banjos and mandolins) use a rigorous grading system. The age of the instrument will affect grading. In short, grades are more lenient for older, more rare instruments. Generally, instruments are graded on their cosmetic condition or finish (checking from strumming and belt buckles, for example), structural integrity (are there serious cracks, rusted frets, broken knobs?), originality (have modifications been made, tuning machines been changed, speakers been replaced?), and rarity. Plus and minus signs are used in this category, too.

M = Mint: Instrument and case as good as new. Unplayed.

NM = Near Mint: All original parts. Very minor scratches or checking (relative to age) under close inspection. One small ding is acceptable. Finish seems perfect at a glance.

EXF = Exceptionally Fine: Essentially the same as near mint.

EXC = Excellent: Light playing wear, no cracks or repairs. Finish has some minor, but not noticeable, defects (scratches, dings). Sold by original owner.

VG = Very Good: More visible wear, missing finish. Has modest repairs and high-quality replacement parts. No major structural improvements.

G = Good: Solid and playable. Noticeable structural repairs well executed.

Music Memorabilia

The same grades that apply to other collectibles, antiques, and celebrity autographs generally apply to music memorabilia as well, because buyers are generally interested in vintage material from past eras. Newer concert memorabilia and merchandise typically go upgraded because they're new, even if secondhand. Memorabilia of historical relevance and high values, such as autographs by Elvis or the Beatles, should be authenticated and sold with a certificate or letter of authenticity on company letterhead, signed by the expert.

A PERSONAL EDGE

One more word to the wise: At some point, you'll need to separate yourself from the pack by developing your own market perspectives instead of just relying on the opinions of others. You'll also want to innovate your own logistical systems and merchandising techniques. (We will explain more on that later.)

Finally, remember that complacency is a killer. In fact, complacency is antithetical to the whole idea of business. So are dated principles and procedures. Market strategies informed by market research and analysis, however, increase market share. Informed market strategies are the hallmark of any successful free-market enterprise. Having time to think and implement new ideas that increase efficiency obviously requires time and planning. It means taking the right risks and making the right investments in staffing and automation. That's where a business plan comes in handy, and that's why we'll cover that next.

PART 2

SELLING MUSIC MERCHANDISE WITH SUCCESS

5

Your Music Category Business Plan

eBay makes starting a business so easy, it's tempting to not write a real business plan for your enterprise. Take this bit of advice, though: If you plan to be in the game for the long run and grow your music business beyond eBay (so that it is just one of several channels), then take the time to write a real business plan, describing your market, customers, competitive edge, and financial goals. If you don't create a real plan for your future success—what it will take to get there (resources and capital) and how long it will take—you're setting yourself up for a fall. You'll not only potentially miss opportunities (because you have not clearly defined your goals and cash flow needs), but you might also go broke before you run the race.

Your first business plan decision regards what kind of plan you need to write. There are several kinds, but generally two to choose from for new businesses: a funding plan or a private internal plan. In other words, your business plan will function as a prospectus for investors or just as a roadmap for your business to help you identify and understand your business's basic success and risk factors—your business's S.W.O.T (Strengths, Weaknesses, Opportunities, and Threats).

In this chapter, we will cover specifically why you should have a business plan and its various applications—how it can be used to further your cause. Next, we'll cover what general elements should be in your business plan and provide a basic outline, whether you're looking to raise capital or just put your strategies down on paper. Additionally, we'll discuss resources for helping you produce a professional plan, which will open doors for you as you attempt to develop key relationships with important business partners, be they investors, suppliers, or other complementary businesses.

THE BIG DEAL ABOUT BUSINESS PLANS

When was the last time you did something and it turned out exactly like you first anticipated? If you are like most people, probably never. Don't assume you have all the answers before you've identified all of the questions and given them some real thought. As the military slogan goes: "Proper preparation prevents piss-poor performance." That, in a nutshell, explains why you should write a business plan. The process of sitting down and satisfying the requirements of a real business plan will provide you an enormously deeper appreciation for the journey you are about to take. The process will show you both opportunities and obstacles you didn't have a clue existed.

This is not to say that writing a business plan will ensure your success. It won't enable you to see the future, and it doesn't mean you won't have to be nimble and make some real, even radical, shifts in your tactics and strategy once you're in the game. The real world is often strikingly different than the imagined ones in our business plans, but the more you can close the gap between the two, the more successful your business will be. When the unexpected does occur, your business plan will at least have prepared you for a problem, if not that exact one. Your plan will give you that problem-solving mindset, that "Eye of the Tiger," if you will, on which you will depend for the entire life of your business.

THE NUTS AND BOLTS OF YOUR PLAN

Many entrepreneurs get their start on eBay because it's cost effective. They're right about that—in the short term. An evolved eBay business, which sells and fulfills orders in volume, requires some real capital, and we'll discuss this topic in Chapter 8. Generally, though, eBay businesses require less overhead than a new brick-and-mortar operation. As a result, most initial eBay business plans will be *internal* plans, not investor plans. That doesn't mean they won't feature detailed projections about your expenses and liabilities; it just means they won't act as both a strategic plan and funding pitch. (They probably will be used in pitches to suppliers, though.) Your eBay plan can be more direct and matter-of-fact than a more sales-oriented funding plan. Your plan should also reflect if you are a startup or continuing business. If you are an existing company and you just want to map out your eBay strategy, then your plan introduction (Executive Summary) will be quite a bit different from that of a new company. Additionally, some plan sections can be shortened or omitted, but you probably know this already.

Last but not least, you have the option of writing a standard-term business plan, forecasting activity for the next 12 months (with general milestones for the next two years), or a long-term business plan, covering the first five years. For the purposes of most eBay businesses, the standard plan is probably best. New businesses need to focus on the here and now, and it's more efficient for existing businesses to revise standard plans than to try to accurately project out five years in the fast-paced, online environment.

So, without further adieu, let's cover the essential components of a comprehensive business plan. (One last note: business plans come in a variety of styles. This is just one approach, familiarizing you with some key terms and elements. Also, this is only a general discussion of the following topics. Your eventual business plan software package or reference will provide many more specific details.)

Cover Page
Table of Contents
Executive Summary
  1.1 *Objectives*
  1.2 *Mission*
  1.3 *Keys to Success*
Company Brief
  2.1 *Company Ownership*
  2.2 *Startup Summary*
Products
Market Analysis
  4.1 *Market Segmentation*
  4.2 *Segmentation Strategy*
  4.3 *Industry Analysis*
Strategy
  5.1 *Competitive Edge*
  5.2 *Marketing Strategy*
  5.3 *Sales Strategy*
      5.3.1 *Sales Forecast*
Management and Personnel
Financials
  7.1 *Break-Even Analysis*
  7.2 *Profit and Loss Statement*
  7.3 *Cash Flow Analysis*
  7.4 *Projected Balance Sheet*
  7.5 *Business Ratios*

Now, let's define exactly what goes into all of these sections. Keep in mind that the financials sections at the end are the most important and most difficult to produce, particularly if you are a startup. Here you estimate your liabilities and profits, based on expenses you haven't incurred and sales you haven't made.

Cover Page: Just like it sounds.

Table of Contents (TOC): The headings above can be turned into your TOC.

Executive Summary: This summarizes what is in your business plan and introduces some important facts about your company, such as its name, location, business, and why it's relevant. If the plan is for investors, include some top-level sales and profit projections and details on your company's competitive advantage. Keep the summary concise—it should just be a couple of paragraphs or a group of bullets. Many people write this summary after finishing the rest of the plan. Some include a break-even analysis chart.

    1.1   *Objectives:* In brief, list your business's three or four main objectives. Keep them specific and measurable. For an eBay music business, think of the number of listings and sales you will do per week or per month, projected gross merchandise sales per quarter, percentage of successful listings, ratios of returns to sales, feedback targets, customer and supplier objectives, and the like.

    1.2   *Mission:* In a brief paragraph, two or three sentences, answer the question, What's the point of your company? Your mission statement is for your employees, suppliers, and customers. It sets the tone and priorities for your company. Though short, it can be difficult to write. In a nutshell, it should express exactly the purpose of your venture and its value proposition.

eBay TIP: Value proposition—what's that? The value proposition summarizes the key benefits you offer your customers at a particular price. You may want to reprise it in your actual listings to drive interest and sales.

    1.3   *Keys to Success:* Bullet the three or four critical factors that will determine if your business is a success or a failure. For eBay music businesses, quality inventory sources would probably merit mention. Expert freight service and warehouse space at low price might be key. Other possible factors: back-end automation, volume selling, and membership in the eBay's Developers Program (*developer.ebay.com/DevPro gram*).

Company Brief: In this brief introductory section, summarize what your company does (e.g., sells authentic rock-n-roll memorabilia to collectors), who owns it, how it's classified (DBA, LLC, S-Corp), and what kind of facilities, assets, and staff it has. This is similar to the Executive Summary, minus the salesmanship. (Note: If your business is established and your plan is for internal use, you can probably skip this section.)

2.1   *Company Ownership:*   Specify what kind of entity you are running. Is it a sole proprietorship (DBA, doing business as), partnership, limited liability corporation, or another kind of corporation (C or S)? Also, give more detail on company ownership, naming the various owners, if you are not the only one, and perhaps their percentage interest.

2.2   *Startup Summary:*   If you are a startup, summarize what your startup costs will be in a few brief paragraphs. Explain if you have secured funding for key assets and expenses or if additional financing is necessary and what steps you're taking to raise the capital. A funding chart and table of assets and expenses usually accompany this summary.

eBay TIP: eBay startup expenses may include: initial listing and final value fees; eBay merchandising; eBay Store membership; eBay co-op advertising; third-party auction management fees; office supplies, equipment, and software (computers, digital cameras, scanners PhotoShop, HomeSite); warehouse space; initial inventory; legal and creative services; and more.

Products: Describe in a few paragraphs and bullets what products you will be selling. Without getting too specific, outline the various product lines and price points in which you will specialize. As this is an eBay business, explain what class of inventory you'll be selling: new, front-line merchandise (class A), B-stock (end-of-life, discontinued or defective, returned, refurbished), used items, or one-of-a-kind collectible objects. Detail also what you hope to offer in the future. If you plan to carry any well-known brands, mention them. Also, explain how you will be sourcing your product and any contingencies you have should your supply be interrupted. (Remember, this is not a pointless exercise. This is reality. Ask yourself hard questions.)

Market Analysis: Introduce this section by explaining why you are entering the market. Why is it an attractive market and what facts or numbers support this? (Do some research at *www.census.gov* and *www.stats.bls.gov.*) Name the three or four different customer segments you are targeting. Give these segments or psychographics creative names ("rock star in training," "Beatles zealot," "vinyl purist"), which give them some identity and reality. Provide a brief description of them. Finally, generally explain why you are focusing on these segments.

eBay TIP: Don't go overboard describing your market segments. Information for information's sake doesn't make you money.

4.1 *Market Segmentation:* Give more detail on the market segments you mentioned in your Market Analysis. Each segment should be described in a short paragraph. Most eBay businesses will base their segments on their customers' buying patterns, but don't ignore more classic methods of market segmentation, such as grouping customers by demographics: age, gender, income, education, and occupation. Applying these demographic categories to your psychographic segments will help you merchandise individual products to your customers more effectively. Your market segmentation is usually accompanied by a segmentation table, which includes segment percentages, and a more visual pie chart.

4.2 *Segmentation Strategy:* Here you outline the strategy behind your segmentation. Give the specific reasons why you have chosen one segment over another, why your chosen segments are your focus, why you have given some more priority than others.

4.3 *Industry Analysis:* In light of your segmentation, provide some industry analysis. Cover the size and concentration of businesses in your industry, how products are distributed, and your core competitors. Finally, detail what factors are most significant in influencing purchases. Is it product quality and selection, price, or convenience? On eBay, same-day shipping, Buy It Now pricing, and seller branding and merchandising might also be noted.

Strategy: Take a paragraph to summarize your business's core strategies in regard to marketing and sales. As an eBay business, don't just say your strategy is to market and resell items on eBay and your Web site. Provide bullets that highlight how you will leverage eBay to merchandise your products and acquire customers on eBay, citing specific eBay tactics, seller tools and products, and merchandising programs. (We'll cover this in Chapters 8 and 9. Also, read Dennis Prince's *How to Sell Anything on eBay . . . and Make a Fortune!*) If you have a Web site, explain how you will drive customers to it to upsell them other products.

5.1   *Competitive Edge:*   What is your competitive advantage over other vendors, including eBay sellers, in your niche? What distinguishes you? What's the dramatic difference between you and others? It could be trade and appraisal experience, proximity to suppliers, brand awareness, reliable cash flow, an evolved shipping apparatus, relationships with local technology integrators and database programmers, insider access to restricted supply. Finally, bullet out why this is a long-term edge and not easily duplicated by competitors.

5.2   *Marketing Strategy:*   Outline your techniques for promoting your merchandise and generating sales leads. Even as an eBay or online business, you might mention advertising in online and print magazines. Bullet what eBay marketing services you'll use (eBay listing upgrades, eBay Keywords, eBay Stores). Describe how you'll drive commerce between your Web site and eBay listings. If you are a brick-and-mortar, explain how you'll integrate eBay into your physical storefront. Finally, remember your different segments will probably require different messages.

5.3   *Sales Strategy:*   Explain how you will turn your customer leads into actual sales. Highlight tactics and customer incentives that will trigger transactions but not erase your margins. Examples: low, convenient Buy It Now pricing within your auction listings; free shipping with premium products; rebates on group purchases. Sales strategy also relates to operations. If you have a team of listing specialists, how will you compensate them to raise performance? If you have a low-margin, value product that needs to be sold in volume, how will you automate ordering and fulfillment so that you can focus on inventory instead of front-end logistics?

     5.3.1 *Sales Forecast:*   A sales forecast table usually accompanies your sales strategy section. This spreadsheet projects your total sales and total product costs (subtotal of direct costs per sale) by month, quarter, or year. It often includes these projections:

         1   Unit sales: Estimated number of units sold per category

         2   Unit prices: Your price per unit of a product

         3   Direct unit costs: Your cost per unit of a product

         4   Sales/Total Sales: Your total earnings per product or line

         5   Direct costs per sale: Your total cost per product or line

The result: you estimate your monthly, quarterly, or annual revenue (total sales minus total direct costs).

eBay TIP: Strategy takes thought. It has to be specific enough to provide focus for your employees on a few manageable priorities. It also can't be so narrow that it stifles creative thinking and action. Take some time with this.

Management and Personnel: If you're looking for private funding or a loan, you might need to sell your management team and also provide a table that includes their names and salaries. If not, this section is more about helping you project your payroll. For clarity, discuss your organizational structure (departments, jobs, number of employees, and salaries) in a short paragraph and then table the information. Be sure to estimate the cost of unfilled positions. Don't set yourself up for a surprise. Think ahead.

Financials: A plan without financials is not a basis for business. In fact, it's not a plan. The financials section features several critical spreadsheets or tables that illustrate the profitability of your business by comparing sales to expenses. They include a projected break-even analysis, profit and loss statement, projected cash flow analysis, projected balance sheet, and business ratios analysis. We could dedicate a chapter to each, so we'll quit while we're ahead and just introduce what each one is for and point you to some online resources to learn more. Review these various forms in eBay's latest financial report: *http://investor.ebay.com/financial.cfm.*

    7.1   *Break-Even Analysis:*   Essentially, this illustrates when you will start earning a return on your initial investment.

    7.2   *Profit and Loss Statement:*   This statement enables you to calculate your business's "bottom line" or annual net earnings. It features the following components: total sales, cost of goods sold, gross margins, operating expenses, earnings before interest and taxes (EBIT) or gross profit, and more.

eBay TIP: Projected profit and loss tables also are referred to as pro forma income statements. Pro forma means projected in accounting lingo. The familiar term *bottom line* refers to the final line of a profit and loss statement.

    7.3   *Cash Flow Analysis:*   This table projects your business cash flow month to month (the amount of liquid capital in your bank account). This is critical, because profits don't equal cash, which you'll need on hand to pay your employees (if you have any) and, well, eat. At times you may have low cash *flow*, but you should never have a negative cash *balance*. As an eBay seller, a company with low cash flow can be a great supplier.

7.4   *Projected Balance Sheet:*   This is your end-of-the-month or end-of-the-year accounting of your assets, liabilities (debts), and capital (earnings). It's called a balance sheet because your earnings are your assets less your liabilities. Components include cash, inventory, accounts payable, accounts receivable, accumulated depreciation, current borrowing, retained earnings, and more.

7.5   *Business Ratios:*   This is a complex topic you'll want to do some reading on, but essentially ratios enable you to compare the performance of your business to the industry average. There are profitability ratios, activity ratios, liquidity ratios, debt ratios, and many more.

Before we start talking about how to use your business plan, here are a few other interesting components you might want to incorporate into your plan, if your are heading into a crowded, competitive market, of which eBay music is one. One is called a S.W.O.T. analysis, outlining your company's core *S*trengths, *W*eaknesses, *O*pportunities, and *T*hreats. This analysis can be presented in a chart or in four brief paragraphs. It fits nicely in your Company or Strategy sections. You might also want to have a Controls section, featuring among other highlights a Milestones table, which features important project dates for you to hit, and a Contingency Planning section. If your general assumptions about your market, competitors, sales, and expenses are wrong, what will you do? Well, give it some thought now and provide yourself an answer.

THE BENEFITS OF YOUR PLAN

Business plans serve a number of purposes that new eBay entrepreneurs need to keep in mind. As previously mentioned, they can greatly enhance an entrepreneur's understanding of his or her business and its real prospects. It's better to get a reality check about your business before you start it than while you are running it. Plans also are a prerequisite for investment, even from family and friends. People don't like to throw good money after bad. (They did that in 1999.) These days even your dog will want to see your numbers, talk it over, think some more, and then *maybe* invest. Cozy fireside chats help, but they won't seal deals.

What else? Good business plans don't just get written and put on the shelf. If they include milestones and pro forma financials, they are living documents that help your realize your goals. Your plan is your way of measuring your projections against your real results and gauging your success out of the gate. It thus becomes one of your most valuable motivational tools, helping you push yourself and rally your troops in order to realize your plan objectives. If you hadn't put your financial goals down on paper, how would you know how to grade your performance? You might not, and that could spell disaster. There's a difference between successful and unsuccessful businesses. The successful ones don't stop evaluating their progress and refining their strategies, tactics, and processes.

Good business plans also help you forge vital relationships with important partners, most notably suppliers. Some distributors will sell you product on the spot if you have a resale license and good credit, but most supplier relationships are not forged in an afternoon over the phone. According to one prominent off-price CD PowerSeller, there's no shortcut or substitute for hard work when winning over new suppliers. "That's where I spend all my time and resources," says this top music seller. "It could be the end of the year before you have your first meeting with a person. It can take that long to build a rapport with someone."

Besides being a good introduction and pitch, business plans are often the yardsticks by which many suppliers measure potential resellers. Why? Well, distributors are business people, and they know that writing a business plan isn't easy. Business plans aren't something you bang out in an afternoon in front of the ball game over a few beers. In essence, good plans show that you are serious about your enterprise and that you understand issues that matter, namely, the costs and liabilities of running your business and its potential profitability.

"The first thing I tell new businesses is write a business plan, do a feasibility study, do your homework and figure out where the opportunity is," explains Scott Robertson, director of marketing and communications at the International Music Products Association, also known as NAMM. "It's important to understand who you are and who you are not. I think too many Internet businesses open up and want to be everything to everyone."

Suppliers also appreciate a good plan because it enables them to do some due diligence before they get too involved with a reseller. If your plan adds up, it will give potential distributors some confidence that you can actually meet their minimum orders and create enough cash flow to pay them, according to their terms. Even more important, it will suggest to them that you want to do business with them for the long haul and that you'll have strong inventory turn and be filling orders regularly. "I think all distributors are interested in building long-term partnerships," agrees Robertson. "You make it about their business, as well as your own."

Just like retailers, distributors are under pressure to turn their inventory in order to satisfy customers (other suppliers and manufacturers), recoup their costs, create cash, and pay their bills, not to mention make room for new shipments. The faster you can sell their merchandise, the happier and more profitable they'll be. Why? Because that probably means you'll be ordering more.

A well-presented business plan will be invaluable at important trade shows in conversation with suppliers. It will provide you a means of introduction and give you the professional edge you need over other buyers. Moreover, if you have nothing to leave with an important contact at a booth, what's the likelihood they'll call you or remember you when you follow up? Pretty slim. If you are able to schedule sit-downs with distributors at events, you'll need something to present, preferably your business plan (with sharp charts, graphs, and tables) on a laptop. You may want to simplify it into a PowerPoint executive summary, but you will have something to work from only if you have written a plan.

RESOURCES YOU CAN TRUST

From software packages to books and Web sites, business plan resources abound. Take advantage of them; they will make the plan process much easier and help you craft a polished, well-organized product that isn't missing any key components. Here are some of the best sites on the Web.

- *www.business.com*
- *www.allbusiness.com*
- *www.paloaltosoftware.com*
- *www.quicken.com*

Remember, business plans are not exercises. They are a means to an end: your success.

6

Strategies for Building Your Inventory

Becoming a success on eBay takes hard work and perseverance. Don't be fooled into believing otherwise. To keep your business climbing that stairway to heaven and your employees (if you have them) singing, "We are the champions, we'll keep on fighting till the end," you'll have to avoid scores of minor and major pitfalls. One challenge, though, that most serious sellers claim trumps all the rest is the issue of reliable supply.

Building a successful eBay business from the ground up and sustaining it over the long haul require developing dependable sources of inventory and eventually, in the case of commodity-oriented products (recorded CDs and the like), swimming upstream of your initial suppliers to reduce your costs.

"My biggest problem is getting enough merchandise to sell," explains eBay music memorabilia PowerSeller Larry Lancit, president of U.S. Trade Discount (eBay ID: axop). Located in Naples, Florida, Lancit is also involved in concert event management and promotion. "Authentic autographed items are hard to come by, and have to be verified with photographs. I could probably sell much more and create all kinds of campaigns to increase sales, but I might run out of items to sell, and disappoint larger customers."

Dennis Sullivan of value guitar reseller MusicLandCentral (eBay ID: dsull31068) is one of the top sellers of Jay Turser guitars in the United States. He gives a similar answer when asked the inventory question. "That's probably the hardest part of the whole thing, getting somebody to sell to you," says Sullivan. "I think it took us seven months to find a manufacturer to start working with us."

Geff Ratcheson of Dandylion Records (eBay ID: dandylion_records) also understands the difficulties of sourcing product in his niche—out-of-print and import CDs. "Now, there's considerable competition for inventory sources in CDs," he says. "Acquiring unique value-priced product is becoming more difficult as competition keeps increasing."

Figure 6-1   Sourcing exciting items, like this vintage Slingerland drum set, signed by Buddy Rich, doesn't happen every day.

Vintage vinyl PowerSeller Robert Bergmann of Boogie Bob's Records (eBay ID: boogiebobsrecords) wouldn't argue with that assessment. His advice: "Buy whatever you have in your area and are fortunate enough to locate."

Procurement doesn't have to be the bane of your business. After all, millions of items are sold on eBay every day. Tens of thousands of resellers are obviously meeting the challenge. Having enough supply just requires focus and knowledge. This chapter will cover the basics of supply and the advantages of buying from different types of sources; how to locate quality sources in our three areas; what's required to do business with various kinds of suppliers and dealers; and finally, how to be a good partner and maintain strong relationships (see Figure 6-1).

BASICS OF SUPPLY

One of the keys to procurement in the music industry (and any industry, for that matter) is identifying what supply nodes (or links) in the chain, from manufacture to liquidation, are best for your business and customers. After all, not every business has to sell "Class A" inventory to satisfy its market segment. Some buyers might have other priorities, namely, they prefer a low price over bells and whistles or even condition. You don't need a Steinway Grand if you're still trying to master playing "Chopsticks" on the piano, for instance. By the same token, it doesn't matter how inexpensively you can source a product if it doesn't meet your customers' expectations or if it's inappropriate for your business's brand. "Even if you can buy something for X, if you can only sell it for Y, it might not be worth the money," notes MusicLandCentral's Sullivan.

The goal is to identify suppliers that meet your and your customers' needs at the lowest cost. That means understanding the various nodes in your industry's supply chain and how they can give you an edge. Of course, if your business is in rare items and collectibles, you have a different set of challenges, namely, identifying a niche in which supply is restricted, but not too restricted. Before we get too far afield, though, let's look at the major nodes for practical goods and collectibles.

Music Manufacturers

Manufacturers are actually somewhere in the middle of most supply chains. Upstream of manufacturers are producers of raw materials and components (from silicon chips and amp tubes to compact discs), distributors of these raw materials, and component-finishing companies. Once a product is ready for sale, it's either sold directly to consumers or sold to another set of middlemen who get it to market. From a reseller standpoint, buying direct from a manufacturer is arguably the best bet for building your inventory. Why? Because your unit costs will be lower since no other middleman has added margin to the product.

UPSIDE: Authorized dealers pay lower per-unit costs, enabling them to compete on price and still earn a reasonable per-unit gross margin. Sellers who buy directly from them also can offer their items with warranties, increasing their credibility with customers. "Partnerships with manufacturers is key," says Kevin Sanderson of instruments reseller MusicYo Direct (eBay ID: musicyo_direct), which specializes in budget guitars, starter percussion, and music apparel that it sources from overseas suppliers (Korea, China). "We travel at least four times per year to Asia to continually strengthen the relationships we have had for many years."

 eBay TIP: If you develop a name for yourself in music memorabilia, some record labels and artist management operations will sell merchandising memorabilia to you. More valuable memorabilia, original objects, and music equipment are reserved for large traditional auction houses.

"You have to build a reputation," says Darren Julien, memorabilia expert and owner of renowned entertainment memorabilia auction house Julien Entertainment. "Authentic entertainment memorabilia is a hard thing to get into, but once you're in, it's a tight-knit community. Hollywood's a small town. If you do something right, they hear about you; if you do something wrong, they really hear about you." He adds, "It's almost better to come out of the entertainment industry and then get into memorabilia because you'll have relationships on the inside."

Finally, dealers often get financial help with advertising and can buy significant quantities of supply on credit. "Most of these manufacturers will open up credit accounts for their dealers—they're not having to go out and get any personal backing," notes PowerSeller Eric McKenna of BoogieStreet WorldWide Guitar Sales (eBay ID: www.boogiestreet.com), one of eBay's largest premium guitar resellers. "I've never had any of that—I'm completely self-funded. It would be fantastic if a manufacturer came to me and said we want you to be a dealer and you can sell on the Internet, and by the way, we'll extend you $40,000 of credit for 45 to 60 days to sell our product."

DOWNSIDE: The majority of music products manufacturers have strict policies against dealers selling new inventory on eBay or the Internet, for that matter, in order to protect their dealers' regional prices. "A lot of companies still have that philosophy. They want nothing to do with the Internet," says PowerSeller David Brown of Pro Gear Warehouse (eBay ID: progearwarehouse), which specializes in pro audio equipment. "At our first NAMM show four years ago, we'd say Internet and they'd say, 'Well, it's been nice talking to you.' I mean extreme cold shoulder." Manufacturers tend to be more lenient with overstock and closeout or discontinued product, depending on the importance or size of that dealer's business. "In our experience, the attitude on B-stock has been that you can sell it for what you want, but you've got to clearly label it as refurbished or B," says Pro Gear Warehouse's Brown (see Figure 6-2). The same goes for discontinued products, according to Brown. "They'll let us sell it for whatever," he says. "Typically, we also buy that at a better price because the manufacturer is trying to close it out and just get it off the shelf."

Many manufacturers also require dealers to have physical storefronts or be what's called "stocking distributors," with stock already on the shelf. Initial inventory buy-ins and minimum orders can be steep for small businesses. Some manufacturers additionally require dealers to meet monthly, quarterly, or annual purchasing quotas. Most important, as alluded to above, they don't permit dealers to sell below a minimum advertised price, or MAP, to prevent channel conflict.

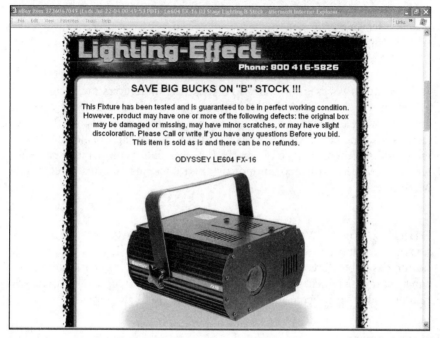

Figure 6-2 If you are selling a distributor's or dealer's overstock, often called B-stock, it's wise to advertise that in your listing.

Last but not least, some manufacturers more than others pressure dealers to support all of their products and marketing campaigns. "When you do finally get a supplier, they usually try to push you toward certain items in their line," explains MusicLandCentral's Sullivan. "The biggest mistake I think people make is buying into this and getting too much product or product that isn't selling real well. Avoiding this is probably the most critical part of your first order."

eBay TIP: The following music product manufacturers have policies against dealers selling new in-box merchandise online in order to protect their minimum advertised pricing.

- Fender (Guild)
- Gibson
- Grestch
- Martin
- Neumann
- Newmark Products

- Paul Reed Smith
- Schecter
- Shure
- Yamaha

Products you see on eBay from these manufacturers are secondhand manufacturer closeout, or dealer B-stock, the latter sold "sideways" by dealers to remarketers, who resell the product without a warranty. NetEnforcer .com is just one new company policing unauthorized sales of new front-line merchandise. Interestingly enough, the Big Five record companies (see Chapter 3) have been pressured by industry and consumer groups to eliminate MAP pricing.

OTHER FACTORS: When you work with music manufacturers, expect a a no-nonsense credit check (by the likes of Dun & Bradstreet). There are limited opportunities to buy direct in the recorded music industry. New music collectibles can be purchased direct and sold in volume. One example: new guitars, records, photos, and other ephemera with authentic in-person autographs.

Music Distributors

Distributors perform two essential services: they *aggregate* product and make it more *accessible* to resellers, shipping or trucking it to regional distribution centers. This increases efficiency and lowers costs for retailers, particularly those that are part of "highly visible" collaborative supply chains, which establish agreements with upstream suppliers, allowing them to share demand data and sales forecasts. Collaborative supply chains allow resellers to carry less burdensome "just-in-case" inventory, which can languish and become surplus, and sell more "just-in-time" inventory, which can be drop-shipped or purchased in the right amount initially.

There are an array of different types of distributors, so many, in fact, that it becomes a little problematic to discuss them all, but we'll try. There are logistics/transportation companies, such as Atlas Logistics, which refine supply chains and transport cargo to ports, distribution centers, and retailer warehouses by truck, plane, and train; importers, which arrange the transport of goods across borders with the help of freighters; and wholesalers, catalogers, or mail-order companies, which generally aggregate products for bulk purchasing, but don't take part in the transportation piece, but may drop-ship product to customers. One-stops also are an important supply node for small resellers in the recorded music industry. These are regional wholesalers that carry a variety of releases from multiple distributors, designed specifically for independents not large enough to open accounts with larger distributors. They not only supply but also help resellers with selection and merchandising. We won't go into rack jobbers, which set up in-store merchandising, such as paid end-caps, but they're another component.

e B a y   T I P :   NARM uses three criteria to grade one-stops: service, fill, and price—in that order of importance. *Service* is the one-stop's ability to provide timely information about new releases via mail, e-mail, and phone. *Fill* refers to the quality and depth of a one-stop's inventory and the rate at which it successfully fills reseller orders. A fill rate of 90 percent is good. *Price* relates to costs per unit. Service and fill generally decline as price improves.

One-stops to know:
- Alliance Entertainment (AEC) *www.aent.com*
- Baker & Taylor *www.btol.com*
- Super D *www.sdcd.com*

UPSIDE: Distributors provide resellers selection and value. This is particularly true in the recorded music category (see Figure 6-3). The *Music Products* category is still generally dealer oriented with a less robust distributor component, though independent reps do fill this role. Many distributors will drop-ship product to your customers, so that you don't actually have to carry product. This can lead to negative feedback on eBay, though, if you don't have a dependable manufacturer partner and shipments arrive behind schedule. If a manufacturer can't fill a rush order, a regional distributor can often deliver in the clutch. "There are some manufacturers who will not drop-ship, you have to bring the product into stock, even if you're trying to correct an error," says Pro Gear Warehouse's Dave Brown. "That's where having a few wholesale sources, selling the same products, can come in handy. You won't make as much money but your customer will be happy."

DOWNSIDE: Your costs increase and pricing position weakens as more middlemen handle your product. Many music sellers try to discover the suppliers and importers upstream of their sources for this reason. Like manufacturers, some distributors require fairly substantial buy-ins, minimum orders, and annual purchasing quotas. High-profile distributors can be choosy and deny small resellers. They prefer to support a select group of large accounts as opposed to a lot of little ones. Bigger buyers often get preferential treatment, reducing supply for small buyers—one reason not to drop-ship. And as with manufacturers, only volume buyers get discounts.

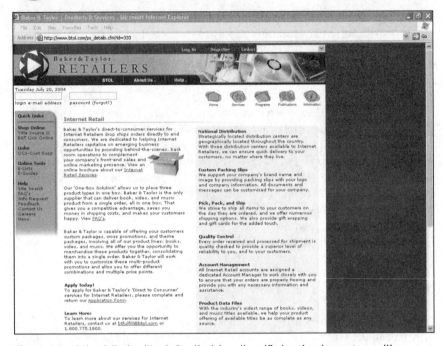

Figure 6-3   Baker & Taylor (North Carolina) is a diversified national one-stop, selling everything from books to CDs to DVDs.

OTHER FACTORS: You will need to pass a credit check. You'll also need facilities to receive shipments by the carton, pallet, and truckload.

Music Retailers and Dealers

We all know this link in the chain—the online and offline businesses that sell new stuff, Class A releases, front-line merchandise. Music products are still sold by a variety of retailers, from massive chains to corner stores, but channel share in the recorded music space is shifting dramatically to electronics chains and mass merchandisers, diminishing the role of small businesses. Also, music downloading—legal and illegal—is reducing new CD sales. "I'm more worried about paid downloads than file sharing," notes Dandylion Records' Ratcheson. "File sharing has mostly affected music for young people. If something like the iPod succeeds on a major scale, it could significantly reduce my collector market."

On the brighter note, NARM says online buying of recorded music is increasing dramatically. Consolidation in the music products industry by the large "full-line" stores (Guitar Center, Sam Ash, Brooks May Music), who can make volume purchases and negotiate lower MAP pricing, are putting pressure on small regional dealers.

UPSIDE: If you are a music remarketer, the retail node can be a great supply source for you. Regional retailers who are in a pinch to increase their cash flow will often sell overstock and remainders (still in box) to other resellers at or near cost. That's new product at a great savings without the restrictions of MAP pricing (or benefit of warranties). "I've partnered with a lot of dealers across the country that will move their product to me sideways," says BoogieStreet WorldWide Guitars' Eric McKenna. "I take their unsold inventory and put it on eBay new in the box, unplayed—the whole bit—and then price it pretty competitively compared to what people can find it for in a store. That's actually how I began to really grow my business." Retailers are eager to develop relationships with bulk buyers who have ready cash and the infrastructure to make these transactions fast and efficient.

DOWNSIDE: Off-price remarketers can't sell authorized dealers' overstock or discontinued product with factory warranties. Sellers that pretend to be authorized dealers are in VeRO's sites (eBay's Verified Rights Owner program). Small stores and regional chains will liquidate surplus to online resellers, but larger chains generally sell their "shelf-offs" and close-outs to liquidators and remarketing companies, which specialize in reselling off-price merchandise.

eBay TIP: Here are some common supply terms that get tossed around.
- Closeout: Remaindered stock that is discounted to clear it from inventory
- Discontinued: Remainder stock no longer being produced or distributed in the same packaging
- Refurbished: Secondhand product that has been refurbished in order to be remarketed
- Return: A returned product being remarketed by a manufacturer, distributor, or reseller
- Salvage: Damaged or end-of-life product sold in bulk at a steep discount

Remarketers, Outlets

The Internet has enabled many manufacturers and retailers to reap higher returns on refurbished, discontinued, and end-of-life product. Not surprisingly, eBay has become a major part of this business, as manufacturers and distributors diversify their surplus sales, selling their most attractive unit (sometimes referred to as Class B) through their own branded Web outlets (DellAuction is an excellent example) and selling the rest on eBay and other marketplaces, privately or under a separate brand (so as not to diminish their front-line identity) with the help of a third-party remarketing service.

UPSIDE: This is the eBay sweet spot, so rather than buying from these folks, you should be joining their ranks. If you can buy from them in bulk at a reduced cost, they might be a viable sourcing alternative. The larger the remarketing company the more realistic that is.

DOWNSIDE: Their pricing is usually for consumers, not businesses, preventing resellers from making a legitimate return on remarketer material.

Liquidators and Product Disposition Companies

Some surplus reaches a point at which it cannot be sold on per-unit basis for a profit. Marketing costs for individual products prohibit any real return. This product is often sold in bulk to a liquidator, which then sells it for a very modest return in bulk to another discounter or one-stop, which has to separate and remarket the pieces individually or again auction them in bulk.

UPSIDE: These types of buys are inexpensive. If you are a good merchandiser and skilled at making markets in unusual, niche material or exotica, liquidation loads can be a good source of material (see Figure 6-4). This is particularly applicable in the recorded music and new music novelty/collectibles categories, which support an incredibly broad range of tastes and lifestyle niches. For example, if you are a lifestyle dealer who sells your own lines of music apparel, buy a load of plain T-shirts cheaply and silkscreen them yourself with your own stylized designs.

DOWNSIDE: All goods through this type of channel are sold "As Is" and all sales are final. Most liquidators must be paid cash (that also includes checks). Items are sold without warranties or guarantees. Sometimes loads will have a high percentage of unmarketable material. True liquidation loads are generally not a good source for fragile, complex music products, unless you can recycle device components. Sideways dealer sales are best for nonauthorized music products sellers. Liquidators don't really play favorites and won't hold material for buyers.

Figure 6-4   Probably more than a few of these "one cent" CDs were purchased from liquidators.

OTHER FACTORS: The material is always sold in bulk on a first-come, first-served basis, often without a manifest or document elaborating what is in the load and the items' original pricing.

eBay TIP: Want to know what is in a liquidation load without a manifest (i.e., the list of what is included)? Consider the source—that is, buy loads from the same source. Material in loads from the same source will often repeat itself.

Auctioneers and Secondary Market Dealers

There are all kinds of auctioneers, from regional companies, auctioning business assets, to international fine art and antiques auctioneers (Sotheby's, Christie's, Bonhams & Butterfields) to specialty auction companies with focuses in sports memorabilia and Americana (Julien Entertainment, Lelands, MastroNet).

All of these auctioneers have something in common: They use dynamic pricing to establish an item's current market price, either because its value is unknown (due to age and condition) or because the item is special and will generate competitive bidding.

Secondary market dealers include regional dealer-brokers (who have relationships with collectors, estate sale reps, and other kinds of wholesalers) and open-air vendors (flea-markets, fairs, and collector shows), shows which deal in secondhand collectibles and practicals. (Open-air dealers that duplicate and resell copyrighted material, such as CDs and DVDs, prints and photos, and knock-offs of various kinds, are breaking the law. The risk they run depends on the tenacity of the affected rights owner. Most products have an individual use license, meaning you have the right to resell the product, but just once.) Finally, estate representatives are a kind of secondary-market dealer, selling property from estates for family heirs. A simple Internet search, such as "estate sales" −real +San Francisco, will locate companies in your area. Estate sale reps have something in common with the wholesalers and retailers discussed above. They are all sitting on inventory they need to move. That spells profit for you.

UPSIDE: No hassles—anybody can buy from an outdoor market or estate sale. Small Americana auction houses can be a good bet for buying and consigning. "My suggestion to new music memorabilia dealers is to buy on eBay or at auctions that aren't publicized very well and then consign their best material to higher-profile auction companies," says Darren Julien, owner of Julien Entertainment, which works with the likes of Madonna and Barbra Streisand. "That's where they'll probably get the most money." Business liquidation auctions are an inexpensive means of sourcing saleable product. (Get there early, though.)

DOWNSIDE: Liquidation auctions, flea markets, and other collector shows are open to the public, increasing competition. Product can be mixed and unreliable at open-air sales. Major auction houses can set steep reserves. Buyer premiums can be high.

OTHER FACTORS: Some estate sale companies have relationships with dealers and will sell property in advance of public sales. Get on agent and lists in your area.

Supplier Evaluation

Once you identify some suppliers, don't just start calling them haphazardly. Create a short list based on some key criteria, which we'll discuss now. A variety of factors make a good supplier, not just how low their prices are (though that is probably the most important element). When rating the bene-fits of a particular supplier, consider the following:

- *Product Quality:* Will the supplier's products meet your niche's standards and expectations? Will the products sell themselves or will they require excessive merchandising and positioning? Product quality is subjective, depending on your customers, but inexpensive is good only if your items sell at an acceptable gross margin and create cash flow. Remember this: if you use third-party sales management services and PayPal, fees can account for about 7 percent of your sales.
- *Catalog Strength/Variety:* Consider how diverse the items are in the manufacturer or supplier's catalog or dealer's inventory or collec-tion and if they will satisfy your eBay customers' needs in the short and long term. The last thing you want to do is promise a customer something that's on backorder or has already been sold. Before en-tering a relationship, make sure the supplier won't have chronic shortages.

eBay TIP: Finding suppliers takes some detective work. For-tunately, we have the Internet to help us out. When searching, try this formula, enabling you to search Web page titles.
- intitle: "[term]" –[conflicting term] –[conflicting term]
- intitle: "music distributors"
- intitle: "wholesale music"
- intitle: "woodwind distributors" –CD
- intitle: "music memorabilia" –sports –ebay –vinyl

The key: experiment and refine. To reduce unwanted results, pick out unrelated words on the results page and enter them into your search field with a minus sign, as above.

- *Product Price:* Before you buy, consider if you can still make a net profit on your purchase after you've subtracted your expenses and considered your competitors' pricing. Also, know that volume buy-ers get volume discounts. Additionally, keep in mind that if you are buying from a manufacturer or distributor, you might have to keep up with regular quotas. Be realistic about your real sales potential. Better not to agree to terms if you can't meet them due to the com-pany's pricing.
- *Terms, Commitments, and Restrictions:* Understand that your terms might be less favorable at the start of a relationship. Be careful of accepting terms that put you in a compromised position, requir-ing you to purchase product that's not right for your business or to

execute inappropriate merchandising schemes and campaigns. Do some homework before you convince a supplier to work with you. Don't agree in a panic to a program that's not right for your brand. That'll be bad for you and for them.

- *Incentives:* Consider if the supplier provides you incentives to purchase in volume, such as lines of credit, percentage discounts, or free drop-shipping. Find out if the supplier wants to make you a collaborative supply partner that shares demand data, enabling both of you to have a just-in-time inventory model.

- *Supplier Location/Distribution Points:* Location of your supplier is important, probably more than most people think. Don't rack up major costs shipping your product to where you keep your inventory (whether it's your house or a warehouse). Go the extra mile to find one-stops that are in your immediate vicinity. Pick the closest suppliers that meet your product and cost requirements. You might even consider drop-shipping, but this can complicate customer service. The closer the supplier, the faster you can get products into your inventory and into your customers' hands. Don't get caught out-of-stock, or S.O.L., as they say.

eBay TIP: Things to think about:
- How much to order
- How much inventory to hold (safety stock)
- If you should drop-ship (manufacturer or distributor ships your orders)
- If you are able to carry "just-in-time" inventory (inventory by order)

SUPPLY FROM THE INSIDE: STRATEGIES TO CONSIDER

Enough theory, let's hear from some successful eBay PowerSellers on how they uncover new sources, maintain supplier relationships, and protect themselves during the buying process. This is just a sample. We'll discuss more specifics on this topic in our industry-intensive chapters to come (Chapters 11–13).

Establishing Relationships

In the new instruments trade, buying direct from manufacturers is the norm, but that doesn't means it's easy to do. Even in value-priced instruments, which have proliferated on eBay (for better or worse), it's getting tough to become an authorized dealer, particularly because the word is out that overseas manufacturers have generally embraced the Internet (including eBay) as a front-line channel. Moreover, some factories are selling direct online themselves. According to Sullivan of MusicLandCentral, eBay sellers who specialize in this category need to become a sleuth and dig up factories that have not ventured onto eBay (see Figure 6-5). "My suggestion to anybody starting out is to find a supplier that doesn't have a whole lot on eBay already and try to sell them on that fact," he says. "Tell them, you can move a lot of product on eBay and that you want to build a relationship." You might even try to convince them to supply only a few eBay marketers to control their supply on eBay. According to eBay PowerSeller David Brown of Pro Gear Warehouse, quite a few mail-order companies in the pro audio and DJ space haven't taken the plunge onto the Internet. "They don't quite have the knowledge and/or they haven't invested the time and money to do it," says Brown. "Also, selling online had a bad ring for awhile and they didn't want to be associated with something that people perceived as dragging the industry down. I think that's changing."

Another strategy for establishing relationships is to make a presentation to a supplier and prove that you can market and merchandise their inventory

Figure 6-5   MusicLandCentral now offers its own brand of value-priced guitars, Sanatoga.

better than somebody else (all's fair in love and business). "There are a lot of people on eBay that don't do a real good job of presenting some suppliers' products; they don't put a whole lot of effort into their listings," says Sullivan. "Find someone who isn't selling a manufacturer's product real well and do a pitch to that company. Tell them 'Look, I have the ability to do it like this, I think your product will sell better if we present it like this.'"

People trying to source resale property in the vintage instrument trade will benefit from a physical storefront, says Mark Morse of Mark's Guitar Shop (eBay ID: marksguitarshop), who has also invented his own brand of guitar slide used by greats such as Steve Miller, Billy Gibbons (ZZ Top), and Pete Anderson (Dwight Yoakam). Essentially, storefronts provide an entry point for secondhand gear from hobbyists, musicians, and other dealers. "As far as the used stuff goes, a lot of it just walks in the front door," says Morse. "I buy stuff off the street almost every day, paying far better than the pawns do, keeping my selling customers happy." It also pays to advertise that you buy these types of instruments, according to Morse. "We advertise that on the radio, we advertise it on the front of the store, we advertise it in newsprint, we advertise it on eBay, we advertise it everywhere," he says.

Leveraging his store (which he pictures in all of his eBay listings) also has been more effective than attending guitar shows. "Shows are mildly important; I don't go to too many anymore," says Morse. "Everybody selling wants too much money and buyers don't want to spend any money." What about buying products on eBay to resell on the site? He says this works "A little bit, but not too often because the prices are too high. You've really got to buy right so that you can sell at the right price. If your profit margin is only ten percent and six to seven percent of the sale goes to the eBay/PayPal machine, you're not going to make squat." He adds: "When I do buy on eBay, I use a bid sniper [an auction utility that automatically makes last-second bids on items]. It does the work for you with pinpoint accuracy." When quoting an offer to a seller, Morse usually knocks 30 percent off his eventual price.

eBay PowerSeller Larry Lancit of U.S. Trade Discount has outside associates who help him source his specialized merchandise. "My primary sources of inventory are the people out there 'running' after autographs," he says. "They are a special kind of person, who will overcome all obstacles to get the authentic goods. I also buy some of my autographed albums from longtime collectors, but in all cases, I am very particular about who they are and where the pieces have come from. I prefer to deal with sources that are in the business of getting autographs regularly, who can provide me photographic proof and also are willing to swear by affidavit that the merchandise is real. Sellers on eBay who can provide the volume and variety of authentic product that I need are frankly not there."

Maintaining Relationships

Besides just being a marketplace, eBay is one of the Internet's best resources for current pricing data. Use what you learn about current values to develop mutually beneficial relationships with your suppliers. If your business is large enough, consider investing in software and technology that enable you to share demand data with your suppliers so that they can make smart sourcing and manufacturing decisions, too.

That's what MusicLand has done with its prime guitar manufacturer Jay Turser, which markets instruments from Asia. "We are watching patterns they can't see; they're very interested in that," says Sullivan. For example, MusicLandCentral shares sales data on popular colors, options, and even prototypes with Turser. "We are so big with them now we're almost partners," says Sullivan. "When they are getting ready to do their monthly orders, we sit in on that call." Another way to earn points with suppliers is to show an interest in servicing their product, says Brown of Pro Gear Warehouse. "I always inquire about product training, so I'm showing an interest in learning the product," he explains. Having experience selling online via eBay and other sites also makes a big difference. "I've learned how to sell my products online, so I have a sales history to back me up."

If your strategy is buying excess inventory from retailers and dealers (a practice some appreciate and some don't), your approach fills a need in itself. That's the way Eric McKenna of BoogieStreet WorldWide looks at it. "There are a lot of dealers out there that have new stock in their stores they can't sell," he says. "They're dying to get rid of it at cost or lower. I come in and provide an outlet for their headaches." Turning sourcing into service also often earns buyers greater leverage in their relationships with distributors and retailers. "I see product that we've turned down go to somebody else, and it doesn't do well," notes one volume CD seller, who preferred to go nameless.

In the vintage vinyl business, Robert Bergmann's advice is to return favors (see Figure 6-6). "Treat your sources fairly," he says. "A lot of auction houses and estate sale people don't have a clue as to the value of records. If you buy something cheap from them and it sells big, then you should take care of them the next time you buy from them." He adds: "When buying in bulk, pay a fair price for the items you know you can move right away and take the rest as a favor to the seller."

Buying Smart

Authenticating collectible objects and grading the sales potential of new products is another major supply challenge, of course. Dandylion Records' Geff Ratcheson does the following when vetting his secondhand, off-price CDs. "I check CD's under regular light bulbs for scratches," he says. "Fluo-

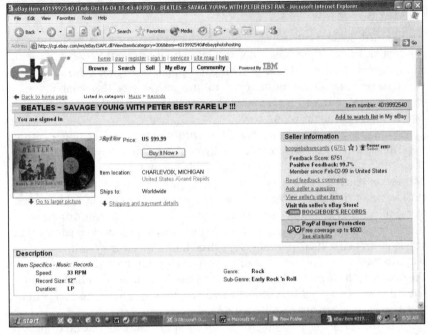

Figure 6-6   Boogie Bob's Records sources much of its vinyl from estate sales.

rescent lights and sunlight are useless; both hide scratches. This may be the most important thing I can mention for new sellers." Ratcheson also tracks prices generally before going out to buy: "I'll check eBay sales histories for given items before buying and offering them," he explains, referring to the two-week sales histories that eBay makes available to registered users. Vintage guitar dealer Morse uses eBay's completed items search as a tool for researching Blue-Book pricing on inventory as it comes through the door. "That's probably the most useful feature on the whole site," he says. "I'd rather learn from somebody else's mistake than my own. If something isn't selling, I don't try to reinvent it or sell it."

What about authenticating potential stock? That comes with experience and revisiting your references, online and in print (see Chapters 10–12). "It's like if you're going to sell cars, you've got to go out and look at them. You've got to know where to find the Bondo," says Morse. "You have to get in the trenches and try to remember everything you see and learn from it." If you do make mistakes, don't worry too much, Morse adds. It happens. "You will get burned once or twice, but just deal with it," says Morse. "It's not as rampant as you might think, but there is some good fraud out there." Vinyl dealer Bergmann buys sure bets or items that are just different. "I buy what I know we have sold in the past and what I haven't seen before," he says. "Do not overstock on common items." His advice for new sellers: "Buy cheap. Price items cheap. If you feel they should sell higher, then use a reserve auction."

Music memorabilia eBay PowerSeller beatle421 doesn't draw unnecessary attention to himself when buying. "Keep your knowledge to yourself and make little of being a dealer," he says.

MusicYo Direct's Kevin Sanderson considers how his customers might feel when buying music equipment. "It comes down to the question would I be willing to accept this if I were purchasing it," he says. "Occasionally, we will offer returned, blemished items, but they're noted as blemished." MusicYo also makes limited buys in new items before it invests significantly in them: "We test any new item on our Web site before implementing them on eBay about 90 percent of the time."

You can come up for air now. Did you get all of that? Don't worry, there's more information on building your inventory in our industry chapters in Part 3. For now, we're going to move on to targeting actual customers on eBay. How do you get them to notice the stuff you're selling? With more than half a million music-related items on eBay every day, that can be challenging. Fortunately, there are some creative solutions to this head scratcher, which you'll learn now.

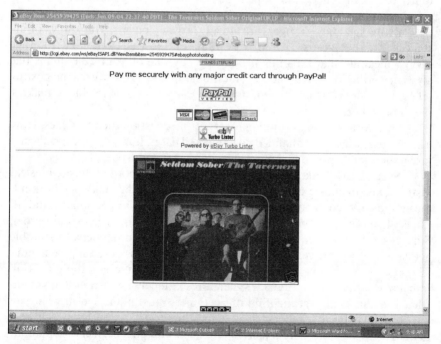

Figure 6-7 Now, here's a U.K. LP you don't find every day, but perhaps not the credo busy eBay sellers should live by.

7

Targeting Music Customers

Every day (and night), thousands upon thousands of music fans seek out items in eBay's three core music categories—the new CD by Usher, a Selmer Mark VI tenor sax, an original psychedelic poster by Stanley Mouse, and much more. This is one of eBay's core benefits: it provides a built-in customer base. For sellers, the "Open" sign is always on, guaranteeing them a certain number of potential buyers.

Better yet, eBay shoppers are already targeted buyers. You know, for instance, that they are registered with eBay and at least somewhat Internet savvy—meaning that they might not only buy one of your eBay items but also later go to your Web site for additional merchandise where the cost of selling is lower. Most important, most are ready, willing, and able to make a purchase online.

Once you're up and running on eBay, the question then becomes, How can you reach the *right* qualified customers? That is, how can you specifically target those buyers who will most likely purchase your specialty items?

Specialty is the key word here. As a seller of recorded music, musical instruments, or music memorabilia, you have a specific customer in mind: music fans and collectors, recording enthusiasts and professionals, and all kinds of musicians (students, part-timers, collectors, and even studio pros). Sure, it's nice to get an occasional surprise buyer who happens to stumble across one of your items, but those sales should be considered supplemental. Think about it: If you are looking for a mattress, you're not going to walk into a piano showroom, right? It's therefore extremely important that you do what you can to attract the kind of customers most interested in what you have to sell. To do this, sellers rely on a few time-tested strategies, which we'll discuss in this chapter. We'll also highlight several effective services that attract buyers. By chapter's end, you'll have a better idea of how to market your listings and target the people who are most likely to make a purchase from little ol' you.

CALLING ALL CUSTOMERS

Before you start marketing your business and items, devise a system of tracking your sales and reviewing the performance of individual products in your inventory. Why? Well, you want to be able to evaluate if your eBay marketing and merchandising is working. Sometimes you can find that out only by actually listing what you have and reviewing the results. Review your sales data for a few quarters to determine if everything in your inventory appropriate for your customers and if some units require more specialized marketing strategies. It's quite probable that you'll drop a few items after doing some analysis or shift some items to fixed pricing in your eBay Store. "Every quarter we go in and look at what's selling, where it's selling, and even at what time it's selling," explains Greg Niekerk, sales and promotion coordinator at sheet music retailer WindMusic Plus, which uses Microsoft Access to database its sales.

If you're unfamiliar with database software (Microsoft Access or File-Maker Pro), then look into one of the third-party sales-management applications from companies such as Andale, Channel Advisor, Infopia, Marketworks, and Vendio. These applications generally feature sales-reporting functionality. In other words, these programs actually track how specific items are doing for you. Additionally, off-the-shelf accounting or inventory management programs, such as QuickBooks and PeachTree Accounting, have sales report capabilities that help you track how various items are trending on a daily, monthly, or quarterly basis. (Having a real accounting package is advisable, if you plan to go far.) Another option: online "back office" services, such as NetSuite.com, which provide online business applications and secure data storage.

"You can't do this on paper, you've got to embrace technology," explains Eric McKenna, owner of BoogieStreet WorldWide Guitar Sales (eBay ID: www.boogiestreet.com). "In Quickbooks, I track every expense I have as well as final net margin on all my pieces. Once a month, I run a report and review where my guitars are trending. Back in 2000, I made $580 on one of my custom guitars. Now I'm making $900 on it."

MUSIC CATEGORIES MATTER

Once you are able to accurately and effectively record your sales data, you can really start listing. That means listing your items in the proper merchandise categories and subcategories. That may sound like a no-brainer, but you'd be surprised how often merchandise gets mislisted on eBay—and thus winds up unnoticed and unsold. While the majority of buyers use eBay's search tool, many still browse by category. If you're selling a Miyazawa or Sankyo sterling flute, then you don't want to list it in, say, *Brass*, because the most qualified buyers will likely never see it. And if they do, they'll probably not believe it's the real McCoy. Carefully consider category selection. Which one best suits your item? Which one will help you reach the most buyers?

Niekerk of WindMusic Plus found his company was best served by listing its sheet music in the most general sheet music category and related wind instrument categories. "I used to list in a lot of the sheet music categories, but not much really sold. I realized that not many of our customers are looking to buy sheet music specifically," he explains. "They're usually parents or players browsing for other things, such as a mouthpiece or some horn oil, and then they happen on one of our pieces and buy it."

Understanding your categories is especially important as eBay continues to expand and redefine its category structure. Make a point of keeping abreast of recent changes. (As a music seller, you can do that by bookmarking the following page: *http://forums.ebay.com/db1/forum.jsp?forum=38*). (See Figure 7-1.) eBay is adding categories on a regular basis as buyers and sellers demonstrate increased demand in new areas. Additionally, eBay's Item Specifics tool, already

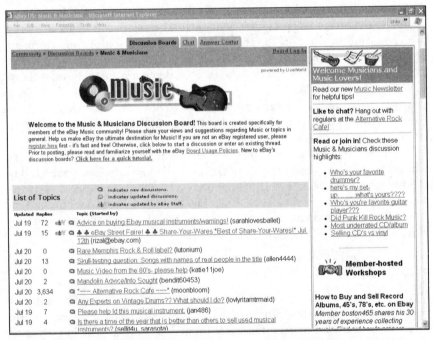

Figure 7-1 Make a habit of visiting eBay's Music and Musicians forum to track category changes and attend useful workshops.

available in *Music*, is reshaping many categories by providing sellers new, more specific categories in which to list. Consider this: back in January of 1997, *Music Memorabilia* wasn't even a Level II category. It was represented by a few small categories in *Books, Movies & Music*.

e Bay   T I P :   If possible, avoid eBay's *Other* categories, offered in almost all of eBay's categories. eBay has done some research on this vague category and found it's a poor performer. In fact, it has started to warn sellers that listings in this nebulous category are less likely to sell.

In some cases, two categories might be appropriate for a particular item. If this is the case, consider cross-listing in a second category. That way, you target two different customer segments and increase the chances of a sale. eBay's Listing in Two Categories option allows you to easily do this and, in turn, attain a larger, select audience. This is particularly effective if your item appeals to two different types of buyers, for example, Beatles enthusiasts and autograph collectors, or Gibson Les Paul fans, looking to complement their ax with a vintage Marshall stack.

According to a study by The Parthenon Group (commissioned by eBay), the Listing in Two Categories enhancement can increase bidding and price by 15 and 18 percent, respectively. The catch: this "listing upgrade" doubles your insertion fees. It's really only wise to use when you have a sure-fire hit in both categories, which will attract competitive bidding.

TARGETING WITH TITLES

Another way to target customers on eBay is to make the most of your listing titles. Again, this is pretty straightforward. A seller's titles should alert would-be buyers to the pertinent product information—what you're selling, its condition, its history, and other important facts. Take the time to craft informative and professional titles. Strive to be accurate, to be comprehensive, and to convey your passion for your product.

e Bay   T I P :   eBay listings now appear in general Internet search results. As a result, popular search terms in your titles and descriptions will increase the exposure of your eBay listings with buyers on and off eBay. MusicLandCentral (eBay ID: dsull31068) buys sponsored placements on Google and other search engines partly so that it can gain access to their search term reports, which show what terms in different categories and industries are most popular with Internet users. You can do the same. The terms inform your sourcing (see the previous chapter) and also provide you keywords to put in your titles and descriptions to attract search traffic. Of course, only include terms that relate to what you're selling. Adding terms erroneously to steal traffic is known as keyword spamming.

Titles are like billboards for your music goods. If they don't communicate the proper information, then people will not bother to stop and take a look—the very people you're trying to target. Write titles that are brief but informative. Most important, at the end of the day, include relevant keywords for buyer searches. If someone is a Pink fan, and you only list the name of her CD in your title and fail to mention her Pink-ness, your potential customer will get his or her Pink fix from someone else.

Avoid typos, too, unless you know the misspellings are often mistakenly used as search terms. Titles and descriptions marred by typos not only appear unprofessional but also prevent buyers from finding your listing when they do a search. For example, a search for recording software from "Cakewalk" won't do you any good if your title mistakenly says "Cake Walk."

Rock memorabilia PowerSeller Roger Pavey (eBay ID: thewyzyrd) doesn't take any chances when targeting his listings at potential customers (see Figure 7-2). "I'll write, for example, 'Beatles 1964 Concert Tour Program

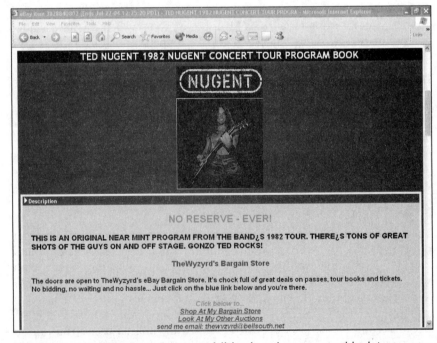

Figure 7-2 PowerSeller Roger Pavey, specializing in rock programs and backstage passes, captures multiple searches by including multiple search keywords in his listing titles.

Book,'" he says. "It's pretty redundant, but if someone is looking for a program, it'll get there, if someone is looking for a tour book, it'll get there, and if somebody is looking for a concert book, it'll get there. You've got to kind of play that game."

Devise your own visual style for your listing titles, creatively applying different characters and capital letters. This will brand your listings and give your buyers a visual cue when browsing search results or index pages. Here are some good examples from several eBay music sellers. A few tweaks can make all the difference. Notice how TastyCDs includes dates to differentiate its listings.

- SMASH MOUTH CD Get The Picture? (Kent's Source for CDs)
- Beatles: George & Ringo 1962 AUTOGRAPHS + Prov & COA (mtmworldwide)
- ALBERTA HUNTER—AMTRAK BLUES—NEW CD (Nambca Music Plus)
- PINK FLOYD The Wall 1982 1 sheet Movie POSTER (uforick-posters)
- Music Of Many Colours—Fela Kuti (CD 1996) (TastyCDs)

"I make all my titles look the same, I make all my ads look the same," notes PowerSeller Pavey. "Buyers might not always recognize it's me, but something will be familiar to them and that could encourage them to click on my listing."

THE RIGHT DESCRIPTION IS CRUCIAL

When targeting customers, it's also crucial to understand the value of your descriptions. This is significant eBay real estate at your disposal. (Each of our intensive industry chapters—Chapters 10–12—gives tips on listing content.) Here's your chance to go into detail and offer more information about your item, as well as give an overview of your sales policies, in regard to payment and shipping. (For more on developing good general terms of service, pick up Dennis L. Prince's *How to Sell Anything on eBay . . . and Make a Fortune!*) Customers can then zero in and see if this is in fact what they're looking for.

Of course, it also is imperative to demonstrate your expertise in your listings. Why? As we discussed in Chapter 4, buyers feel more comfortable purchasing goods from someone who's an expert in their field. Showcase your command of the merchandise you're selling. In your description, include product specifications, trade-specific terminology, precise product grades, facts about provenance, and, when appropriate, references to identification guides. For example, if you are selling a vintage Fender telecaster, you might want to provide an image of the stamp on the body-end of the guitar's neck, proving that it's an original neck. For added credibility, you also could provide a reference and page number that authenticate the stamp. (Richard R. Smith's *Fender, The Sound Heard 'Round the World* has such a photo, p. 289. See Figure 7-3.)

When appropriate (if you're not a volume seller), pepper your descriptions with interesting historical facts and notes that add color. This, too, targets customers, in that they'll know you're a seller who can educate them about your products and guide them through the buying process. When customers feel safe and secure, there's a greater chance that they'll buy. Showing yourself to be an expert also will attract buyers who are interested in forming long-term relationships—you know, those *repeat* buyers.

Take your listings to the next level by developing a listing template that is tailored for specific types of buyers. This is a great way to appeal to buyers' tastes, and it affirms your status as a leader in your field. Understand that different items, namely, those that are vintage or antique with lots of components, need to be more heavily illustrated than others. Review other sellers' listings in your area to see what lengths you should go to. If your listings are not on par with your competitors', lacking, for example, close-up photos for authentication, then qualified customers will probably ignore your listings,

Figure 7-3 Example of the stamps used to date the production of Fender's guitar necks. Earlier Fender necks also featured the guitar tech's initials.

reducing your sales. Sometimes you do have to keep up with the Joneses to target the best customers. In contrast, if you're selling generic items, such as CD-Rs, you don't even need photos. (Tailoring listing templates and photos will be covered in more detail in our industry chapters, Chapters 10–12.)

A LITTLE HELP FROM eBAY

When it comes to targeting customers on eBay, you don't have to go it alone. eBay offers several tools and services that will assist you in reaching out to the kind of customers you're after. Although it began as an online auction site, eBay now lets sellers offer items at a fixed-price as well. Individual items can be listed with Buy It Now, whereby the seller selects a set price, and once a buyer agrees to pay that price, the auction ends, and the sale is then completed. Sellers also can open their own online storefront, called an eBay Store, where items can be listed at a fixed price for 30 days and longer. (Good Til Canceled listings last indefinitely, if their listing fees are maintained monthly. They end only when purchased or manually ended.) Storefronts have become a major component of many volume sellers' eBay strategies, enabling them to effectively merchandise diverse product lines and also establish credible brands on eBay. Upgrading to a Featured Store (for $49.95 a month) makes this even more feasible, providing sellers valuable links and promotion on category index pages (in the left-hand margin) and on related eBay Store directory pages (see Figure 7-4). Upgrading from a basic to featured subscription is probably more advisable for music sellers with broad product lines that depend on volume sales.

"My whole strategy is predicated on moving people to my Store," explains Pavey. "That's what my goal is, not necessarily making money from my auctions. And, it's really beginning to work. I would say 15 to 20 percent of my sales are now in my Store. I couldn't have said that last year."

BoogieStreet WorldWide's McKenna is a little more conservative: "For anybody starting out, I think an eBay Store is imperative to have, but I also believe it's important to post all of your items in the general listing area." Presenting buyers with different pricing options—auctions as well as fixed-price items—will broaden your opportunities. Some buyers prefer the fun and excitement of an auction, while others would rather complete the transaction as soon as possible. By providing both types of listings, you appeal to both types of customers. Additionally, you can use your regular eBay listings to drive traffic to your eBay Store, where you can up-sell buyers other items—variations, complementary products, or accessories—that you also are currently carrying, not to mention give customers the ability to search your Store inventory, free of competing listings.

Your Store's cross-promotion tool (previously dubbed the Merchandising Manager), which comes standard with all subscription levels, makes this even easier. It allows you to merchandise four other items from your inven-

	Michael Jackson RARE CD Box set of ALL his solo albums	$373.62	-	Jul-26 07:25
	5 Complete Karaoke CDG Sets 152 CD+G Disc's 2200 Songs Sweet Georgia Brown-Country Karaoke-Hip Tracks-Nutech	$369.99 $374.99	- =BuyItNow	Jul-25 20:00
	5 Complete Karaoke CDG Sets 152 CD+G Disc's 2200 Songs Sweet Georgia Brown-Country Karaoke-Hip Tracks-Nutech	$369.99 $374.99	- =BuyItNow	Jul-20 20:00
	SOUND CHOICE KARAOKE FOUNDATION 1 SERIES .NEW New ...Unopened..Great Price!	$365.00	=BuyItNow	Jul-20 20:17
	SOUND CHOICE KARAOKE FOUNDATION 2 SERIES .NEW New ...Unopened..Great Price!	$365.00	=BuyItNow	Jul-21 05:37
	Queen 20 CD RARE wall mountable boxset	$350.00 $450.00	- =BuyItNow	Jul-27 06:37
	THE CARPENTERS-JAPANESE BOX SET RARE CD SET	$325.00 $350.00	- =BuyItNow	Jul-25 13:34
	DEPECHE MODE ~ MEGA RARE, "SONGS OF....", PROMO BOX ! !	$305.00 $850.00	8 =BuyItNow	Jul-24 06:30
	LED ZEPPELIN-JAPAN LP SLEEVE BOX SET RARE	$300.00 $350.00	- =BuyItNow	Jul-24 14:17
	THE MOODY BLUES JAPANESE PROMO LP SLEEVE CD BOX JAPAN	$300.00 $350.00	- =BuyItNow	Jul-24 17:20
	Alphaville Dreamscapes Boxset, Rare, Autographed!	$300.00	-	Jul-23 12:43
	500 Different CD Lot Collection - $299 Instant Collection! All 500 CDs are DIFFERENT! $299	$299.99	=BuyItNow	Jul-26 11:00
	David Sylvian - Weatherbox (MINT COND.)	$280.22	-	Jul-22 19:21

Figure 7-4 This Featured Store placement can increase your company's visibility rapidly. Of course, it'll cost you.

tory in other Store listings and, even better, your regular auction and Buy It Now listings. You can set up the cross-promotion tool to run on autopilot and randomly place items in the listing placement (at the bottom of your listings) or get more hands-on and match specific items with other items, such as XLR microphone cables with digital recording interfaces from the likes of M-Audio, Fostex, or Tascam.

eBay TIP: Driving buyers to your Store can significantly lower your eBay costs, particularly if you are a volume seller of commodity-style goods. With Store listing fees (for now) still just five cents and standard eBay insertion fees ranging from $0.30 to $4.80, based on your item's opening value, Store sales are quite a bit kinder on your margins. In fact, some volume sellers are using their auctions just as advertising for their Store listings to reap this cost benefit.

Four spots aren't enough for some sellers and they develop their own merchandising tables and placements in their HTML listing templates, showcasing additional deals and accessories. Some sellers are also now embedding their Store search box directly in their listings, so that users can search for additional items directly from a listing. The idea: once you have captured a qualified buyer (one who has clicked on one of your listings), try not to let them go—keep them in *your* universe. We'll delve deeper into this idea in our industry chapters. Your Store provides several other innovative customer-marketing tools, including the ability to export your Store listings and data (via an XML file, extendable markup language file) to a third party to be published on another Web site, for example, such as a product search engine.

eBay TIP: Up-selling is merchandising complementary products to a customer at the point of sale. Product accessories are typically up-sold with bigger ticket items, such as additional packs of strings or a guitar stand with a new guitar.

eBay Keywords

Keywords on eBay are, well, key, and they're the basis for another interesting eBay service, designed to help sellers generate qualified leads for their material. Almost 80 million times a day, someone types a keyword into eBay's search box. eBay Keywords operated in conjunction with AdMarketplace (*https://ebay.admarketplace.net/ebay/servlet/ebay*) takes advantage of that fact. It works like this: First, sellers select specific words or phrases that they believe buyers will use to search for their items. Then, when a user performs a search and there's a match, a targeted banner ad—linking to a specific item or eBay Store—appears above the buyer's search results (see Figure 7-5). Nice? You bet. This high-visibility advertising links you directly with qualified buyers who want the type of merchandise you're offering. (Interestingly, sellers bid on how much they'll pay for a banner click. The higher a bid, the more likely the banner ad will appear. Also, sellers can control the total amount they're willing to spend for a particular campaign.)

Speaking of high visibility: eBay's Gallery listings also remain a popular and effective way to reel in more customers. One of several available listing upgrades, Gallery inserts a thumbnail photo next to your listing on category index and search result pages. At a glance, buyers can see a picture of the item you're selling. You also get placement on the "Gallery View" pages. (According to eBay statistics, Gallery listings can potentially increase final sale prices by 12 percent. They also are 10 percent more likely to sell.) Other listing upgrades include Gallery Featured (premium placement in "Gallery View" and a photo that's twice as big as a normal Gallery photo), Featured Plus (places your listing in the "Featured Items" area that appears on index and search result pages), and Bold (adds boldface type to your list-

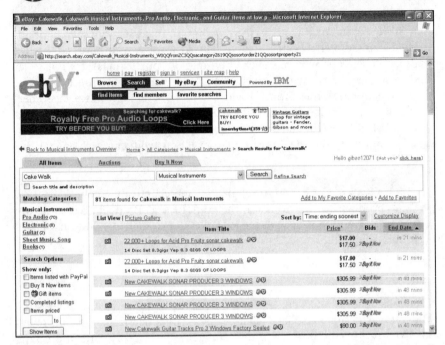

Figure 7-5 Here's an example of an eBay Keywords banner ad, advertising Cakewalk computer-recording software.

ing title). All of these services involve additional fees, but they promote your goods and attract more buyers. It's an investment that many eBay sellers find well worth the cost. The new Subtitle upgrade ($0.50), for example, is getting to be a favorite of David Brown of Pro Gear Warehouse because of the length of his product names. "By the time you get done putting in the manufacturer name, the part number, and 'New' in your title, you don't have much space left," he explains. "So, subtitle is becoming important."

Not all sellers invest in upgrades, though. Like all of eBay's fee-based services, upgrades get to be expensive, particularly when PayPal transaction and third-party auction management fees are factored in. "A lot of times, the upgrade isn't worth the cost," says Brown of the more traditional listing enhancements. "If you're trying to drive people to your Store to find other things, then it is advantageous to use them."

Generally, this is autograph PowerSeller Larry Lancit's (eBay ID: axop) view, as well: "We have done this from time to time, and it has brought more people to our other listings and to our Web site, so it seems to be a nice feature for the right kind of special item."

As an alternative, many sellers just list more items, which can generate a buzz all by itself (particularly if they have a unique look). Of course, for this to work you have to have enough items to list, which can be difficult if you're a dealer in one-of-a-kind items. Our advice: use upgrades to get some initial visibility for your eBay brand and then let your listings speak for themselves.

eBay TIP: To validate its listing upgrades, eBay commissioned a study by the Parthenon Group, analyzing the benefit of upgrades on bidding, final price, and sales conversion. During the study:

- Bold ($1) was shown to increase final price by an average of 25 percent
- Featured Plus! ($19.95) was shown to increase sales by 28 percent
- Gallery ($0.25) was shown to increase final price by an average of 11 percent
- Highlight ($5) was shown to increase bids by an average of 12 percent and price by 15 percent

A free way to increase your listing traffic and sales is by filling out your Item Specifics, so that buyers can search for items more precisely. It increases sales by 10 percent, according to eBay numbers.

Give Them a Second Chance

Another eBay service helping sellers cultivate relationships with buyers who might otherwise slip away is Second Chance Offer. Second Chance Offer works just like it sounds, providing nonwinning bidders (the folks who lost one of your auctions to its final winning bidder) a second chance to buy from you. The service consists of an automated form, provided by eBay, that is sent to nonwinning bidders if (1) the winning bidder backs out of the sale, (2) the reserve price is not met, or (3) a seller has a duplicate item that a buyer might want to know about. The service is free, and Second Chance Offers can be sent up to 60 days after a listing ends. For Brown's business with significant supplies of duplicate products, Second Chance Offer has become a valuable sales-generation tool. Of course, we're not trying to toe the company line here. If you're smart enough to embed your company's phone number in your listing templates, About Me page, and Store descriptions, then buyers will probably just call you to inquire about another duplicate listing.

What about targeting customers outside eBay? That's an option, too, thanks to eBay's Co-Op Advertising Program (*http://www.ebaycoop advertising.com*). Under the program, eBay pays part of your advertising costs when you run ads in offline print media, such as magazines, newspapers, newsletters, catalogs, and even handbills at major shows which promote and advertise your eBay business. For its part, eBay will reimburse you 25 percent of your advertising insertion fees. To be eligible for the program, you must be a PowerSeller and have an eBay Store or participate in the Trading Assistant Program.

eBay will even help you build your ad with its Ad Creation Wizard. One of the program's benefits is that it provides targeted promotion in the venues where you're likely to locate your core customers—music aficionados, musicians, and so on. In addition, you might pick up new customers who previously were not familiar with eBay. Unfortunately, the Co-Op program does not support online advertising yet. A related kind of program is eBay's Store Referral Credit (*http://pages.ebay.com/storefronts/referral-credit-steps.html*). If, by promoting your eBay Store in materials *off* eBay (e-mails, printed materials, and other Web sites), you generate sales of a Store item, then eBay will credit you 50 percent of that item's final value fee, good toward future final value fees (see Figure 7-6).

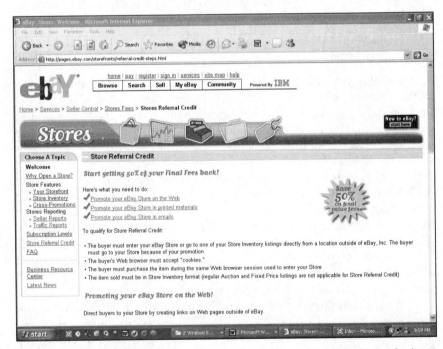

Figure 7-6   eBay's Store Referral Credit program can reduce an item's final value fee by 50 percent.

RETURN TO SELLER

So whether you expand your audience (and save some money) with a Co-Op ad or snare a buyer with a Second Chance Offer, you have many smart ways to target your customers. It's all part of a seller's job. Getting the word out about your eBay sales takes time, effort, and money, but in the end you'll be rewarded with a bigger, better customer base.

Of course, once you target and draw in the customers you want, the next step is keeping them. Offering perks and incentives, such as free shipping, can nudge a buyer back in your direction. Still, the best way to turn a customer into a repeat customer is to impress him or her with a smooth, successful transaction. That means answering queries and shipping in a timely manner and exuding an air of professionalism at all times, among other things. Remember: One successful sale leads to other successful sales. Impress them the first time around and there will be a second time . . . and third . . . and fourth . . .

8

Tips for Boosting Sales

Now for the fun part: completing some real sales. It's time to get people to buy what you're selling en masse (or in profitable amounts, at least). In this chapter, we'll talk about fine-tuning your sales efforts and turning up the wattage on your sales—taking those customer leads, generated by your eBay marketing and off-site networking and advertising (perhaps through eBay's Co-Op advertising program), and converting them into actual transactions. That's often easier said than done. Earning customers' trust online can be a challenge for the simple reason that the customers can't actually hold your products in their hands and vet them in person. Also, you don't have the opportunity to look the customers in the eye, shake their hands, and make your pitch in person. Thanks to the ceaseless white noise of Internet marketers, bombarding users with junk mail, pop-ups, and faux Web sites, buyer fatigue is another problem. Quite a few customers suffer from Internet exhaustion even before they arrive on eBay. As a result, they can be cranky, apprehensive, and impatient.

You often have a small window to make the right impression in your eBay listings. So how do you overcome these inherent obstacles? You develop quality customer policies and marketing practices, which demonstrate that your business is honest and transparent and that you offer true value—a great product at a good price. The worst move you can make on eBay is to leave details to your buyers' imaginations. Online buyers don't really give sellers the benefit of the doubt. More often than not, you're guilty until proven innocent on the Web and on eBay.

So, let's get to it. Let's isolate some important strategies and tactics that make your business and items more attractive to prospective customers, give them the confidence to make a purchase, and help you build a repeat customer base. The following rules apply to all kinds of sellers, whether they're selling the San Francisco Symphony's latest concert CDs, mass-merchandised KISS action figures, or handmade Breedlove banjos and mandolins. Some of these strategies and tactics are just common sense, and some might surprise you. Both have the desired result: more cash in your register.

ERRORS AND OMISSIONS

Before we get to the strategies, let's quickly cover some common pitfalls you should know about before you get serious about your eBay sales. For starters, don't underestimate the work required to make your eBay business a success, particularly if you intend to build and maintain a Web site that complements your eBay enterprise. (Launching a Web site in tandem with your eBay effort or soon after you start selling will enable you to use eBay as an advertising vehicle for your company and brand.) You'll be surprised how time-consuming eBay really is. Talk to a few experienced sellers and that's exactly what they'll tell you. Even if you are automating your operation with one of the third-party or eBay sales-management tools, making the most of the eBay opportunity still requires real diligence and attention. It can take over your house, take over your life, and keep you busy morning to night, if you're not organized and smart about it. From sourcing inventory and bulk-listing product to communicating with buyers and fulfilling orders to refining your processes, listings, and Web site, often there are not enough hours in the day to get everything done.

"It's tremendously time consuming," agrees vintage Hammond B3 specialist Dennis Delzer (eBay ID: oldspeed), who boasts one of the world's largest collections of original, living-room-ready B3s (see Figure 8-1). "If you're retired, forget it. You're not retired anymore when you start doing eBay." Delzer spent more than a year designing and launching his top-notch Web site (*www.b3hammond.com*) to complement his eBay listings.

One of the main reasons an eBay business is time-consuming is that the customer comes first. You often have to drop what you're doing and go out of your way to make the customer happy. (Of course, this is only true if you care about eBay feedback, and you should.) Also, putting out one fire can cause flare-ups somewhere else, which can throw you off schedule. You don't want to get into that vicious cycle and jeopardize your credibility. That's one reason to hire an assistant or two to help carry the load and master each step of the eBay process. "You need to have a talented, knowledgeable sales staff," agrees MusicYo Direct's Kevin Sanderson (eBay ID: musicyo_direct). "People tend to think they can build a Web page and start taking orders. It's not as easy as it looks or seems."

Another efficiency idea: bring in a local technology consultant and a software or database engineer. They're not cheap, but they can help you integrate your back-end systems with eBay to reduce manual data entry, not to

Figure 8-1 Dennis Delzer's Hammond B3 auction photos are second to none, but there's a reason for that. He puts a lot of effort into them.

mention automate checkout via your Web site (where you can up-sell other items and product accessories). These folks also can help you take advantage of the eBay Developers Program and the eBay API (application programming interface), which provides you a more direct, fail-safe link to eBay's servers. This is important for a number of reasons, but one of the most important is that it insulates your business from changes eBay makes to its site architecture, which otherwise might force you to redo listings and recue them in your listing tool. For some sellers, that can be a major burden, forcing them to retouch hundreds if not thousands of listings. Just ask PowerSeller Stephen Benbrook, owner of popular Zion's Gate Records (eBay ID: zionsgate) in Seattle, Washington. Early in 2004, Benbrook had to manually relist thousands of items because of an eBay format change. He's still trying to get back to his listing peak. Also, his sales dropped 50 percent for a few months. "It's definitely a lot of work, blood, sweat, and tears," says Benbrook with a laugh. "Most people assume it's the Internet and it's boom, boom, boom, and you're done. It's just not that way. Running an eBay business is definitely a daunting task and you are never done."

e Bay TIP: To learn how you can further automate your eBay business, explore the new Solutions Directory, aggregating a great variety of applications from scores of certified eBay developers. Just click on the *Service* link at the top of any eBay page to access it.

But It's Time Well Spent

Fortunately, time invested in eBay is usually time well spent, according to Pro Audio and DJ PowerSeller Brad Hagen of Musician's Advocate (eBay ID: musiciansadvocate), an authorized dealer of AKG, Mackie, Midiman, and Neumann products, among others. Doing the little extras, such as reflecting on sales policies, polishing listing templates, refining corporate identity, and mastering new eBay services, does pay dividends. "Using tools like the Merchandising Manager, setting up accessories in your eBay Store, cross-referencing products—it's tedious and it's extra work, but it's definitely worth doing. It's worth putting in that extra hour."

Another mistake to avoid is being overbearing with your customers. After all, one sale isn't worth tarnishing your rep. Rock memorabilia dealer Jeff Gold, owner of *Record*mecca.com (eBay ID: recordmecca) as well as a one-time senior executive at Warner Bros. and A&M Records, follows that oldest of customer adages (though he doesn't shy away from giving deadbeat bidders negative feedback). "The customer is always right, no matter what," he says. "In the short run, that seems stupid, but in the long run, it's the only way to do business." He adds, "If people are thrilled with you, they'll come back. If people have a so-so experience, they won't."

Hagen of Musician's Advocate also strives to be customer friendly and do what the other guy might not: "What people forget is that you have to take chances in this business, and, more importantly, you have to do whatever it takes to get ahead. There's a lot of competition," he says. "You have to take any kind of payment; you have to be willing to ship anywhere in the world (if permitted by the manufacturer); you have to be willing to go the extra mile. How many times can I say, 'Yes'—that's the policy around here. That's what separates the people that win from the people that are on eBay a few months, don't make any money, and quit." (See Figure 8-2.)

Another prerequisite for success is grasping the realities of the eBay market. For one, conversion rates are generally better for items with lower price points. "I sell lower end stuff on eBay, but higher-end material tends not to do as well because eBay is a bargain hunter's paradise," explains Gold of *Record*mecca.com. "I sell that stuff on my Web site." Equally important, items in so-so condition are more problematic on eBay, dramatically increas-

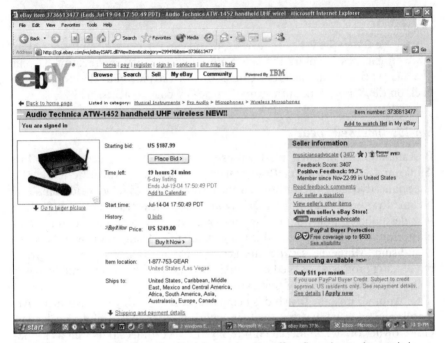

Figure 8-2 To go the extra mile, Musician's Advocate offers financing and extended warranties with its products on eBay.

ing phone and e-mail time. (Of course, if you are looking to generate inquiries, then putting up a hot item that will need some explaining isn't such a bad idea.) Some buyers just ignore items with problems because they can't review them in person. That's why guitar dealer Mark Morse of Mark's Guitar Shop lists only his clean inventory on eBay, items that aren't too problematic to photograph well. "There are plenty of guitars in my store that I could sell to people walking through the door that I wouldn't put up on eBay," he explains. "If a piece has issues, you need to be able to hand the item to the customer and explain the issues in person. You don't get that on eBay." David Brown of Pro Gear Warehouse (eBay ID: progearwarehouse) favors selling brand-name items on eBay over generic versions because buyers can't vet them in person. "On the Internet, I believe people feel better buying brands because they can't put their hands on the product," he says. "Now, if they were in a store, that might not be the case. Potentially, they could see one is as good as the other."

Another no-no is being dependent on drop-shipping. This means you don't actually stock the item. A distributor or manufacturer retains the product and ships it to your customer. The problem with this is that it puts the success and credibility of your business in someone else's hands. It does reduce stocking expenses, but it also increases your inventory costs and jeopardizes your ability to deliver in a timely fashion, which can lead to excessive negative feedback. Our suggestion is to keep a good stock of items and drop-ship when you are in a pinch.

> **eBay TIP:** Brad Hagen, Musician's Advocate: "For us, eBay is really an advertising and marketing expense. As well as being a marketplace, it drives traffic to our phones, to our e-mail, and our Web site. That's where eBay is most powerful."

If you are new to selling on eBay, it's important that you don't expect everything you list to sell the first time around. If you sell 50 to 75 percent of what you list, you are probably above average. Some argue that sell-through rates are plateauing, as more vendors enter the eBay fray. This is particularly true in CD sales, making it even more vital to have a complementary Web site, so that you can widen you net. In fact, the more you're able to leverage eBay as advertising, the further your eBay dollars will go. "eBay is an advertising vehicle that makes money," notes Zion's Gate Records' Stephen Benbrook. "I'm paying 50 cents each week to advertise this record and it sells 50 percent of the time."

Ditto for Brown of Pro Gear Warehouse: "I view eBay as an advertising mechanism. I mean we sell some stuff, too, but I'm more hoping the phone rings and we meet customers. And eBay really helps us do that."

Finally, don't play fast and loose with eBay's rules or your dealer agreements. The fastest way to derail your business is to get your eBay account suspended. "Basically, we walk very softly," says Hagen. "When in doubt, don't do it—that's our motto." At the end of the day, eBay is an automated, somewhat impersonal operation because it has to be. It has too many customers to really play favorites. That means you'll have to go through official channels, for example, e-mail, to get your concerns and issues addressed. If your account is suspended, it will take some time for your appeal to float to the top (even though eBay has hundreds of customer support reps). In the meantime, your business will suffer. Keep that in mind when you're considering something borderline. Save yourself some grief and follow the rules closely. If your eBay biz gets shut down, your crafty maneuvers won't do you any good. Finally, don't thumb your nose at your manufacturer's minimum advertised price policies. Unless they are legally challenged, you need to comply with them to maintain supplier relationships. Before you sign a dealer agreement, study it. Some manufacturers don't allow sales outside the United States or Canada or on the Internet, for that matter.

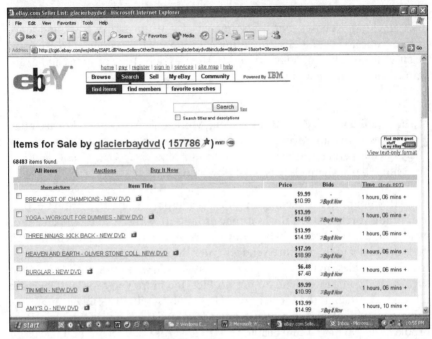

Figure 8-3   Notice Glacier Bay DVD's feedback rating at the top of the screen. Now, that's a lot of happy customers.

HIGH FEEDBACK

Positive feedback arguably will be one of the most important factors in your success on eBay. Having a few negatives isn't the end of the world, but it is critical to have an impressive feedback record (see Figure 8-3). Most highly automated volume sellers of music CDs do have some negatives; however, they also usually have a *lot* of feedback. It's not uncommon for sellers of commodity products to have tens of thousands of post-sale comments. As a result, their percentage of positive feedback can be very high despite having more negatives than the next guy. At the end of the day, both buyers and seller are imperfect. The important thing is to have an acceptable rating, at least 99 percent. As you dip into the 98 and 97 percent range, your sales will probably dip, too. "Feedback is incredibly important, I believe," notes eBay PowerSeller Roger Pavey (eBay ID: thewyzyrd). "Other than the item, it is the next most important thing. Then comes shipping and the price."

Remember, feedback is your reputation and your credibility. Take it seriously and your customers will take you seriously. "Buying online can be a very scary thing for a lot of people, especially when you put a comma in the price tag," notes specialty drum eBay PowerSeller Barry Knain of Indoor Storm (eBay ID: indoor_storm1), based in Raleigh, North Carolina. "The better your feedback, the safer your customer is going to feel."

What if you're new and you don't have a sales record? How do you prove you're a great seller before you've done enough business on eBay to garner significant positive feedback? Well, being a real business with a physical storefront, warehouse, or Web site helps. Guitar dealer Mark Morse (eBay ID: marksguitarshop) suggests doing some heavy buying on eBay and earning some positives from other sellers. David Brown of Pro Gear Warehouse did some simple extracurricular selling. "I bought a whole bunch of karaoke CDs really cheap and sold them really cheap," he says. "The goal was not to make money. The goal was to sell a whole bunch of them and earn a whole bunch of feedback."

Another question you should ask is, What's more important, having great feedback or being a PowerSeller? "It's more important that your percentage of positive feedback is high," notes Robert Bergmann of BoogieBob's Records (eBay ID: boogiebobsrecrods). Roger Pavey has another take: "I don't think being a PowerSeller really matters," he says. "The best thing about it is that you get access to a phone number so you can actually call someone at eBay." Our take is it's better to be a PowerSeller than not to be one. We prefer buying from PowerSellers. After all, PowerSellers earned this distinction because they've maintained a good feedback rating and a high volume of sales.

AUTOMATION

Automating your business processes is one of the best things you can do for your eBay business. There's no reason not to do it, unless you are just selling a few premium-priced items a month. For most eBay businesses, it makes a lot of sense to automate listing, post-sale communications, payment and shipment confirmations (with carrier tracking numbers), and the printing of invoices and shipping labels, not to mention the bulk posting of feedback and non-paying-bidder (NPB) requests. Both eBay's online and offline seller applications (Selling Manager and Auction Assistant) are solid tools for automating your business. Moreover, there are third-party sales-management tools that serve the same purpose (see Figure 8-4). Even if you are only listing 50 items per week, why not standardize your listings offline and then list them with one click of the mouse? It makes a lot more sense than listing every item individually via eBay's Sell Your Item page. All of these programs also have preset listing templates, which you can customize to your liking. In short, they make your listings look far more professional. (Of course, if you have existing Web site HTML and graphics, you should leverage those in your template.)

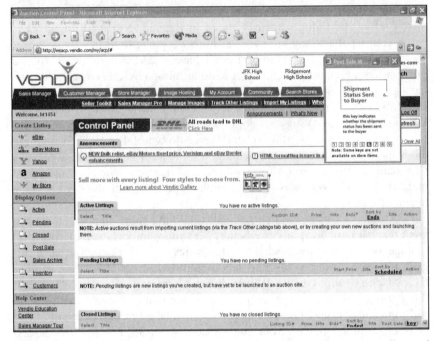

Figure 8-4 Vendio's Sales Manager tool effectively displays a seller's current, pending, and closed listings. The closed-listing key shows what stage a transaction is at.

 eBay TIP: Prominent Seller-Services Providers:

- Andale *www.andale.com*
- Auctiva *www.auctiva.com*
- Channel Advisor *www.channeladvisor.com*
- Infopia *www.infopia.com*
- Marketworks *www.marketworks.com*
- SpareDollar *www.sparedollar.com*
- Vendio *www.vendio.com*

Probably most important, these automation programs allow you to bulk schedule the launch of your listings offline. The listings then post automatically whenever you want. This way, you can set your auctions to close at desirable times, usually when users in multiple time zones are able to bid. Vinyl dealer Bergmann uses Auctiva's bulk lister to quickly upload his entire month's listings at once. "We list 1,500 to 2,000 items so customers have an opportunity to buy more than one item," he explains. "We try to schedule our launches so that customers on the West Coast can bid as late in the day as possible." In the final analysis, automating your back end enables you to spend more time on other critical aspects of your business, namely, improving your supply relationships and identifying new sources of product.

Using eBay's or another company's tool set is really just the beginning, too. If you are a recorded music or value instrument seller, listing hundreds or thousands of items a month, explore the aforementioned eBay Developers Program. MusicYo Direct has become a certified eBay developer. "Being certified allows us to combine all of our business systems with eBay for a smooth seamless shopping experience," notes MusicYo's Sanderson.

In brief, the eBay Developers Program helps vendors integrate the eBay API and make database calls to eBay's servers outside the site's standard listing forms. The result: they can list items and collect data related to their sales directly from eBay in real-time. One implication is that sellers are able to respond to customer demand more nimbly and fulfill orders more rapidly with fewer people. The program also offers a software development kit, or SDK, which among other things can enable bigger sellers to integrate their company's back end systems, such as a database or accounting and inventory package, with eBay via a Web-based checkout system (created, for example with Microsoft ASP—active server page).

In broad strokes, this would allow them to further automate order taking and reduce manual keying of orders into their accounting and inventory system. More advanced systems allow customers to communicate directly with a seller's back end system (via an ASP Web interface) and write orders directly to their accounting software's internal data files, eliminating the need for orders to be manually transferred from a post-sale management application. Scripts also are written to automate the listing of new inventory as the accounting and inventory system records sales. Yeah, pretty heady stuff. The downside: the eBay Developers program costs money (more than most small sellers can afford), and you need to be a developer to leverage it or have some IT people.

TRANSPARENCY

Successful sellers don't hide from their buyers. You'd think that would be common sense, but a lot of eBay sellers choose to remain anonymous and don't provide their potential customers a way to effectively communicate with them. This is a good way to reduce your sales. Buyers, especially those considering an item more than the price of a CD, generally want to get to know a seller before buying. Seriously consider including your phone number and address in your listings as well as on any of your other eBay pages. Also consider including a photo of your physical store, your warehouse, and a picture of you and your staff, if your business is at this level. Make your business real or people will have some doubt that it is.

"I always include all my information so they can call me," says Delzer of B3Hammond.com. "Call me, talk to me, I'm available. It's all about communication and availability." Percussion specialist McGinnis of Indoor Storm is also a believer in giving eBay buyers the ability to make contact before bidding and question them about the particulars of their business and merchandise. "A lot of people like the anonymity of e-mail, and that's cool, but a lot of people also want that peace of mind that there is someone on the other end of the computer screen," he says. "And, I welcome their calls. I make no secrets about what we do here."

 eBay TIP: Design a graphical header for your listing template that includes an image of your physical location and your phone number to connect with customers.

BRAND IDENTITY

You can have a great product, but if you don't have a great brand or recognizable identity on eBay, you won't go as far as you'd like. "In this game, it's all about marketing," notes Eric McKenna of BoogieStreet WorldWide Guitar Sales. "If someone isn't market savvy, they're not going to be able to do it."

The first place to begin is your business's name, which gets effectively promoted at the top of each listing once you open an eBay Store. "I think the name you have is important," says rock memorabilia dealer Pavey, who modeled his user name, thewyzyrd, after Lynyrd Skynyrd. "I don't think you can just blow that off. You have to come up with something that sticks in people's minds." Spend some time on your name. It's an opportunity that shouldn't be wasted. If you have a Web site, incorporate the URL into your name, sans the dot-com. Your name shouldn't be your e-mail, if you're doing this as a business, particularly if you use one of the Web e-mail services.

You should also design a compelling logo and corporate identity that communicate your value. You won't be taken very seriously without them. Eric McKenna felt so strongly about this that he hired someone to design a logo for him, only to later design his own, which he still uses. "When people see that BoogieStreet logo now, it's comforting to them," he says. "It sounds crazy, but it's true." At one point, McKenna even had a company mascot, his Dalmatian, Shelby. "He was at the bottom of every auction," recalls McKenna. "It sounds corny, but people started e-mailing me about it."

A word of advice about your identity and logo: don't live and die by them. If your business changes and your logo isn't sending the right message, give it a makeover. That's what McKenna did when his international sales become a significant component of his business. Today, he's BoogieStreet *Worldwide* Guitar Sales. Leading guitar effects PowerSeller Ryan Nixon also wasn't married to his initial identity and strategy; they evolved with his business, which has transitioned from discount to retail pricing. Once Effectsforless.com, he's now GuitarEffectsPedals.com. His eBay ID reflects the change, too. The change has paid off, though. He's replaced ineffective e-mail-for-price links with shopping cart functionality on his Web site and his sales have jumped, even though his prices are now higher. The moral of the story: customers are willing to pay a premium for convenience and privacy (see Figure 8-5).

Consider also extending the colors in your logo into your listing template to drive home your branding. Also consider developing a catchy slogan for your company, which spells out why buyers should pick you over the competition. Musician's Advocate has made this move. Its customer e-mails and listings often include: "JUST SAY NO!!! to the Megastores!!!!" If you come up with something truly memorable, stick it in your logo, in

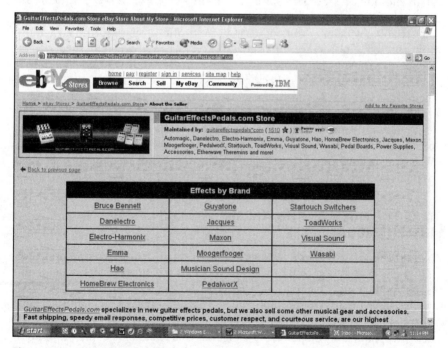

Figure 8-5 When eBay PowerSeller Ryan Nixon changed his business's name from Effectsfor less.com to GuitarEffectsPedals.com, he also updated his eBay username.

your listing template, on your About Me page, in your product news bulletins, everywhere.

eBay Stores also are important to your eBay identity and building customer awareness for your products. Why? They enable you to economically merchandise a spectrum of your products. As a result, customers can see how broad—or specialized—your brand is. This is key for tastemakers such as Zion's Gate Records, which sells a variety of different genres, from jungle to heavy metal to reggae. "Look at our eBay store, there's 22 categories of music," says owner Benbrook. "It's basically a virtual record store. And, it's driving a lot of people to our Web site. Our Web site hits doubled last month, which is really a big deal." As mentioned in Chapter 7, you can also upgrade your Store to increase its exposure. This also nets you valuable eBay marketplace reports, providing important stats and metrics on the general performance of your category. Before upgrading, get your store ready for prime time. Spend some time refining your categories, writing a compelling Store description, and designing an exciting logo. It's a waste of money to upgrade if your Store is generic and uninteresting.

It is critically important to take advantage of your About Me page. Try to keep your info focused on your business's mission, products, and history. (This shouldn't be too hard since you've already written a business plan. See Chapter 5.) In our view, descriptions of your pets and even your kids (unless they're actually helping you out) detract from your business identity. It's more powerful to include images of your staff and facility, if you have them. If you are set up to answer phone calls and receive mail, include your information. If you are a member of any collector groups, societies, or trade groups, include their logos on your About Me page. You can also turn your About Me page into a jump page for your Web site. Include links on the page to actual content pages on your Web site. Violinslover.com (eBay ID: violinslover) does a beautiful job at this. It's hard to see where its About Me page ends and its Web site begins, and that's exactly what you want—uniform, consistent branding on and off eBay.

TAKE THE MUSIC TO THE WORLD: INTERNATIONAL SALES

Not everybody sells music products internationally, but those who do generally think it's the best thing since sliced bread. If your business is small and isolated, then eBay's global audience can be a minor miracle. "You reach more people on eBay faster than anywhere else on the planet," notes musical instruments dealer Bobby Boyles, owner of BestPriceGuitar.com (eBay ID: bestpriceguitar). "I can put an item on eBay and 800 or so people will see it in three days. I can put it up somewhere else and eight or ten people will see it. I can put it in my store and two or three people will see it."

eBay TIP: If your dealer agreement allows you to sell internationally, make sure your products are compliant with overseas power sources.

International shipping can be more time consuming and risky, with the complications of customs forms and credit card charge backs, but once you master the steps, it can be a tremendous benefit to your bottom line. "You know shipping is the biggest hassle on eBay, but it's worth it," says Hagen of Musician's Advocate, adding that he has only about one bad international experience per year.

Music dealers that specialize in flatter, smaller goods, such as new or off-price CDs, collectible vinyl, instructional videos, sheet music and songbooks, and certain types of music memorabilia, are probably best positioned for international selling. Not only are these items less expensive to ship, they also aren't as readily available overseas. Even items that are saturated in the States can sell well internationally where such items are not readily available.

PRODUCT POSITIONING

Your brand isn't the only aspect of your business that gives you credibility. How you position your business and products gives you credibility, too. For starters, you have to expose each potential customer to as much of your inventory as possible. Give them as many options and choices as you can. They'll probably surprise you and buy items you wouldn't associate with the same buyer. "We've been sending out reggae and metal to the same person," says Benbrook of Zion's Gate Records. "There are people that are looking for totally different genres of music."

Your attitude on customer returns also will have a major bearing on your business's positioning. Because of this, we strongly advise you to guarantee your products and offer a no-questions-asked return policy. That's becoming the norm, particularly for music product sellers who cannot offer online buyers a hands-on demo. If you don't give buyers that opportunity, it's unlikely they will seriously consider your items. Knain of Indoor Storm provides a 48-hour trial period on his high-end drum kits. Antique violin PowerSeller Jaap van Wesel (eBay ID: jwesel) provides a money-back guarantee minus expenses. "You really have to play and hear an instrument," says van Wesel. "People can't make a truly informed decision from a description and a photograph."

Hagen also supports liberal return policies. "I see a lot of 'All Sales Final' out there and these sellers are only hurting themselves," he says. "If you sell good products and describe them accurately and answer questions in a

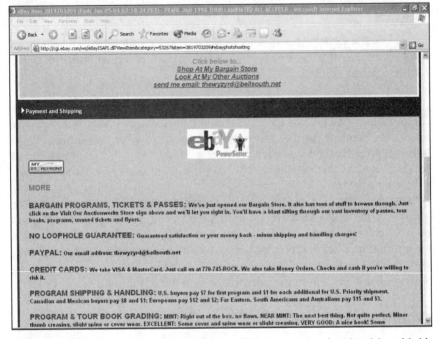

Figure 8-6 The Wyzyrd, Roger Pavey, offers a lifetime warranty of authenticity with his items, which he calls the "No Loophole" guarantee.

timely manner, 99 percent of your sales are going to stick." In the memorabilia business, a money-back guarantee is essential, particularly for items of significant value that collectors will want to authenticate post-sale. In fact, memorabilia dealers Roger Pavey and Jeff Gold offer *lifetime* money-back warranties of authenticity (see Figure 8-6). "I'm not in this business to sell you one thing, I'm in this business to have repeat business and have satisfied customers," says Gold. "If anybody is unhappy with anything they buy from me they can send it back. I don't care why, I'll take it back."

Recorded music sellers can probably get away with not offering a money-back guarantee, but economically that's probably the wrong route to go. A nice return policy will boost a seller's volume more than it will increase returns and refunds.

What else is important in regard to positioning? If you are part of a franchise, plug your dealership on all of your eBay pages and customer communications. In fact, this should be at the top of all of your listings, just below your description headline. Better yet, design a dealership promo into your template header or create a colorful seal that plugs it. If a buyer can't touch what you're selling, they'll want to know they can get it repaired if it malfunctions. This is particularly vital in the music products space. Of course, if you're not an authorized dealer, then don't pretend you are one. You not only run the risk of being arrested, you'll also be part of a group of unscrupulous sellers giving Internet sales a bad name. Nevertheless, according to Eric McKenna's experience, it is possible to sell instruments without warranties if they are new in box and guaranteed.

 eBay TIP: If you have a physical location, merchandise special items in your store and on eBay. If an auction ends without a bid, offer it to someone local who might have expressed interest in it.

Last but not least, if you have a click-and-mortar operation or just a Web site, make this clear to your eBay buyers. Like Mark Morse, include a photo of your store in your logo and listing header. This can do wonders for your initial reception on eBay. Why? Well, buyers are looking to buy from existing businesses. Also, they'll feel that they have some recourse if a problem emerges. They'll have someone to call or visit, not just a dead-end Hotmail address. For sellers without storefronts or Web sites, here's an alternative: include a small, tasteful picture of yourself in your listing. If you are a member of an important association with a legitimate code of ethics, include its logo and your membership number in your descriptions and eBay business graphics. The point, as previously mentioned, is to make your business less anonymous.

LISTING FORMATS

Some eBay listing formats work better with some items than others. Experiment to discover what formats are best for your specific products. You'll find similar items don't always perform the same way. "Very few times have I gotten concert passes involved in the auction process," notes Roger Pavey. "However, the reverse is true of programs."

To determine the best format, the first question to ask is, Will I make more money selling a particular item in volume at an attractive fixed price (and possibly not eke out every nickel once in awhile) or will I make more money on it when my customers determine its price (meaning I might lose money from time to time)? Conventional wisdom says that rare items should be listed as auctions to encourage competitive bidding and that low-priced items should be listed at a fixed price or as auction with a Buy It Now option. Unfortunately, eBay's new reserve fee derails this logic. At $5 a pop, reserves aren't very affordable for most sellers. (Just think: if you do 100 reserve auctions a month, you'll pay $500.) The reserve increase has encouraged many sellers to use Buy It Now pricing even for one-of-a-kind items, from custom guitars to authentic handbills.

In the final analysis, how much you invested in an item dictates how you list. If your price was low, you can probably afford to open low in order to attract bidders. If your margin is narrow and your price is close to retail, it's probably wise to open slightly above your cost and offer a Buy It Now at retail. Shoppers who appreciate convenience might go for the Buy It Now. Bargain hunters might bid, and that could initiate some competition, which is always good. Or you might just get one opening bid and make the minimum. Any way you look at it, you're protected. In the case of collectibles, you could also be more aggressive and open at about 75 percent of your desired price. You'll either capture serious bidders or just find out the item isn't worth as much as you thought, which is good to know.

Buy It Now pricing is particularly effective for sellers who have to comply with manufacturer minimum advertised prices but who also want to compete. The prevailing wisdom is to set your Buy It Now at MAP but start the bidding at a more attractive price, which still doesn't devalue the item's perceived value (see Figure 8-7). The wrong move would be to list ten of a MAP item in a Dutch auction, $50 below MAP. That'll earn you a call from your rep.

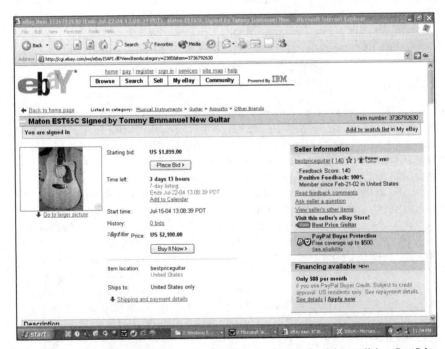

Figure 8-7 To comply with its suppliers' minimum advertised pricing policies, BestPrice Guitar.com lists its items with Buy It Now prices at the MAP.

Of course, there are Store items, too, eBay's best value. This format is ideal for economically selling slow movers or low-margin accessories. "You can switch an item over to your eBay Store for three cents a month and just sit on it until it sells—it's a no brainer," says Benbrook. Indoor Storm's Barry Knain agrees. "I do the smaller accessories, such as drum keys, there," he explains. "It just doesn't make any sense to pay $1 to list that kind of product."

A new trend is using auctions and Store items in tandem, enabling sellers to lower their eBay fees and also accessorize their sales. Here's how it works. List all your inventory in your Store. Then list your most popular items in eBay's general listing area. In each listing, provide links and other entry points to your Store. (Mark Morse provides a Store bookmarking link.) Before you know it, people will start going straight to your Store to buy, increasing your per-unit profits. Ideally, they'll also start to buy more of your accessories and product variations, cross-promoted with the Merchandising Manager in your Store and auction listings.

LISTING VOLUME

Most sellers also believe it's important to maintain a consistent and fairly high volume of auction listings to remain visible and attract new buyers. This is particularly important during the holiday months and post-Christmas sale season. "More product, more sales—there's a direct and obvious correlation," says Benbrook. Boyles of BestPriceGuitar.com is also on board with that. "The more hooks you have in the water, the more fish you catch," he says.

Besides keeping a presence in eBay's general listing area, it pays to offer some variety with your volume. This not only attracts new eyeballs, it also prevents your existing customers from getting bored. "You've got to mix it up and put up new stuff," advises Benbrook. "If I didn't do that, my repeat sellers wouldn't do as well. A wider array of products brings in a wider array of customers."

LISTING CONTENT AND PRESENTATION

Sloppily designed listings will get you nowhere fast. Give your listings and photos a unique, polished look and buyers will be more inclined to believe you're legitimate. While listing templates vary dramatically in style, those that make the right impression have a few things in common. For one, they don't feature massive blocks of impenetrable text. They have an appealing HTML layout, organizing and tabling different elements and pieces of information, from your item description and photos to your policies. The goal is to establish a hierarchy of information so that buyers don't miss what's important about your item and terms. Different-sized headers and subheads often accomplish this. The cooler templates also feature header navigation so buyers can quickly jump to specific sections, such as your shipping and handling fees or a merchandising box. Special features, such as a custom search box, are also possible with HMTL.

Powerful listings also don't give too much or too little information. They strike the right balance, so bidders are not left with more questions than answers or forced to scroll and scroll. The right *targeted* information also will reduce your e-mail. Effective listings feature practical details, not vague statements such as "Works Great!" or "Mint." Valuable descriptions note when an item was purchased, how much it was used, what's been repaired or replaced, if it's new in box, and what application it's best suited for. "Typically when people go on eBay to look at things they know what the product is. They don't need a two-page description of what it does," says L&M Music's (eBay ID: lmauctions) keyboard specialist Jacob McGinnis. "What they do want to know is, what's the deal: where did it come from, what kind of condition is it in, who had it, how much was it played, that kind of thing."

A stock dealer photo is fine for new, warranted music products. Likewise, eBay's Pre-Filled Item feature is a good bet for CD sellers. Used products need to be shot from all angles with good lighting, preferably against a backdrop or screen. Labels, serial numbers, distinguishing features, and any defects must be shot at close range. The guts of musical devices should be pictured as well, if removing the top doesn't cause damage. MusicYo Direct has a photo set and employs a staff photographer for its auction images. Boyles' team at BestPriceGuitar.com spends about an hour on photos for each listing. "I've got to do that photograph so that can the buyer can almost smell it," says Boyles. A few bells and whistles are worth adding, too. "We offer sound files of our drums to minimize hesitation on the buyer's part," explains Indoor Storm's Knain (see Figure 8-8).

COMMUNICATION AND FAST, RELIABLE SHIPPING

Frequent communication with buyers and fast, discounted shipping cannot be underestimated. Almost all the sellers we talked to ranked post-sale communication with buyers as vital to building a trusted repeat customer base. "E-mail, e-mail, e-mail—people want to know you've got their money, they want to know their item has been shipped out," explains Benbrook. That's another reason to use an automated sales-management tool. GuitarEffects Pedals.com has increased its prices and sales dramatically by offering buyers free Priority Mail shipping. WindMusic Plus offers free shipping to buyers who purchase additional items from its Web sites. That's been a great way to drive additional low-cost sales.

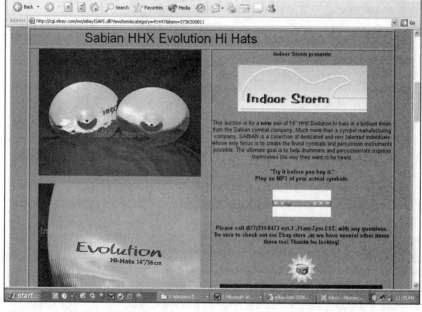

Figure 8-8 Here's a cool listing feature: embedded MP3s that allow buyers to listen to an instrument before bidding.

Musician's Advocate has a team of packers so that it can get its customers' items out the day they pay. "Usually, if we get an order by 1 p.m., we can get it out the same day. Also, we always e-mail tracking numbers and send follow-up e-mails. Follow through is the key in this business. People aren't just going to trust you, that's the reality."

9

Packing and Shipping Music Products

There's nothing like ringing up an eBay sale. Your efforts—finding inventory, researching the market, targeting customers—have paid off. But just because the cash register went *ka-ching* doesn't mean you can kick back and relax, flip that Miles reissue on the Hi-Fi, and sip your mint julep. The hard work in many ways really begins after a customer agrees to buy one (or more) of your products.

We're talking now, of course, about packing and shipping, one of the most challenging aspects of the sales process, especially for those who specialize in large or fragile three-dimensional objects, from record awards and Fab Four toys to Moog synthesizers and vintage Gretsch snares—any piece of recording or musical equipment, for that matter. If an item arrives damaged because it was poorly packaged or improperly shipped, an otherwise successful transaction turns sour. Fallout ensues—namely, unsatisfied customers and negative feedback. But fear not: the perils of packing and shipping needn't be your Achilles' heel. As with all facets of eBay selling, packing and shipping just require some thought and planning. By investing some time and effort, you can learn how to become a professional packer and shipper, no matter the size or fragility of your items. Proper shipping and handling obviously have their rewards as well.

"Shipping is one of the things that helps you most in this business. It's one of the main things that sets you apart from the Mom and Pops," says music memorabilia Powerseller Roger Pavey (eBay ID: thewyzyrd). "Ship everything as if you were going to ship it to yourself—keep everything uniform and professional. That basically tells the buyer that you believe the item inside is actually worth money. The subliminal message to them is 'Gee, this must be worth the money I just spent.'"

Before transforming yourself into a master of bubble wrap, though, you first want to do some prep work. Many sellers find it helpful to designate a specific room or space in their home or warehouse as their main shipping area. This streamlines the packing and shipping process, keeping all your necessary materials together in one convenient place. Create a packing assembly line—a place to prepare an item, wrap it, pack it, apply a shipping label, and so on. (Speaking of shipping labels: one way to save time is to use automated software that automatically prints out labels once an order is received.) Obviously, the more space the better, but even having a table or large desk devoted to all things packing and shipping makes a big difference.

Once that's done, go out and establish some relationships with local businesses that are looking to get rid of boxes you can recycle. Memorabilia PowerSeller Roger Pavey has a relationship with a Costco and Sam's Warehouse in Atlanta where his business is located. He takes long pieces of cardboard, used in pallet-size product shipments off their hands for free, cuts them up, and makes his own boxes. Mark Morse of Mark's Guitar Shop is also an avid recycler, reusing his manufacturer guitar boxes and packing supplies from local businesses as well as his own. "We always try to recycle instead of creating new garbage," he says. "There's a trophy shop across the street. When its trophies come in, they're packed in thousands of peanuts. The owner gives me bags and bags of the stuff for free."

At the end of the day, most sellers rely on a mixture of recycled and store-bought supplies. "Typically, I'll have to go out and buy some boxes and other materials a couple times a year," explains PowerSeller Eric McKenna of BoogieStreet WorldWide Guitar Sales. "It's a necessary expense."

With that in mind, you should locate a good retail outlet you can depend on, such as a UPS Store or any local office supply store. It's good to have the following on hand at all times: boxes, mailing tubes, padded envelopes, scissors, tape, butcher paper, markers and pens, an Exacto knife, a scale, newspaper, foam peanuts, and, yes, bubble wrap. If you want to avoid those long lines at the post office and further streamline the shipping process, think about purchasing online postage at places like Endicia.com, Stamps.com, and Pitney-Bowes.com, through the U.S. Postal Service's PC Postage® program (see Figure 9-1). This will allow you to print out postage on your own computer, saving both time (no more lines) and money (less gas). Once you start selling your CDs, '80s heavy metal T-shirts, digital workstations, or whatever it is you specialize in, consider bringing in a part-time shipping assistant (perhaps a local high-school student or retiree), who can work afternoons, packing and preparing your packages for delivery by one of the major carriers—often the best bet. "We have a specialist who has years of experience packing fragile items," says rock memorabilia PowerSeller Larry Lancit of U.S. Trade Discount. "We pack our items so that they can withstand the roughest handling

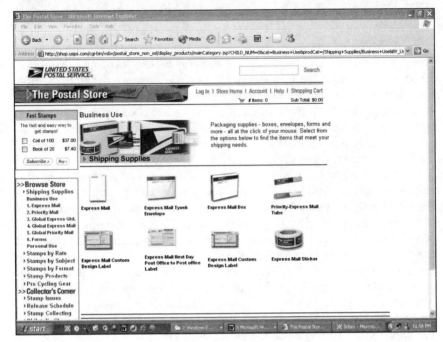

Figure 9-1 Order your U.S. Postal Service Priority Mail supplies online to save time and trips to the post office.

you can expect from shipping companies. We use lots of bubble wrap, styrofoam, and strong cartons. We rarely have problems. All of our labels are automatically printed by our FedEx software."

Of course, if you just sell pricey, one-of-a-kind items in fairly low volume, roll up your own sleeves and skip this expense. It's all about efficiency. Automate your packing and shipping system as best you can, so that when an order comes in it goes out quickly, competently, and professionally. The money you invest in your shipping process will be earned back ten-fold.

eBay TIP: Negotiate with the major overnight and ground shippers, such as UPS, FedEx, and DHL. If you ship enough volume, they expect it. "When FedEx and UPS wouldn't give me any discount on my international shipments, though I was doing some decent volume for a small business, I went to DHL," says Eric McKenna of BoogieStreet WorldWide Guitar Sales. "Much to my surprise, they were willing to work with me. Now, I can provide better pricing to my customers internationally."

PACKING SCHOOL

Next it's time to work on your packing technique. Like anything else, it will take some practice before you earn your packing wings. Even if wrapping Christmas presents has always been a struggle, it's still possible to become a top-notch packer.

First things first: box or envelope? Determine which is best for the item. Padded envelopes, or bubble mailers, are appropriate for CDs and small, flat items but won't work well for larger, more unruly (and more breakable) items. After experimenting with his packing options, Geff Richardson of Dandylion Records now uses only solid cardboard boxes: "We got numerous complaints when we used bubble mailers," he reports. Use a box that's corrugated and the right size for the item. If you choose a box that's either too big or too small, you run the risk of your merchandise getting damaged and not arriving intact, no matter how well you think you've secured it. (Boxes should display the maximum weight they'll hold, usually on a flap; don't exceed the stated amount.) Surround and cushion the item with packing material so that it will remain in place during its journey to the buyer. "I use a lot of large bubble pack for support and cushioning," explains vintage musical-equipment dealer Atoyboy, who works for Audio Toyshop.com in the United Kingdom. "For some items, such as old amps, I order special 3-ply cardboard boxes to pack them in."

But be careful to not overdo it with packing materials; if you overstuff a box, it might actually explode (and that's not good) if it gets mishandled. Interior packing should be sufficient enough to secure an item, but it should not cause a box to bulge. Another option is to cut your box or envelope to the size of your item. That's what Roger Pavey does with his Priority Mail boxes, free from the post office, in which he ships his delicate vintage concert programs. First, he places the program in a padded envelope and then further secures it by inserting two properly sized pieces of cardboard on each side of the program. "Then I cut the Priority boxes to fit the item," he says. "That way, they don't run around anywhere and there is less chance anything can happen to them." His worst fear: sealed envelopes and boxes opening as heat rises in mail trucks during transport. Items that aren't snug in their box can get free in a truck and be destroyed.

If you are sending more than one item in a box, then wrap them individually (with bubble wrap, foam, tissue, or newspaper) and secure with masking or other tape. If the items are especially fragile, it's best to put them in smaller individual boxes within the larger box. "You've got to wrap each individual thing," agrees Pavey. "You've got to make them stable. If you don't, the buyer is going to be disappointed. And, I don't want the buyer to be disappointed. I want them to be happy because I want them to come back . . . because there's a lot of competition."

Remember that looks count, too. Customers don't want an item to arrive and look like it's something that could be found in a dumpster. Avoid using damaged boxes or envelopes. Seal packages carefully. Tape with straight lines. If you write on the package, do so legibly. Better yet, use printed return and shipping labels for a more professional look. This is particularly important with items that have sentimental value for their buyers, from retirees buying '50s vinyl to relive their sock-hop days to Aerosmith junkies craving that "Toys in the Attic" tour T-shirt or program that got away. "This is something they have a memory wrapped up in and it's important to them," notes Pavey. "You have to keep that in mind and give the package that kind of importance."

Sometimes there might be a packing job that requires more skill and fortitude than you possess. Hard-to-pack items can be, well, hard to pack. In that case, there's always the option of hiring shipping experts—either as an employee, if your company is big enough, or on a case-by-case basis when the expertise is required. "I have never come across anything too fragile to be sent yet, but any very large and fragile items I usually give to a local specialist packer who is used to fragile electronic items," says Audio Toyshop.com's Atoyboy.

eBay TIP: Here are some of the leading carriers you might work with.

- Craters and Freighters *www.cratersandfreighters.com*
- Creightfreight.com *www.creightfreight.com*
- DHL *www.dhl.com*
- Federal Express *www.fedex.com*
- United Parcel Service *www.ups.com*
- United States Postal Service *www.usps.com*

SHIPPING MUSIC PRODUCTS

Now, once your work area is set up and you have refined your packing prowess, you've got some choices to make. Post office or an independent carrier? Should you hire a shipping company that specializes in large items? Are you going to gently (or not so gently) bump up your shipping fees to cover your packaging material costs and perhaps even earn a little something extra for your efforts? Having choices is nice, but it also means there's more to consider.

The most important shipping-related decision you'll make is which carrier or shipping company to go with. The old standbys are the U.S. Postal Service (USPS), United Parcel Service (UPS), Federal Express (FedEx), and DHL. When it comes to selecting a carrier, it's wise to do some comparison-shopping. Get quotes. Do your research. Then, after you've used one of the major shipping providers once or twice, evaluate the cost and service, and decide which will work best for you in the future. "I use UPS to the U.S. and FedEx to Asia," says Atoyboy. "I think they all offer about the same standard of service. My choices are based on rates rather than any other factors."

BoogieStreet's Eric McKenna has a different take: "I use UPS Ground because FedEx hasn't really reached the level of quality yet that I'd be comfortable with." Brown of Pro Gear Warehouse has similar thoughts on the subject: "UPS is who we're using at the moment, though, there's ever a battle there. UPS has done a better job than FedEx, overall, mainly on the delivery side. The software is pretty much equal. Pricing wise, FedEx is probably a little better, but getting product where it needs to be, particularly remote areas, UPS has won."

For Pavey, the good old post office is the best bet for his small, flat items. "The post office is the most reliable, the cheapest, and they give you all of the supplies," he says. "I ship almost everything First Class with Delivery Confirmation or Priority with Delivery Confirmation."

Regardless of what carrier you choose, guitar dealer Mark Morse advises sellers to follow carriers' shipping rules to the letter. "You've got to follow the rules, such as packing guitars with two inches of foam," he says, "or your UPS or FedEx insurance isn't worth buying."

Large, heavy, and awkward items, such as some musical devices and instruments, deserve special consideration. The best solution is to reuse boxes and packing materials obtained directly from manufacturers or those obtained from dealer sources. If this isn't an option, then you might need to buy your boxes in bulk from a box manufacturer or shipping company that specializes in big, bulky items. That's what Pro Gear Warehouse decided to do, enabling them also to do some advertising on their packages. "We have a local company that supplies all our boxes and all the packaging supplies," Pro Gear's Brown explains. "We had them make several boxes to our size specifications. Our name also goes out inked on every box," says Brown. "It's like if you were getting a box from Hewlett Packard. We view that as a little bit of advertising. And, at this point, we're buying enough boxes that it doesn't really cost us extra."

Shipping companies like the ones mentioned above sometimes have size and weight restrictions. Rules vary from company to company, but if you're shipping a particularly large and problematic item, such as an upright piano or set of large stage speakers, you might not be able to use their service. In these instances, you'll need to turn to a freight company, such as Freightquite .com, Craters and Freighters (*www.cratersandfreighters.com*), and FedEx Freight, which offers less-than-truckload (LTL) service throughout the United States. These services will crate and blanket-wrap your oversized item and ship it to your buyer's door or a transport terminal, such as an airport. In short, the size and complexity of the merchandise you're shipping can often dictate how it gets shipped. Consider the logistical requirements of fulfilling certain products before specializing in them.

> **eBay TIP:** eBay has some useful shipping resources, which give good pointers on properly shipping abroad.
> - International Trading *pages.ebay.com/internationaltrading/index .html*
> - The Shipping Center *pages.ebay.com/services/buyandsell/shipping .html*

What else? You'll need to decide whether you want to ship internationally. Some sellers prefer to ship domestically only because of the added logistics involved in shipping overseas (more paperwork, customs forms, etc.). Mark Morse is one dealer who believes it is more trouble than it's worth: "The shipping is always more expensive and the customer always complains about how much it is," he says. "If I had to do it I probably would, but I don't, so I don't. The lower 48 states keep us plenty busy!"

Other sellers we talked with, however, were bullish on the overseas opportunity. "eBay has provided us an international sales base and increased sales ten-fold," says PowerSeller Robert Bergmann, owner of Boogie Bob's Records. BoogieStreet Guitars renamed itself BoogieStreet WorldWide Guitar Sales because its international sales, particularly to Australia, have surged. According to Kevin Sanderson of MusicYo Direct, shipping globally yields new customers and more sales, and you don't necessarily have to worry about altering your packing process. "We use the same shipping techniques when shipping domestically or internationally," he explains. "By standardizing the technique, you eliminate any potential packing error."

WHAT WORKS BEST FOR YOU?

As a seller of recorded music, you have some packing and shipping advantages. Most significantly, the merchandise you sell (CDs, vinyl, tapes) is uniformly sized. This means you can easily streamline the packing and shipping process. Since you know the exact size and weight of a CD, for example, you can order a steady supply of the same-sized envelope or box (see Figure 9-2). You'll also know beforehand how much it will cost to ship—no variables or guesstimating.

For the most part, your best shipping option for small items such as CDs will likely be the USPS. Overall, it's less expensive than FedEx and UPS, and, despite those lingering stories of packages getting famously lost in the mail, it's reliable. Many sellers ship merchandise via Priority Mail, which is convenient and fast. Packages arrive in two to three days, with the cost starting at $3.85. Among the perks: the USPS provides free boxes and envelopes for items sent Priority Mail. Moreover, you can order these supplies ahead of time by

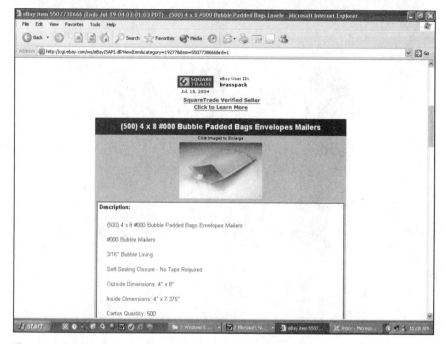

Figure 9-2   These padded envelopes are made specifically for CDs.

mail. Another popular (though lesser known) option is Media Mail. The delivery time takes longer, but the service also costs less ($1.84 for up to two pounds). Many CD sellers prefer Media because it keeps the shipping costs low—something that buyers appreciate. Only certain goods can be sent Media Mail, including books, sound recordings, recorded video tapes, printed music, and recorded computer-readable media (CDs, DVDs, and diskettes).

"We get some customer resistance to the high Priority postage rates," says Richardson of Dandylion Records. "But I use Priority for two reasons: One, the free boxes; and two, the USPS seems to lose Media Mail and surface mail more often than First Class and Priority." In some cases, First Class may even be cheaper than Media Mail. That's what one seller reported in a post on eBay's message boards: "A single CD in a jewel case mailed in a bubble envelope can be sent by First Class mail for either $1.06 or $1.29 (depending on the particular CD's inserts) which is about the same as the Media rate and much quicker and more reliable. I send almost all my CDs by First Class mail although I do offer Priority as a more expensive option. It is generally only one day quicker than First Class mail even for mail sent from coast to coast and is a total waste for people who live close to you. Priority Mail is good for multiple CDs (more than two) as an alternative to the much slower Media Mail."

Figure 9-3   Some items need more care to pack and ship than others.

If, on the other hand, you are selling music memorabilia, you'll have more of a challenge (see Figure 9-3). As you know, memorabilia comes in all sizes and shapes, from ticket stubs to concert pins and posters to fragile housewares. (The value of items can vary, too. For higher-priced items, you should consider shipping insurance, by either buying it yourself or having your buyer cover the cost.) The USPS will work fine for most memorabilia items, but so will FedEx (offering Express, Ground, and Home Delivery services) and UPS (offering Next Day Air, Second Day Air, Ground, and so on). Prices vary depending on the weight and size of the item and its destination. As far as the actual packing of memorabilia goes, Larry Lancit, president of memorabilia seller U.S. Trade Discount Inc., shares this bit of advice: "We carefully bubble wrap each item, then double box it if appropriate with Styrofoam corners, then tape securely." (Lancit, by the way, prefers using FedEx over the other carriers "by a mile.")

Perhaps the best approach to shipping recorded music and music memorabilia, as suggested by one of the sellers quoted above, is to let buyers choose for themselves. That way, they can decide whether they want to pay the extra cost for, say, Priority, and thus receive the item faster, or they can pay less if they don't mind receiving their merchandise a little later (see Figure 9-4).

If your main inventory is musical instruments, then you have the most challenging of the three types of merchandise under consideration. But don't panic. There are options here as well. In many cases, you'll still be able to use the USPS, FedEx, or UPS. A lot depends on the weight and size of the instrument or equipment. To cite one example: the maximum weight for Priority Mail is 70 pounds, while the maximum size is 108 inches (calculated as the length of the package plus the circumference of its thickest part). Have a shipment that's even larger? Then turn to a freighting company, like the ones mentioned previously. You'll also definitely want to insure, and it's probably best, too, if you don't provide the buyer with a choice of shipping options for large, breakable items. Insurance isn't an excuse to let your packaging slide.

What if, for example, you need to ship a guitar? It might seem daunting at first, but once you have a system it's quite simple. For starters, you'll want to use two boxes—one an outer and one an inner. That's what MusicYo Direct's Sanderson does. "Guitars are considered oversized by the carriers, yet only weigh 14 pounds," he says. "We take the original factory carton, with additional padding, and place it in a larger outer carton for added protection."

Atoyboy at Audio Toyshop.com also has some great suggestions for guitars and amps: "Guitar necks must be well supported with foam or bubble

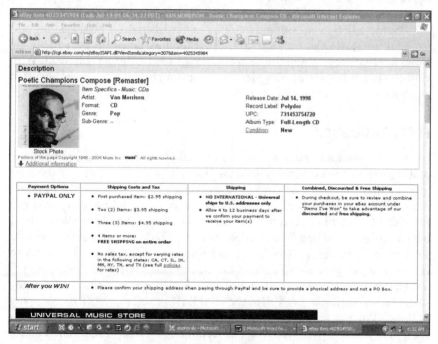

Figure 9-4 Describing your shipping policy effectively in your listings can be as important as what you're selling. You'll find more on this in Chapters 10–12.

pack and strings are slackened. Any bits that can fly off are bagged inside the case pocket, such as Stratocaster tremola arms and bridge covers. I have seen a few vintage finishes ruined by flying trem arms, which have not been properly bagged inside the case. Amps have the tubes taken out and labeled. AC cords and any footswitches are bagged with bubble pack. Some old Vox's have their chassis supported with large poster tubes, too."

And what about finding boxes for guitars? (See Figure 9-5.) Well, sometimes that can be a bit problematic. But here's a possible solution: check your local guitar store. Some stores sell or will even give away boxes. Remember, though, that they're probably selling on eBay, too, and using all their extras. "Just get friendly with a local music store as they usually trash a lot of good cardboard boxes which used to contain guitars," says Audio Toyshop.com's Atoyboy. "Amp boxes are more difficult and I sometimes have to order these in."

eBay TIP: More thoughts on shipping guitars from Atoyboy of Audio Toyshop.com: "Gibson, original reverse body Firebirds must have the tuners taken off and bagged or else the headstock may break. The case is then surrounded in bubble pack and packed in a cardboard guitar box, then sealed."

Some sellers avoid shipping guitars in hardshell cases because they add size and weight to the package, and often the instrument doesn't fit snugly enough inside the case and thus is more likely to move during shipment. With vintage guitars this is obviously less of an option, because the cases are often a valuable component of the sale.

FINAL THOUGHTS

It's a fairly common practice to pass along additional shipping and handling costs to the customer. Some sellers, for example, will "round up." If the total packing and shipping cost is $3.25, they'll charge $4. However, the question is, How much is too much? While buyers expect to pay a little extra, you run the risk of alienating customers if you go too far. "Shipping should be a breakeven point at best," advises Sanderson. "You may make money on a small percentage that outweighs the amount you lose on others. If you try to derive revenue, your shipping fees are not in line with your competition." That's the point of view of BoogieStreet's McKenna, as well. "I told a guy yesterday in Australia that I'm in the GUITAR business—NOT the shipping business. I'm not making money off the shipping—I'm making money off the guitar you're buying from me," he recounts. "He really appreciated that."

Instead of overcharging for shipping, there are many ways to cut costs and reduce your packing and shipping expenses. Buy packing supplies in

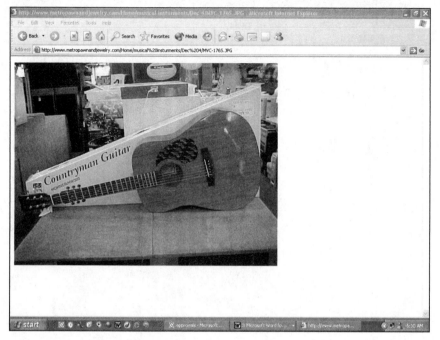

Figure 9-5 Your typical guitar box.

bulk. Take advantage of the free boxes when you ship Priority Mail. Work with manufacturers to increase the quality of *their* packing, so there's less of a need for repacking. It's also possible to try to negotiate better rates with your carrier.

Communication with customers is key, too. Once an item is shipped, try to keep the customer in the loop. If possible, send an e-mail confirming shipment. Consider sending a tracking number to the buyer so they can follow a delivery's progress. Keep in mind that the period between the conclusion of a sale and the arrival of an item can be a murky time for buyers. They wait. They wonder. If you can keep them up to date on the status of their purchase, they'll feel better and be more inclined to buy from you in the future.

If a problem should arise, however, work with the customer to resolve the situation. Items do arrive late or damaged, and it might not be your fault. Buyers can, at times, be unreasonable. But the bottom line is this: it's up to you to make it right. Most problems can be easily remedied through effective communication and maintaining a professional, respectful dialogue. Of course, the most effective way to defuse a sticky situation is to ensure that it doesn't happen in the first place. By properly packing and shipping your merchandise, you're less likely to have to deal with an uncomfortable aftermath.

PART 3

BECOMING A
MUSIC SPECIALIST

10

Becoming a Recorded Music Specialist

We've covered the basics of sourcing, merchandising, and selling music products on eBay. Now let's start getting in-depth and discuss becoming a specialist in our three categories. First on the agenda: recorded music. Then it's on to musical instruments and music memorabilia in Chapters 11 and 12.

In this chapter, we'll cover both new music sales of CDs and other recorded music formats as well as collectible music, most notably vintage vinyl. Our first order of business is to study the structure of eBay's music category and highlight what items are being bought and sold in the greatest numbers. Having an appreciation for the architecture of the *Music* category is important because it reveals where the music market is strongest at large. Why? Well, eBay's categories reflect the interests of its users, its buyers and sellers, and the category structure evolves in step with the eBay community.

After breaking down the category, we will take a closer look at the industry in general, highlighting the recording industry's major record companies and labels to help you track tomorrow's important releases. Here we'll also identify important one-stop distributors that you might just buy from in the future. Next we'll provide an overview of the existing market, exploring some of the forces that drive demand in specific categories. Finally we'll tackle a number of other important topics, including Internet destinations for additional market research, advertising opportunities off eBay, important buyer search terms that can inform your sourcing, listing content and design, photos that get results, and customer incentives that increase value and customer satisfaction with music enthusiasts and collectors.

ANATOMY OF A CATEGORY

Music is popular on eBay for the same reason it's popular on the Internet at large. CDs and records are well suited to eBay. They can be effectively merchandised online (via photos and sound files) and they're light, uniformly sized, and easy to ship. Plus, CDs are an inexpensive, low-risk proposition for most consumers.

That in mind, let's review the scope of the category and which areas are most significant. As you read this section keep in mind that categories are prone to change as interest in one fades and interest in another increases.

Music—found at *http://music.ebay.com*—is organized by music format. Not surprisingly, the industry's dominant category, *CDs*, is also the largest eBay music category, usually featuring more than 200,000 items on any given day. The *Records* category is also significant, catering largely to collectors, DJs, and thrifty music lovers.

Music (Level I)

Accessories (Level II)	DVD Audio	Other Formats
Cassettes	Records	
CDs	Super Audio CDs	

Each of the main Level II categories (*Accessories*, *Cassettes*, *CDs*, and *Records*) is subdivided into Level III categories, which are organized by genre and other unique subcategories particular to their format, such as duration, size, and speed in *Records* and album type in *CDs* (box set, single). We won't break out the *DVD Audio* and *Super Audio CD* categories because they do not have unique Level III categories. (These subcategories are actually part of the *Other Formats* Level II categories.) We assume eBay managers have included them in the Level II list because they expect them to grow—on and off eBay—in the future. The jury is still out on that, though, and that might make you think twice about sourcing these formats aggressively. According to eBay's Hot List, demand is not greater than supply in these categories. (We've included listing numbers from a recent day on eBay to highlight listing volumes per category.)

CDs (Level II)

Genre (Level III):

Blues (3,606)	Easy Listening (4,531)	New Age (2,634)
Children (1,414)	Folk (2,707)	Pop (32,657)
Classical (7,890)	Holiday (843)	R&B (12,124)
Comedy (1,286)	Jazz (10,484)	Rap, Hip-Hop (10,053)
Country (14,749)	Karaoke (2,661)	Reggae, Ska (1,953)
DJ, Dance (13,586)	Metal (13,661)	Religious (7,268)

Rock (76,924)   Spoken Word (328)   Other (20,703)
Soundtrack (12,240)   World Music (6,706)

Album Type (Level III)
Box Set (10,100)   Single, EP (24,913)
Full-Length CD (172,758)   Other (31,269)

Condition (Level III)
New (116,507)   Used (101,286)

Records

Genre (Level III)
Same as above.

Speed (Level III)
16 RPM (43)   45 RPM (53,189)   Other (639)
33 RPM (115,480)   78 RPM (4,916)

Figure 10-1   Imported CD box sets from Japan can earn you a nice profit. Watch fluctuations in *Music* category numbers.

<u>Record Size</u> (Level III)
7" (46,030)	12" (115,865)
10" (18,163)	Other (1,453)

<u>Duration</u> (Level III)
EP (7,037)	Single (37,178)
LP (73,521)	Other (1,364)

<u>Other Formats</u> (Level II)
8-Track Tape (1,954) (Level III) Reel-to-Reel Tape (1,071) Other (175)
DVD Audio (596)   Super Audio CD (172)

<u>Wholesale Lots</u> (Level II)
Cassettes (106) (Level III)	Records (546)
CDs (895)	Other Formats (100)

Things start to get very specific in eBay's Level IV categories. When deciding which category to list in, remember there's a fine line between accurately categorizing your material and burying it. Determine what's best for your product by experimenting. It might be better to list your items in the more general Level III categories for sellers who browse. Most Level IV categories are subgenre categories.

Only *CDs* and *Records* feature subgenres, which goes to show where most of the action in the category is taking place. It also suggests where there might be a need that is not being met, spelling opportunity for you. The relatively diminutive *Cassettes* and *Other Formats* categories do not feature subgenres.

The *Wholesale* category is a category unto itself. Level IV *Wholesale* categories refer to product quantities. *Wholesale* is such a small category, though, we decided to not break it out. The important thing to note in the following list is which Level III genre categories have Level IV subgenres. By noting this, you can see which categories will likely be the building blocks for your business.

CDs & Records

<u>Blues</u> (Level III)
Acoustic (750) (Level IV)	Vocalists (368)
Electric (971)	Other (468)

<u>Children</u>
Sing-Along (199)	Stories (54)
Songs (593)	Other (314)

Classical
Ballet, Dance (57)   Opera (1,345)   Other (1,442)
Chamber Music (562)   Piano (693)
Choral (427)   Symphonic (1,980)

Country
Alternative (636)   Honky-Tonk (532)   Other (1,114)
Bluegrass (1,094)   Mainstream (8,669)

DJ, Dance
Ambient, Trip Hop   Hardcore, Rave (226) Techno,
  (622)   House (216)   Electro
Disco (778)   Industrial (1,229)   (2,211)
Drum 'n Bass (305)   Lounge, Downtempo Trance (1,016)
Electronica (1,347)   (266)   Other (1,496)

Jazz
Big Band, Swing (1,468) Fusion, Acid (660)   Other (4,153)
Bop (828)   Latin (180)

Metal
Black, Death (2,604)   Thrash, Speed (1,613)
Nu Metal (670)   Other (5,946)

New Age
Instrumental (1,085)   Vocalists (221)   Other (675)

Pop
Pre-1970 (1,582)   1980s (4,630)   2000–Now
1970s (1,484)   1990s (9,362)   (8,135)

R&B
Doo-Wop (257)   Mainstream (5,224) Soul (2,067)
Funk (605)   Motown (619)   Other (1,403)

Rap, Hip-Hop
Freestyle (311)   Hip-Hop (3,010)   Other (693)
Gangsta, Hardcore   Old School (388)
  (2,858)

Reggae, Ska
Dancehall (275)   Roots (378)   Other (306)
Dub (94)   Ska (336)

Figure 10-2   One of Metallica's early albums on vinyl, now more than 20 years old!

Religious
Christian (5,604)   Gospel (1,256)   Other (221)

Rock
Alternative (20,231)   Glamrock (550)   Punk (4,952)
Classic: Acid (1,932)   Gothic (1,066)   Surf & Garage
Classic: Other (11,702)   Grunge (1,266)   (580)
Classic: Symphonic (512)   Hard Rock (9,916)   Other (6,887)
Early Rock 'n Roll   New Wave (1,910)
  (2,457)

Soundtrack
Cabaret (89)   Musical Cast (1,253)   Other (2,198)
Film (7,124)   Television (716)

World
African (256)   Indian (146)   Russian (435)
Celtic (678)   Latin (2,020)   Other (2,337)

MAJOR SOURCES

To help you source product in the most viable subcategories in the *Music* category, let's look at the industry's primary record companies and distributors, including one-stops. For the sake of brevity, we have omitted international labels here. Let's first take a look at the Big Five:

1. Universal Music Group

www.universalmusic.com
    Owned by Vivendi Universal, a subsidiary of NBC Universal.

- DreamWorks Records, DW Nashville
- Geffen Records
  - Decca Music Group
    Decca Records
    Philips
  - Deutsche Grammophon
  - ECM
- Island Def Jam Music Group
  - American
  - Def Jam Records
  - Def Jam Soul
  - Island
  - INC. Records
  - Roadrunner Records
  - Roc-A-Fella Records
- Interscope Geffen A&M
- Lost Highway Records

- MCA Nashville
- Mercury Nashville
- Motown Records
- Polydor UK
- Universal Classics
- Verve Music Group
  - Blue Thumb Music
  - GRP
  - Impulse
  - Verve
- Universal Records
  - Bad Boy Records
  - Blackground Records
  - Casablanca Records
  - Cash Money Records
  - Republic Records
  - SRC
  - Strummer Recordings

2. Warner Music Group

www.wmg.group
    Recently sold by Time Warner to a group of investors led by Edgar Bronfman, Jr.

- Atlantic Records Group
  - Atlantic Records
  - Elecktra
  - Lava

- Warner Bros. Records
  - Maverick
  - Nonesuch
  - Reprise

- – Ruffnation
- – Sire
- – Warner Bros. Jazz
- – Warner Bros. Nashville
- – Word Records

- • Warner Strategic Marketing US
- – Rhino
- • Word Distribution
- – Curb
- – Word Records

eBay TIP: Make regular visits to the Big Five record companies' Web sites. This will help you identify who their "A" artists are and see where they are putting their promotional dollars.

3. The EMI Group

www.emigroup.com

Global music production and publishing company; originally Electric and Musical Industries.

- • Angel Records
- • Astralwerks
- • Back Porch Records
- • Blue Note Records
- • Capitol Records US
- • Capitol Records Nashville
- • Caroline Records
- • EMI Classics
- • EMI Latin
- • EMI Nashville

- • Forefront Records
- • Higher Octave Music
- • Narada
- • Positiva Records
- • Priority Records
- • Real World US
- • Shak Tire Records
- • Sparrow Records
- • Virgin Records America
- • Virgin UK

4. Sony Music Entertainment (U.S.)

www.sonymusic.com

Owned by Sony Corporation of America, a subsidiary of the Sony Corporation. (Sony Music and BMG have merged forming Sony BMG Music Entertainment. However, the merger has yet to be approved in the United States.)

- • Columbia Records
- • Epic Records
- • Legacy Recordings
- – Odyssey
- • Sony Classical

- • Sony Nashville
- – Epic-Monument Records
- – Lucky Dog Records
- • Sony Wonder

Figure 10-3   BMG owns the rights to RCA's incredible catalog of jazz and classical music.

5. BMG North America

www.bmg.com

Owned by German media transnational Bertelsmann AG (see Figure 10-3). (Sony Music and BMG have merged forming Sony BMG Music Entertainment. However, the merger has yet to be approved in the U.S.)

- BMG Strategic Marketing
  - BMG Heritage
- RCA Label Group—Nashville
  - Arista Nashville
  - BNA Records
  - RCA Nashville
- RCA Music Group
  - Arista
  - J Records
  - RCA Records
- RCA Victor Group
  - Bluebird

- Private Music
- RCA Red Seal
- RCA Victor
- Windham Hill
- Zomba Label Group
  - Jive Records
  - LaFace
  - Provident Music Group
  - So So Def
  - Verity
  - Violator Records
  - Volcano

Here are some of the significant distributors and one-stops that you should be aware of before you start your eBay music business and which you might buy from in the future, if you decide not to sell retailer overstock.

Major and Minor Distributors

- Albany Music Distributors
- Allegro Corporation *www.allegro-music.com*
- Alternative Distribution Alliance *www.ada-music.com*
- BMG Distribution *www.bmg.com*
- Caroline Distribution *www.carolinedist.com*
- Carrot Top Distribution *www.ctdltd.com*
- Chordant Distribution Group *www.chordant.com*
- Crosstalk (Downtemp, nu Jazz) *www.crosstalkchicago.com*
- EMI North America *www.emi.com*
- Groove Distribution (nu Jazz) *www.groovedis.com*
- Handleman Company *www.handleman.com*
- Harmonia Mundi *www.harmoniamundi.com*
- Innovative Distribution Network *www.idndist.com*
- Koch Entertainment Distribution *www.kochint.com*
- Navarre Corporation *www.navarre.com*
- Page Music *www.pagemusic.com*
- Pinnacle Entertainment (U.K.) *www.pinnacle-records.co.uk*
- Premier Music Distributors (Classical) *www.premieremusic.net*
- Proper Music Distribution (U.K.) *www.properdistribution.com*
- Provident Music Group *www.providentmusic.com*
- RED Distribution *www.redmusic.com*
- Redeye Distribution *www.redeyeusa.com*
- Ryko Distribution *www.rykodistribution.net*
- Sidestreet Distributing (Acoustic) *www.elderly.com/sidestreet*
- Sony Discos *www.sonydiscos.com*
- Sony Music Distribution *www.sonymusic.com*
- Sound Choice *www.soundchoice.com*
- Southern Music Distribution *www.southernmusic.org*
- Surefire Distribution *www.surefiredistribution.com*
- TVT Distribution *www.tvtrecords.com*
- Universal Music & Video Distribution *new.umusic.com*
- Watts (dance, DJ) *www.wattsmusic.com*
- WEA Corporation *www.wea.com*
- World Serpent Distribution (Goth) *www.worldserpent.com*

eBay Tip: Try to identify one-stops in your area that you can source product from in person. That will reduce your procurement costs.

Major and Minor One-Stops

- Allegiant Marketing *www.wholesalemusiccds.com*
- Alliance Entertainment (AEC) *www.aent.com*
- ATM Distributing *www.arrdis.com*
- Baker & Taylor *www.btol.com*
- Big Daddy Music Distribution *www.bigdaddymusic.com*
- City Hall Records *www.cityhallrecords.com*
- DV&A *www.dvacloseouts.com*
- Galaxy Music Distributors *www.galaxymusic.com*
- Horizons *www.cdlps.com*
- J's Records & Tapes *www.jsrecord.com*
- Moonlight Sales *www.moonlightsales.com*
- Music City Record Distributors *www.mcrd.com*
- MusicSelection *www.wmimusic.com*
- Northeast One Stop (800-289-4487)
- Norwalk Distributors *www.norwalkdist.com*
- Prajin1Stop Distributors (Latin) *www.prajin1stop.com*
- Smash Distribution *www.smashdist.com*
- Southwest Wholesale (800-275-4799)
- Super D *www.sdcd.com*
- TRC Distribution (Hip-Hop, DJ) *www.trcdistribution.com*

Major Independents

There are also a number of "independent" record companies, which are independently operated as opposed to being subsidiaries of larger media companies. Here are some of the big names you should know. Even if you're buying from one-stops exclusively, it's good to know who's who. Some of the independents will sell direct.

- Ace *www.acerecords.com*
- Adelphi *www.adelphirecords.com*
- Ark21 *www.ark21.com*
- Artemis *www.artemisrecords.com*
- Blizzard *blizzardrecords.com*
- Cherry Red *www.cherryred.co.uk*
- Collectables *www.oldies.com*
- GNP Crescendo *gnpcrescendo.com*
- Halogen *www.halogenrecords.com*

- Koch *www.kochent.com*
- Nettwerk *www.nettwerk.com*
- One Way
  www.onewayrecords.com
- Pyramid
  www.pyramidrecords.com
- Razor & Tie
  www.razorandtie.com
- Rounder Label Group
  www.rounder.com
- Rykodisc *www.rykodisc.com*
- Sanctuary Classics
  sanctuaryclassics.com
- Shanachie *www.shanachie.com*

- Shout Factory
  shoutfactory.com
- Southern Records
  www.southern.com
- Sundazed *www.sundazed.com*
- Telarc *www.telarc.com*
- Texas Music Group
  www.txmusicgroup.com
- TVT Records
  www.tvtrecords.com
- Vanguard
  www.vanguardrecords.com
- YepRoc Records
  www.yeproc.com

Finally, here's a look at some of the small independent labels by genre, so that you know who's who in different styles of music. One note before you read on: try to focus on what's here, not on what's not here. Obviously there are more labels than these, but this is a good place to start. If you must have more, try these sites: *http://www.recordlabelresource.com.* and *http://www.rlabels.com/index.html.*

Blues

- Adelphi
  www.adelphirecords.com
- Alligator *www.alligator.com*
- Antone's *txmusicgroup.com*
- Arcola *www.arcolarecords.com*
- Arhoolie *www.arhoolie.com*
- Biograph
  www.biograph.com (reissue)
- Black & Tan
  www.black-and-tan.com
- Blind Pig *blindpigrecords.com*
- Blue Collar
  www.bluecollarmusic.com
- Blue Suit *www.blue-suit.com*
- Blue Storm Music
  www.bluestormmusic.com
- Blues Planet
  www.bluesplanet.com
- Burnside Records
  www.burnsiderecords.com

- CCR *www.crosscut.de*
  (reissue, various)
- Delmark
  www.delmarkrecords.com
- Fat Possum
  www.fatpossum.com
- Folkways *www.folkways.si.edu*
  (historic)
- Globe Records
  www.globerecords.com
- Hightone
  www.hightone.com (various)
- House of Blues
  www.hob.com
- Landslide
  www.landsliderecords.com
- Malaco Records
  www.malaco.com
- Roesch
  www.roeschrecords.com

- Rooster Blues
  www.bottledmajic.com
- Ruf Records *www.rufrecords.de*
- Shanachie *www.shanachie.com*
- South Side *www.southsidela.net*
- Stony Plain
  www.stonyplainrecords.com

- Telarc *www.telarc.com*
- Tone-cool *www.tonecool.com*
- Yazoo *www.yazoorecords.com*
- Yellow Dog
  www.yellowdogrecords.com

Classical

- Albany
  www.albanyrecords.com
- Arabesque
  www.arabesquerecords.com
- Artegra *www.artegra.org*
- BIS *www.bis.se*
- Cala *www.calarecords.com*

- Capriccio
  www.capricciousa.com
- Cedille *www.cedillerecords.com*
- Centaur
  www.centaurrecords.com
- Chandos
  www.chandos-records.com

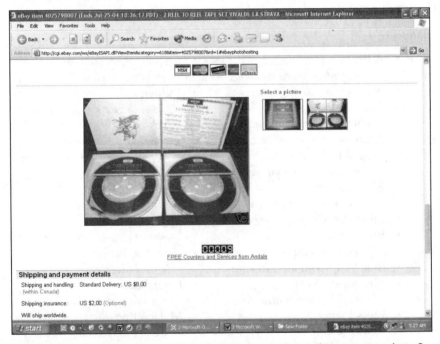

Figure 10-4   Classical music is on all the formats, from reel-to-reel tapes to 8-tracks to Super Audio CDs to DVD Audio.

- Delos *www.delosmus.com*
- Harmonia Mundi
  harmoniamundi.com
- HNH International
  www.hnh.com
- Hyperion Records
  hyperion-records.co.uk

- Marquis Classics
  marquisclassics.com
- Sanctuary Classics
  sanctuaryclassics.com
- Telarc *www.telarc.com*
- Vanguard
  www.vanguardclassics.com

Country and Folk

- Adelphi
  www.adelphirecords.com
- Anti *www.anti.com*
- Bear Family
  www.bear-family.de
- Bloodshot
  www.bloodshotrecords.com
- Bonfire Records
  www.redeyeusa.com
- Folkways *www.folkways.si.edu*
- Hux *www.huxrecords.com*
- Lyric Street
  www.lyricstreet.com
- New West
  www.newwestrecords.com

- Oh Boy Records
  www.ohboy.com
- Okra-tone
  www.bottledmajic.com
- President
  www.president-records.co.uk
- Ragazza *www.ragazza.com*
- Red House
  www.redhouserecords.com
- Rounder *www.rounder.com*
- Shanachie *www.shanachie.com*
- Sugar Hill *sugarhillrecords.com*
  (bluegrass)
- Topic *www.topicrecords.co.uk*
- Vector *www.vectorrecords.com*

eBay TIP: The *Very Hot* and *Hot Music* categories in eBay's June 2004 Hot Categories Report?
- Wholesale Lots > Records > 11-50 (Very Hot)
- Wholesale Lots > CDs > 11-100 (Hot)

The meaning of *very hot*: growth in bids per item (in the category) outpaced growth in listings by 15 to 35 percent. In other words, there's more demand than supply in the category. For more, check out *http://pages.ebay.com/sellercentral/hotitems.pdf*.

DJ and Dance

- 4AD *www.4ad.com*
- Emperor Norton
  www.emperornorton.com
- ESL *www.eslmusic.com*

- Festival Mushroom
  www.fmrecords.com.au
- Naked Music
  www.naked-music.com

- One Little Indian
  www.indian.co.uk
- Secretly Canadian
  www.secretlycanadian.com

- Southern Records
  www.southern.com
- Thump *www.thumprecords.com*
- XL *www.xlrecordings.com*

Jazz

- Delmark
  www.delmarkrecords.com
- Fantasy *www.fantasyjazz.com*
- Folkways
  www.folkways.si.edu
  (historic)

- Marquis
  www.marquisclassics.com
- Naxos Jazz *www.naxos.com*
- Telarc *www.telarc.com*
- Up *www.pagemusic.com*

Metal

- Candlelight
  candlelightrecords.co.uk
- Eclipse *www.eclipserecords.com*

- Roadrunner
  www.roadrun.com
  (Nu Metal)

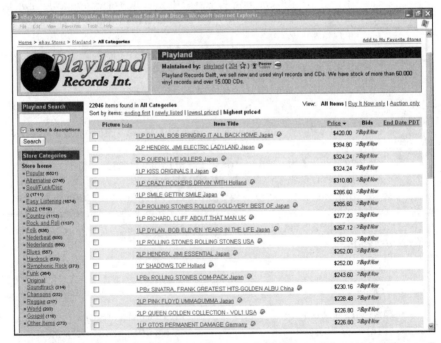

Figure 10-5 Many eBay music businesses, such as Playland Records International, cover all the bases.

New Age

- Nettwerk
  www.nettwerk.com
- President
  www.president-records.co.uk

- Six Degrees
  www.sixdegrees.com
- Source *www.source-records.com*
- Telarc *www.telarc.com*

Pop, R&B, and Soul

- Ecko *www.eckorecords.com*
- Hollywood Records
  www.hollywoodrecords.go.com
- ITP *www.itprecords.com*
- Ministry of Sound
  ministryofsound.com

- Monster Music
  monstermusic.com
- Octone *www.octone.com*
- Telarc *www.telarc.com*
- Yellow Dog
  yellowdogrecords.com

Rap and Hip-Hop

- 4AD *www.4ad.com*
- Octone *www.octone.com*
- Recon *www.reconrecords.com*

- Thump *www.thumprecords.com*
- TVT *www.tvtrecords.com*
- XL *www.xlrecordings*

Reggae and Ska

- Adelphi
  www.adelphirecords.com
- Blood and Fire
  www.bloodandfire.co.uk
- Greensleeves
  greensleeves.easynet.co.uk

- President
  www.president-records.co.uk
- Shanachie *www.shanachie.com*
- Trojan *www.trojan-records.com*
- Tuff Gong *www.tuffgong.com*

Religious

- Ardent *www.ardentrecords.com*
- Benson
  www.bensonrecords.com
- Brentwood
  www.brentwoodrecords.com
- CMR
  *www.crossmovement
  records.com*
- Diademusic
  www.diademusic.com
- Essential
  www.essentialrecords.com

- Fervent
  www.ferventrecords.com
- Gospocentric
  www.gospocentric.com
- New Haven
  www.newhavenrecords.com
- Praise Hymn
  www.praise-hymn.com
- Reunion
  www.reunionrecords.com
- Rocketown
  www.rocketownrecords.com

- Rounder *www.rounder.com*
- Spirit-Led *www.spirit-led.com*
- Verity *www.verityrecords.com*

Distributor
- Provident Music Group
  www.providentmusic.com

Rock

- Bar-None
  www.bar-none.com
- Beggars Banquet
  www.beggars.com (indie)
- Cleopatra *www.cleorecs.com*
  (goth, industrial)
- Del-Fi *www.del-fi.com*
  (surf, hot rod)
- Eleven Thirty Records
  www.redeye.com
- Epitaph *www.epitaph.com*
  (indie, punk)
- Eric *www.ericrecords.com*
  (rock-n-roll)
- Evangeline
  www.evangeline.co.uk (rock)
- Get Hip *www.gethip.com*
  (indie, retro)
- Goldisc *www.goldisc.com*
  (rock-n-roll)
- Gut Records
  www.gutrecords.com (rock)
- Hellcat *www.hell-cat.com*
  (hardcore, p-billy)
- Hollywood
  www.hollywood.com (rock)

- Hux
  www.huxrecords.com
  (U.K., archive)
- Mammoth *www.mammoth.com*
  (rock)
- Matador
  www.matadorrecords.com
  (indie)
- Nervous
  www.nervousrecords.co.uk
  (Rockabilly)
- Norton *www.nortonrecords.com*
  (reissue, retro)
- Radioactive
  www.radioactive.net (rock)
- Southern Records
  www.southern.com
- Subpop *www.subpop.com*
  (alternative, indie)
- Ultimatum
  www.ultimatummusic.com
  (rock)
- Vagrant
  www.vagrantrecords.com
- XL *www.xlrecordings.com*
  (eclectic)

World Music

- Arhoolie *www.arhoolie.com*
- Boosweet *www.boosweet.com*
- Green Linnet
  www.grnlinnet.com
- Karuna *www.karunamusic.com*

- Lanor *www.lanorrecords.com*
- Putamayo *www.putamayo.com*
- Shanachie
  www.shanachie.com
- Triloka *www.triloka.com*

Vintage Vinyl

Sourcing vintage vinyl records is a whole different ballgame than buying new or off-price formats of music from one-stops or existing music shops looking to reduce their overstock. Most vintage vinyl dealers source their items from secondary market suppliers or collectors. The two primary secondhand sources are regional record shows and local estate sales. Here are some leads on the major record shows:

- Aron's Records (Los Angeles, CA) *www.aronsrecords.com*
- Austin Record Convention (Austin, TX) *www.austinrecords.com*
- BRC Record & CD Show (Birmingham, AL) *www.birminghamrecord.com*
- Cincinnati Record & CD Music Mania Expo (Cincinnati, OH) *www.pmshows.com*
- Des Moines Music Collectors Show (IA) *www.zzzrecords.com/recshow*
- Down Home Music 78rpm Swap (El Cerrito, CA) *www.downhomemusic.com*
- Downtown Oakland Record Show (CA) *www.21grand.org/recordsale.html*
- Eugene Record Convention (OR) *www.chromeoxide.com*
- Greater Orange County Monthly Record Show (Buena Park, CA) *www.asavinyl.com/record_show.htm*
- KFJC Record Swap (Los Altos, CA) *www.kfjc.org*
- KSPC CD & Record Expo (Claremont, CA) *www.kspc.org/events.html*
- KUSF RockN'Swap! (San Francisco, CA) *www.kusf.org/rocknswap.shtml*
- Nashville Record & CD Music Mania Expo (TN) *www.chromeoxide.com*
- Northwest Record & CD Collectors Convention (Seattle, WA) *www.nannyagentmusic.com*
- Pasadena City College Flea Market (CA) *www.chromeoxide.com*
- Pennsylvania Music Expo (Lancaster, PA) *www.recordcollectors.org*
- Pittsburgh Record & CD Music Mania Expo (PA) *www.pmshows.com*
- PM Productions *www.pmshows.com*
- Progressive Rock Record and CD Convention (Buena Park, CA) *www.progfest.com*
- Record & CD Show (AK, TN, TX) *www.chromeoxide.com*
- Record Bonanza Record Collectors Show (Canby, OR) *www.chromeoxide.com*
- Record Show (Minneapolis, MN) *www.chromeoxide.com*
- Rhino Records Parking Lot Sale (Westwood, CA) *www.rhinowestwood.com* (see Figure 10-6)

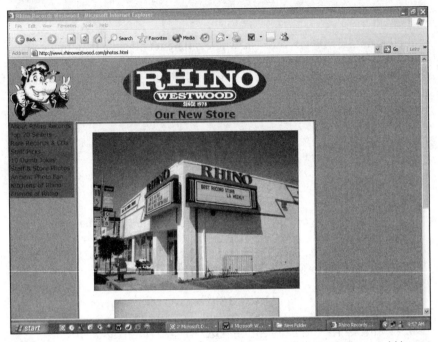

Figure 10-6 Important regional record and CD shops sometimes have swaps and blowout sales, such as Rhino Records in Los Angeles.

- River City Record Club Show (IA) *www.chromeoxide.com*
- Rockin N' Rollin Record Collectors Convention (Newark, CA) *www .chromeoxide.com*
- San Diego Record Show (CA) *www.sandiegorecordshow.com*
- S.F. Bay Area Music Collectors Expo (San Mateo, CA) *www.chrome oxide.com*
- Show Logic Productions *www.showlogic.net*
- Tacoma Music Show (Tacoma, WA) *www.tacomamusicexpo.com*
- Universal Record Show (Universal City, CA) *www.chromeoxide.com*
- Vinyl Only Record Expo (Edison, NJ) *www.chromeoxide.com*
- VRCA Record & CD Show (Vancouver, BC) *www.neptoon.com*
- WMSE 91.7fm Music Meltdown (Milwaukee, WI) *www.wmse.org/ rummage/index.php*
- Wolverines Antique Music Society *www.shellac.org*

At these shows, make it your business to meet genuine collectors. Get their information, too, if possible. You never know when they'll have a collection they might want to sell you when they're strapped for cash.

For estate and business liquidation sales, watch your local newspapers. If you live in a large city, you can also try to search the Web for regional companies and brokers and get on their contact lists. Also, hit *craigslist.com*. Build a rapport with reps and educate them about your niche in the hopes they'll call you first before putting up items for public sale. If you are fair with them on price, they'll call you again. Another way to buy vinyl for resale is to develop relationships with dealers and retailers that own local record stores. If you buy the material they don't want in bulk, then you might be able to get a decent price.

eBay TIP: Check out boston465's excellent workshop on "How to Buy and Sell Record Albums, 45's, 78's, etc." archived in eBay's Discussion Boards: *http://forums.ebay.com/db2/thread.jsp?forum=93&thread=32887&start;=0&msRange=40*

MARKET RESEARCH

Want to know what your customers are listening to and what is on their radar? The first place to hit is the Web, of course. Here's a starter list of music portals, news sites, and newsgroups where you can read up on upcoming releases, find out what new releases are hot, converse with music aficionados, or just read what they have to say, and even listen to new releases and judge them for yourself. Also, bookmark the Web sites of your favorite labels mentioned earlier and don't forget the music magazines we pointed out in Chapter 4.

- All Music Guide *www.allmusic.com*
- CD Universe *www.cduniverse.com*
- Chrome Oxide *www.chromeoxide.com*
- Epitonic *www.epitonic.com*
- GEM *www.gem.com*
- *http://dir.yahoo.com/Entertainment/Music/Charts*
- *http://launch.dir.groups.yahoo.com/dir/Music*
- *http://dir.yahoo.com/Entertainment/Music/News_and_Media/Magazines*
- Launch *launch.yahoo.com*
- Listen.com *www.listen.com*
- Miles of Music *www.milesofmusic.com*
- Live365.com *www.live365.com*
- MP3.com *www.mp3.com*
- MusicStack *www.musicstack.com*

- The Orchard *www.orchard.com*
- *rec.music.marketplace*
- *rec.music.marketplace.cd*
- *rec.music.marketplace.vinyl*
- SecondSpin.com *www.secondspin.com*
- Spinner.com *www.spinner.com*

As you develop a customer base and list, ask them what genres and bands they are most interested in. Their answers will probably surprise you. Include fun trivia questions and polls in your product newsletters and bulletins to garner opinions and insights from existing customers. Offer repeat buyers a couple of free CDs to participate in a survey that features questions regarding your inventory, specifically, what you should carry more of and what you should drop.

ADVERTISING OPPORTUNITIES

Music fans are a passionate lot. When they're not listening to the music they like or going to see it live, a lot of them are reading about it, visiting official band and fan sites, music portals, and various magazine sites. Keeping that in mind, consider complementing the advertising you are already doing on eBay (via your listings and eBay Store) by advertising your eBay Store on these kinds of sites. These, too, can be found by doing some Web research. (See Chapter 4 for a list of important music periodicals in various genres.) This strategy is most appropriate for niche music sellers who are specializing in a few specific genres. If you have a physical storefront, take advantage of eBay's Co-Op advertising program and run some local ads in your city weekly. If you are selling collectible vinyl, Goldmine and Record Collector are still the places to advertise off eBay. Here are some print advertising options:

- Discoveries *www.collect.com*
- Goldmine *www.collect.com*
- Planet Collector *www.planetcollector.com*
- Record Collector *www.recordcollectormag.com*

MARKET FACTORS AND MARKET IMPLICATIONS

Pinpointing what artists and CDs you should sell on eBay is beyond the scope of this book. Plus, people's tastes and interests change. What we suggest today might not be true tomorrow. However, we do want to talk about what market forces are driving music enthusiasts to eBay and how you can identify what kinds of music they are looking for. This should help you formulate your personal eBay music strategy.

Music Is Affordable

It's important to understand that the music business is a low-margin one. Regardless if you are selling full-retail specialty CDs or low-priced overstock, it's critical to list and sell in *volume*. Margins on CDs don't usually exceed 25 percent, and that's for tastemakers, who are selling trendy products to in-the-know enthusiasts. The silver lining is that CDs are mass-produced and in great enough supply that you will be able to buy and sell in large amounts.

Implications: It's critical for your music business to have good cash flow and some liquidity so that you can source product opportunistically. In short, it's important to have cash available to take advantage of unexpected supply opportunities, such as a one-stop clearance sale in your area, a regional going-out-of-business sale, or an offer to buy a truckload of attractive overstock from a distributor at a low price—if you'll pay cash.

It's hard to predict when a great opportunity will crop up, but you can manage your affairs so that you are ready to act when it does. That means pricing your material strategically. It's not enough to just cover your costs. There has to be some room in your margins so that you can reach a level of liquidity that enables you to make the most of your opportunities.

Music Lovers Look for a Deal

Many music buyers head to eBay for one reason and one reason alone: they want a deal. In short, a lot of us don't like to pay much for our music, whether we're a fan of hot, new releases from the pop divas on the charts or more esoteric titles in the back catalogs of small labels. You can blame this phenomenon on a number of different factors, from the in-store pricing strategies of giant stores to Napster, but that's a subject for another date. Buyers shopping for deals on new releases generally want the opportunity to pay less than they would at any mass merchandiser.

When you're talking about new releases, that typically means paying less than $16—the price of a discounted new release (around $13.45), plus ground shipping ($2.70 or so). Quite a few eBay sellers understand this impulse and try to capitalize on it. Take the eBay sellers who were listing Jimmy Buffett's summer release "License to Chill" for $9.99 with a $12.99 Buy It Now option. Even with Priority shipping, buyers had the chance to buy it for less than they would at a discount store's Web site. Of course, if buyers paid the Buy It Now, the price would be higher than Wal-Mart's. Nonetheless, buyers had the opportunity to get the best price.

Another group of sellers capitalizing on people's desire to buy cheap are the site's "one-cent CD" sellers, who make new markets in distributors' and retailers' clearance items and overstock (see Figure 10-7). These volume sellers generate new interest in items that have been all but forgotten by opening them at $0.01 or $0.99 without a reserve. The upside of this strategy: inventory costs are low, conversion and feedback rates are high, and customers are loyal. This strategy has been tremendously effective for PowerSellers Jay and Marie Sinese (eBay ID: jayandmarie).

Implications: If you're selling new mass-market CDs or liquidation stock, you have to be prepared to sell in volume and earn slim margins. That means you also have to develop a very efficient, automated operation with streamlined listing and order fulfillment processes. That takes some investment and know-how. Selling new charting CDs is probably the toughest route you can go. Though they have good visibility, they're not very profitable. Why? Well, you'll probably be buying this material at a fairly high wholesale price from one-stop distributors, but selling it low to compete with Web mass merchandisers and attract eBay's budget-oriented buyers. Instead of just selling new releases, we suggest carrying a diverse inventory of both new releases and classic reissues. Use the new releases to appear in more buyer searches and draw customers into your Store and other higher-margin listings.

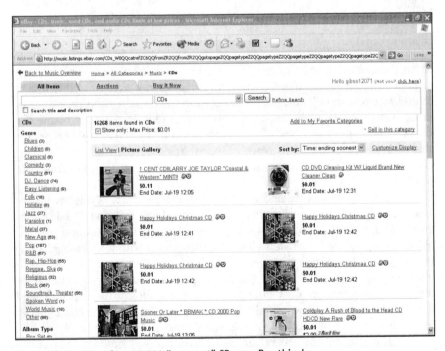

Figure 10-7   More than 16,000 "one-cent" CDs on eBay this day.

eBay TIP: Create a diverse eBay catalog that caters to both casual music buyers—the "tweens" and "teens," "Nascar Dads" and "Soccer Moms"—and more serious music enthusiasts. Also, open an eBay Store where you can effectively target both groups and communicate your value proposition without alienating one or the other.

eBay Is Huge with Music Enthusiasts

One reason why eBay is a destination for music enthusiasts is because it aggregates material that is hard to find elsewhere, such as collectible records, out-of-print vinyl and CDs, or new independent releases that have limited distribution and aren't carried outside major metropolitan areas. Truth be told, you don't *have* to go to eBay find this scarce merchandise. A lot of it, with the exception of eBay's rare records, is available on miscellaneous dealer and retailer Web sites. It's just more efficient and convenient to use eBay than to use a search engine to get to this material. (GEM.com is one marketplace that could give eBay a run for its money in this regard.) Keep in mind that eBay is not just a marketplace, but also an entry point for people wanting to join diverse communities and lifestyles. People realize that there are experts in the topics they're interested in on eBay. They flock to eBay not just to buy from them, but also to meet them.

Implications: Specialty resellers, particularly those with established Web sites and retail stores, who can identify up-and-coming labels and artists (ones that will end up on editor Top Ten lists) as well as trendy out-of-print material and new releases of cult favorites, are well positioned to succeed on eBay. These sellers have the opportunity to build relationships with music enthusiasts, earn higher per-unit margins, and generate more loyal customers than those who just liquidate retailer overstock (see Figure 10-8).

The challenge for niche specialty sellers is finding reliable suppliers that offer reasonable wholesale prices. To give yourself more options, it's probably wise to offer a portfolio of items in your niche, from the classics of your genre to cool reissues to out-of-print exotica to new, lesser known releases from your genre's young lions and new faces.

If you are a true expert in your specialty with an eye for talent (like that of an A&R—artist and repertoire—rep) and a knack for marketing and merchandising, you might even consider buying directly from underground labels and unsigned artists. This increases supply and can attract music aficionados looking for new acts on the rise. Milesofmusic.com is a good source of these kinds of artists in the *Americana, Alternative Country*, and *Rock* categories. Epitonic.com is an excellent source for the *DJ, Electronica*, and *Indie* categories.

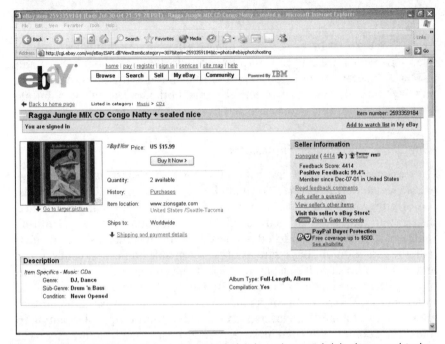

Figure 10-8. Zion's Gate Records is a tastemaker in underground dub, dance, and techno on eBay and at its Web site.

Fans Go to eBay for Hard-to-Find Items

If you are selling clearance items and overstock from distributors and retail stores, note which pieces in your supply are now out of print and market them as such to enthusiasts of that particular band or genre. Because of the size of eBay's user base, one person's cocktail coaster can be another person's essential rarity.

Implications: Be careful when sourcing out-of-print CDs. You don't want to buy a whole load of one out-of-print release (to corner the market) if you believe it might be reissued. If it is, your cool rarity just got un-rare.

TOP BUYER SEARCHES

Why are keywords important? Because they reveal what music buyers are interested in buying, and that tells you what you should be selling. Fortunately, eBay has developed two incredible tools to help track buyer searches:

- Common Keywords *http://keyword-index.ebay.com/A-1.html*
- eBay Keyword *http://buy.ebay.com*

Common Keywords enables sellers to review thousands of common buyer search terms related to their merchandise. As you search or browse the database, you'll notice items and topics that you didn't realize your customers were interested in. Here's an example: look up Ray Charles and you'll recognize that buyers also are searching for jazz musicians Ray Barretto, Ray Brown, Ray Conniff, and Ray Cook, as well as The Doors' Ray Manzarek. Now, that's good information you can use.

It's also effective to use Common Keywords in conjunction with eBay Keyword pages. These pages aggregate all of the listings on eBay that relate to a single search term. In other words, they reveal how popular a given item is. For example, Christina Aguilera might not be your favorite artist, but she is a favorite search term, meaning people are hunting for her CDs on eBay. Keywords also help sellers validate their theories about the market on eBay. Take the term *OOP*, confirming that music enthusiasts are looking for back-catalog material that is no longer in production (i.e., Out of Print). Then there is the term *cd sealed*, revealing that, yes, eBay buyers do prefer new CDs in their original shrink-wrap. Now how about *import*? Yep, people are searching for international releases with original content.

Finally, eBay Keyword pages reveal what new artists in various genres are hot (Dixie Chicks, Jennifer Lopez, Shania Twain) and what super groups from different decades continue to capture the public imagination (Duran Duran—who knew?). Moreover, they highlight what artists and groups from the '90s have started to become established commodities, such as Sound Garden, Phish, and Dave Matthews.

Here's an initial list of music terms that have eBay Keyword pages. For more, go to *http://buy.ebay.com*. To bring up a page, just place one of the keywords after the preceding URL, like this: *http://buy.ebay.com/**acdc***.

ac/dc	cd sealed	elvis
aerosmith	cd single	elvis presley
album	celine dion	eminem
aretha franklin	cher	emo
band	christina aguilera	eric clapton
bb king	clapton	fleetwood mac
beach boys	dave matthews	frank sinatra
beatles	david bowie	goth
billy joel	diana ross	grateful dead
blues	dixie chicks	hendrix
bob dylan	dj	hits
bon jovi	dolly parton	import
britney spears	duran duran	jackson
broadway	dvd	james taylor
bruce springsteen	eagles	jennifer lopez

jimi hendrix

jimmy buffett

joplin

kiss

led zeppelin

limp bizkit

louis armstrong

lp

lyle lovett

metallica

neil diamond

nirvana

nutcracker

oop

parker

pearl jam

phat farm

phish

pink floyd

police

pop

prince

promo

quicksilver
   (messenger service)

ray charles

rem

rockabilly

rolling stones

rush

shania twain

simon garfunkel

soundgarden

streisand

the doors

the rolling stones

tom petty

van morrison

vintage

vinyl

westside story

wings

TRACKING THE MARKET

To be a successful seller in recorded music, you have to keep tabs on what's selling and what's not. That means regularly tracking your realized prices, recording what your customers are buying most, and analyzing what your competitors are carrying. eBay is a fantastic asset in this regard. For starters, eBay's Completed Item search enables sellers to review the last two weeks of completed eBay listings. Quickly, sellers can gauge supply in a particular item, its current market value, and its success rate at different price points.

 eBay TIP: Check out eBay's Solutions Directory under "Services" for third-party applications that enable you to collect historical pricing data for your category.

Sellers can save 100 Completed Item searches to the Favorites area of their My eBay page. In a manner of speaking, this allows music sellers to create their own personal price guides for the titles, artists, genres, and formats they sell. Once their Favorite searches are saved, they simply open their My eBay, run their searches, and evaluate the performance of specific items in their inventory. This is particularly useful for sellers who have a hunch certain items are gaining or losing momentum. Thirty of these Favorite Searches can be linked to an email notification feature. Once a day, sellers receive an e-mail linking them to any new listings related to that search. In essence, this provides a snapshot of the eBay market for that item.

e B a y   T I P :   When setting up your completed searches, select the option "Prices: Highest First." That way, your guide will lead with the last two weeks' highest prices.

eBay also provides sellers a way to collect and review historical market data. Sellers that upgrade to a Featured Store receive a market report, which includes data on their own sales, such as total number of bids, total number of successful auctions, gross sales, and average selling price, as well as the performance of the category as a whole, which sellers can use as a benchmark.

So what kinds of Completed Item searches should music sellers be creating?

New Release Sellers

People selling new releases should consider creating searches for artists currently on the charts. This way they can confirm if these new faces have actually found an audience on eBay and at what price. Also consider tracking hot new artists' back-catalogs and determine if these releases were undersold. If so, explore selling those releases.

Reissue and Overstock Sellers

In this specialty, sellers might create searches for their top-selling artists and titles. The goal: track changes in price and market saturation. They also should design some searches for the rare items that occasionally enter their inventory to keep up-to-date on pricing and identify competing sellers.

Specialty Sellers

These sellers should run searches for the niche styles, based on the terms they use in their listing titles. For example, dealers in vintage 45s might track "northern soul" or "garage"; house and hip-hop sellers might run searches for "Washington go-go"; OOP jazz dealers could try "hard bop" and "Kansas City"; rock sellers might track "classic," "punk," "hot-rod," "surf," and the like (see Figure 10-9). (Don't get too carried away, though; your terms have to match what people are actually searching for.) Niche specialists also will want to run searches for the critical labels that have defined their genre. For instance, if your business is new and old indie/grunge releases, then "sub pop" would be an obvious search.

Collectible Dealers

People in collectibles should run searches for the major albums, artists, and labels they routinely sell or would like to sell. They might also craft searches

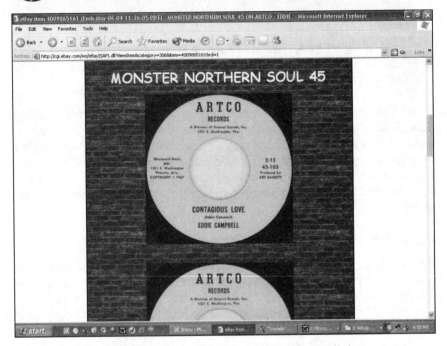

Figure 10-9. In vintage 45s, Northern Soul is one of eBay's hottest little genres.

for certain collectible characteristics that buyers search for, such as OBI (original band intact), Orig, Mono, 2nd State, Import, OOP, 7", 45, and the like. All of the above would help sellers identify new trends and how prices are being affected. If you have some repeat customers with specific tastes, such as Blue Note releases with the Lexington address, Vee-Jay first-pressings, colored '70s vinyl, or demo cassettes from now popular bands, you might want to design searches for these as well. You might find a piece to buy to resell to them. You also might see if other sellers are targeting your kinds of buyers and, if so, how attractive their pricing is.

BOOSTING SALES WITH STELLAR LISTINGS

As we talked about in Chapter 9, how you present and market your material in your music listings can have a real bearing on your success. As a music seller, you don't have to be longwinded or fancy, but there are some key messages you'll want to convey to reassure buyers and raise your credibility. Let's talk about those now.

1. If you are selling overstock or new factory-sealed CDs, your template is going to differ dramatically from that of a collectible seller.

For starters, new CD sellers should consider using eBay's Item Specifics and Pre-Filled Item Information tools. Item Specifics categorizes your items more precisely (so that they appear in more buyer searches) and also places a useful data box at the top of your listings, providing buyers shorthand details about your item, such as its title, format, genre, date, Universal Product Code, and more. Pre-Filled Item Information provides sellers free stock photos and catalog information. Essentially, Pre-Filled Item Information saves sellers time they would have spent photographing CD covers and typing song titles, recording credits, and writing album notes. It even provides access to editorial blurbs from major magazines for your descriptions. If you decide to use eBay's Pre-Filled Item feature, then refrain from offering detailed information about the recording. If there's a major hit on the recording, you may want to call that out, though. This sort of copy might fit the bill:

> Includes hits "Back on the Chain Gang" and "Show Me"

2. Dealers offering collectible material should create their own descriptions and photos, which emphasize the item's condition and the particulars of its issue. They should also consider giving some context for the album, explaining why the album has historical significance—why it's rare and collectible. This is not as necessary for popular reissues, which are widely known and regularly sold. An exception would be new CDs that are from up-and-coming artists in lesser-known subgenres, such as *Electronica*, *New Age*, or *World Music*. The same could be said for listings in the *classical* genre, allowing you to market them to a younger demographic. Provide some background when selling minor artists on important bygone labels, such as Riverside, Checker, and the like.

3. If you're offering an original pressing of a significant album, say, Andy Warhol's "Velvet Underground and Nico" album or Carl Perkins' "Blue Suede Shoes" EP on Sun and it has an interesting history of ownership, then provide some details on the record's provenance (see Figure 10-10). *Record*mecca.com (eBay ID: recordmecca) does this exceptionally well. In fact, it often uses eBay's new Subtitle listing upgrade to highlight an item's provenance. You might also include a simple grading chart in your template that provides buyers a line-by-line explanation of your grades.

  Spend some time reading other vinyl dealers' listings to master condition lingo. Here are a few good phrases: "sleeve has mild scuffing and ring wear," "beautiful glossy vinyl," and "limited surface noise." These extras can make a real difference, substantially increasing your credibility with serious collectors.

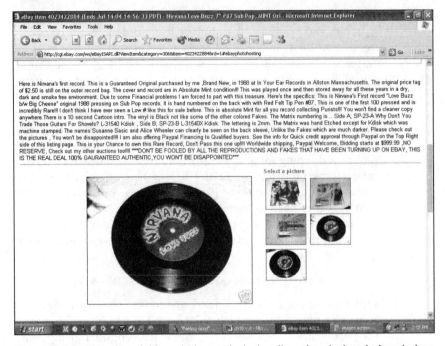

Figure 10-10 The seller of this cool Nirvana single describes where he bought it and when. Good thinking.

4. Regardless of what kind of music seller you are, give your descriptions a good, compelling headline in a reasonably large, bold font. This provides your buyer a place to start and makes reading your description easier. Center the headline and be sure to note the name of the artist or group, the title of the recording, and particulars about the format, such as if it is a CD or record, and then what kind (Gold Disc, box set, EP, 7", 45, etc.). If you want to set off the title from the artist name and other particulars, then consider italicizing it:

The Pretenders—*Learning to Crawl*—New Factory-Sealed CD

If you're selling a collectible recording, you might also want to note the recording's date (1955), pressing number ("first press"/ "orig"), and grade (Mint, VG+, etc.) in the headline. If the recording is out of print or an import, that should be referenced in the headline—replace another detail if need be. Some 7-inch and 45 dealers lead with the item's musical style first, if it is particularly collectible. They often note the song title before the artist and highlight the label. At the end of the day, the elements that make your item most collectible need to be in your listing title and description headline. Here's an example:

Nirvana Love Buzz 7" #87 Sub Pop, MINT Original, NR!!!!

Don't worry if your headline breaks onto two lines, because your font will be bolder and larger than your description text. Another idea is to pare down your headline and include some of the facts in a subhead or deck underneath the headline in a slightly smaller bold font. Here you might call out the recording's catalog number (Columbia 4-42626, The Stereo's "Echo In My Heart/Tick Tack Toe"), its edition number, its style—whatever is of secondary importance for that piece.

eBay TIP: For tips on coding your listings, check out Dennis Prince's *How to Sell Anything on eBay . . . and Make a Fortune!* Also, take advantage of eBay's new listing-form text editor or its Listing Designer, enabling you to add different fonts and colors to your listings.

5. Sellers remarketing retailer or distributor B-stock need to note marks on the product, such as drilled or punched holes and cut corners, which are made to ensure the item isn't resold at full retail price. If the item is totally clean, then mention that, too. Many eBay buyers expect discount CDs, particularly those started at "one-cent," to feature marks. If the CD is factory sealed, then emphasize that. It could increase bidding and interest. Overstock sellers should describe the condition of unsealed CDs' inserts and jewel cases in a subhead or their description's body text.

6. Those specializing in rare or out-of-print CDs and LPs (long play) should take their own photos but should consider leveraging eBay's Pre-Filled Item feature for song lists, credits, album notes, and review blurbs. For credibility's sake, they may want to add a few of their own insights, too. Truly rare, out-of-print material won't be in the Pre-Filled Item database. In these cases, OOP sellers should take the time to include song lists and credits. Jazz sellers also should be sure to note sidemen, as this is important to jazz enthusiasts. Another thought: include star ratings from important music review guides. Also, use the Internet to find compelling quotes from magazine reviews and include them in your descriptions with a credit. Don't bury these in a block of text, either.

7. As for the sales policies portion of your listing, it's best to table this information in three sections: Payment Options, Shipping and

Handling, and Refunds and Returns. You don't have to apply a handling charge or allow refunds and returns. That's up to you, but most agree that returns will increase sales in the long run. In your shipping section be sure to note if you sell internationally or just in the United States. In the payment section, note the state (your home state) in which you collect sales tax. Another approach is including a quick FAQ at the end of your description, which answers common questions about your policies and includes a customer service e-mail. However, this can make your listings long and increase your listing fees.

8. Make sure your template is consistent for all of your listings. This reinforces your branding and helps buyers better assess what you're selling. It also helps you consistently plug your Store and drive sales there. If you have good feedback, tell your prospective buyers to check it—this works!

THE RIGHT PHOTOS

Media sellers offering new products generally have it easy when it comes to item photos. They can use eBay's Pre-Filled Item feature and post stock images, saving the time and the expense of hosting their own images. Those dealing in collectible music aren't so lucky. They have to shoot their items themselves, and do it well to earn the confidence of their buyers. That's what we'll cover here.

1. Vintage record sellers should provide a series of images, including photos of the jacket or gatefold, inside sleeve, record (sides A and B), and label. Use a scanner as much as possible for your flat records at a resolution of 72 DPI (dots per inch). Clean your records before shooting them. (Don't use alcohol-based cleaners on shellac 78s!) Give buyers the opportunity to expand each image so that they can see the images in greater detail. Give some close-ups of any serious wear or damage. Specifically, you might want to shoot rounded sleeve corners, seam splits, or heavy scratches to the vinyl.

2. All of your images need to be sharp, but especially the label image. If the label image is fuzzy, collectors won't bite. They should be able to read all of the fine print on the edges of the label, including the catalog number, the record label's address, and any interesting marketing copy. Close-ups of distinguishing sleeve marks that confirm the authenticity of the item should be included. For example, if you're selling a first press of "The Beatles" album (commonly known as the White album), provide buyers a clear close-up of the catalog number stamped on the front cover.

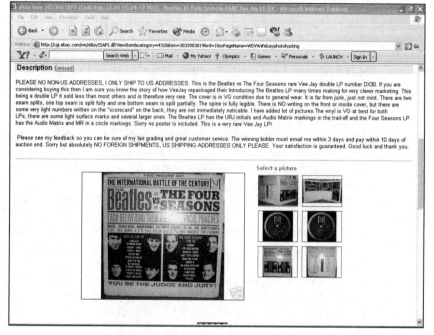

Figure 10-11   Great album, but look at that flash.

3. The record sleeve should be shot front and back to provide serious buyers the ability to verify that your grade is appropriate. If your piece has a box, as in the case of box sets, 8-tracks, and reel-to-reels, be sure to shoot it as well as the inserts and paper band or sash that goes around the box. People collect this material and want to see it.

4. Shoot your records against a neutral background, not on colorful household objects which reduce the buyer's ability to see the item. Don't shoot items from a distance so they look small. Retake shots if you can see your flash's reflection (see Figure 10-11).

CUSTOMER INCENTIVES THAT WORK

Here are some thoughts on getting music enthusiasts to buy more of what you're selling, be that new CDs or collectible formats.

1. In new and used CDs, price matters. You'll find a quite a few sellers now list their CDs for "one-cent" with no reserve, a practice popularized in the *Music* category by PowerSellers Jay and Marie Sinese (eBay ID: jayandmarie). If you want to generate strong bid-

ding on your items and develop a customer base fast, then list your CDs as auctions with a low opening bid, such as $0.01 or $0.99. Of course, this requires you to know your music and understand what overstock items will have niche audiences on eBay. "One-cent CD" also looks great in your listing title. eBay has even started to base merchandising events on this idea.

2. If you're in the budget CD game, combine shipping. In other words, offer buyers a discounted rate on every extra CD they buy. This will encourage customers to buy multiple CDs from you. One approach is to charge only a dollar to ship each extra CD. Another idea: if buyers purchase a certain number of CDs, let's say four or more, then offer them free shipping.

3. List your frontline CDs as auctions with an attractive opening but a higher Buy It Now price. This practice gives buyers the opportunity to get a better deal than they can at Amazon or Wal-Mart.com. Also, you might consider offering free shipping with your Buy It Now, with the caveat that the item will take a week or two to ship.

4. To jazz up an overstock or back catalog item, consider embedding some song sound files in its listing. (This is getting more common and is actually good advice for any CD seller.)

5. To attract true collectors, vintage vinyl dealers should consider offering their buyers a lifetime warranty of authenticity. Include your name, number, e-mail, and address in your listings if you are selling expensive collectible items or large, expensive classical collections. This will work wonders with buyers considering an investment of $1,000 or more. Offer to make special packing, shipping, and insurance arrangements to ensure their purchases are protected. Consider offering buyers PayPal Financing, if you're selling items in the hundreds to thousands of dollars.

6. Sell internationally. Often CDs in your inventory won't be available to buyers overseas. Moreover, items that might not be attractive to domestic customers will be of great interest to buyers abroad.

7. During the holidays, use special offers, such as gift-wrapping, gift cards, and gift-recipient shipping. During the holiday season, keep an eye out for eBay promotions and merchandising events, which can drive traffic to your listings. Here's the music-merchandising calendar: *http://pages.ebay.com/sellercentral/calendar.html.* During busy buying periods, consider using some eBay listing upgrades to garner more visibility for your listings and eBay Store.

8. For more general thoughts on this subject, review Chapter 9.

Ok, that's a wrap. Let's not waste any time—on to musical instruments. There's a lot to cover on that topic.

11

Becoming a Music Products Specialist

Ionian, Dorian, Phrygian, Lydian, Mixolydian, Aeol . . . oh, there you are—you're back. Let's get back to it. Time to stop noodling on that blues-scale and dig a little deeper into your specialty (or, perhaps, your new cross-sell venture): musical instruments. As in our intensive look at recorded music, we'll discuss who's buying on eBay in this category and at what general price points. We'll also highlight some of the factors that are driving demand for instruments and Pro Audio on eBay. Then, we'll talk about Internet destinations for market research, advertising opportunities off eBay, important buyer search terms (that inform your buying), how to list content and photos that will improve your results, and customer incentives that attract instrument buyers. A large part of this chapter also covers the important bygone, boutique, and major manufacturers in each of eBay's core *Musical Instruments* categories, from brass and guitars to percussion and pro audio.

ANATOMY OF A CATEGORY

First, let's take a closer look at the architecture of the *Musical Instruments* category. As previously noted, this gives sellers an initial perspective on what instrument and music product categories are most active on eBay.

- Musical Instruments *http://musicalinstruments.ebay.com*

We won't keep you in suspense. The top five categories are *Guitars* (averaging 45,000 to 50,000 listings per day), *Pro Audio* (in the 25,000 daily listing range), *Sheet Music, Song Books* (15,000 to 20,000), *Percussion* (10,000 and up), and either *String* or *Keyboard, Piano* (usually in the same range as percussion). These numbers are prone to change, of course. That's not to say you can't pursue a very successful business in brass, woodwinds, or harmonicas. Many sellers do, developing brands that cater to just one price point, be it budget to boutique, or a variety of them. Others mix it up, selling several categories of instruments in the two core categories, orchestra or small bands, to appeal to a variety of buyers, from student musicians in orchestras to Joey Ramones in three-chord quartets to serious part-timers in jazz and chamber outfits. We'll discuss this more later. Now on to the categories themselves.

Musical Instruments (Level I)

Brass (Level II)	Pro Audio
Electronic	Sheet Music, Song Books
Equipment	String
Guitar	Wholesale Lots
Harmonica	Woodwind
Keyboard, Piano	Other Instruments
Percussion	

Musical Instruments. Level II categories cover all the major instrument categories, as well as studio and stage equipment (in *Equipment* and *Pro Audio*) and instructional materials in *Sheet Music* and *Song Books.* Unlike the *Music* category, practically each Level III category in *Musical Instruments* has different subcategories, as each instrument family has its own characteristics. Each of the major categories does feature subcategories for *Instruction Books, CDs,* and *Videos* subcategories—an excellent accessory category for dealers specializing in starter instruments or even those selling classic vintage gear, if your media products spotlight the musicians who used the gear that you carry.

Note that a few Level II categories (*Guitar, Percussion*) have thriving *Parts, Accessories* categories. In fact, Guitar > Parts, Accessories is often the largest *Musical Instruments* Level III category of all, though not the largest in gross merchandise sales. (We've included listing numbers for each category from a recent day on eBay to give you a feel for the full volume in each and a reference for the future. We've also starred the top subcategories in the major categories. We've omitted the *Wholesale* and *Other* categories because, at the end of the day, they are not that relevant.)

Brass (Level II)

Baritone, Tuba (388)	Flugelhorn (41)	Trombone (758)
(Level III)	French Horn (324)	Other Brass (431)
Cornet, Trumpet	Instruction Books,	
(2,258)*	CDs, Videos (98)	

Figure 11-1 Even high-end grand pianos are listed on eBay, despite their cost and special shipping requirements.

Electronic

Drum Machines (579)	Samples, Samplers (635)	Synth (908)
		Other (638)

Equipment

Cases (372)	Metronomes (216)	Tuners (144)
Instrument Stands (205)	Music Stands (370)	Other (663)

Guitar

Acoustic (5,441)*	Bass (2,597)	Instruction . . . (2,812)
Acoustic Beginner Packs (754)	Builder, Luthier Kits (371)	Memorabilia (231)
Acoustic Electric (824)	Electric (12,055)	Parts, Accessories (13,447)*
Amplifiers (4,938)	Electric Beginner Packs (183)	Other Guitar (974)

Harmonica

Hohner (406)

Johnson Blues King (11)

Instruction . . . (122)

Other (647)

eBay TIP: The super hot and very hot *Musical Instruments* categories in eBay's June 2004 Hot Categories Report?

- Electronic > Synth > Yamaha (Very Hot)
- Guitar > Amplifiers > Vox (Very Hot)
- Guitar > Bass > Beginner Packs (Super Hot)
- Guitar > Electric > Peavey (Very Hot)

The meaning of *super hot*: growth in bids per item (in the category) outpaced growth in listings by 35 percent. And *very hot*? Growth in bids per item (in the category) outpaced growth in listings by 15 to 35 percent. In other words, there's more demand than supply in these categories. For more, check out *http://pages.ebay.com/sellercentral/hotitems.pdf*.

Keyboard, Piano

Accordion, Concertina (738)

Electric Keyboards (2,536)*

Other Keyboard (550)

Instruction (518)

Organ (775)

Piano Rolls (456)

Piano (1,307)*

Percussion

Bells (82)

Cymbals (1,351)*

Drum Stools, Thrones (82)

Drums (4,362)*

Instruction . . . (414)

Parts, Accessories (2,434)*

Shakers & Blocks (173)

Tambourines (137)

Xylophones . . . (138)

Other Percussion (711)

Pro Audio

Cables (1,607)

Computer Recording (2,455)*

DJ Equipment (5,769)*

Microphones (4,902)*

Monitors (355)

Mixers (1,482)

Multi-Track Records (1,169)

Power Amplifiers (822)

Rack Gear (3,124)

Speakers (1,895)

Other (1,895)

Sheet Music, Song Books

Sheet Music (10,802)

Song Books (5,486)

String

Accessories (325)	Cello (629)	Mandolin (1,005)*
Autoharp, Zither (181)	Harp, Dulcimer (351)	Ukulele (513)
Bass (238)	Instruction . . . (535)	Viola (360)
Banjo (1,013)*		Violin (4,143)*
		Other (440)

Woodwind

Bagpipes (571)	Instruction . . . (192)	Saxophone (2,605)*
Bassoon, Oboe (363)	Piccolo (244)	Other Woodwinds (339)
Clarinet (1,715)*	Recorder (244)	
Flute (1,623)*		

Most eBay Level IV *Musical Instruments* categories relate to instrument or equipment manufacturers. While Level IV categories in *Music* tend to get a little too specific for their own good, Level IV *Musical Instruments* categories are very relevant because qualified buyers know the manufacturers, and many buyers are loyal to certain brands, such as Conn, Fender, Gibson, Gretsch, Hal Leonard, M-Audio, Selmer, Yamaha, and hundreds of others. We've omitted a few categories, such as *Beginner Guitars by Color*, which in our view are not a robust opportunity.

Brass (Level II)

Trumpets (Level III)

Bach (146) (Level IV)	Yamaha (82)	Other Brands (1,380)
Conn, King (98)		

Trombone

Bach, Selmer (53)	Parts, Accessories (103)	Other Brands (586)
Conn, King (85)		

Electronic

Drum Machines (581)

Alesis (50)	Roland (127)	Other Brands (251)
Boss (87)	Yamaha (66)	

Synth (911)

Korg (104)	Yamaha (99)	Other Brands (495)
Roland (213)		

Guitar

Acoustic

Alvarez (135)
Epiphone (81)
Fender (135)
Gibson (278)

Johnson (144)
Martin (500)*
Ovation (173)
Takamine (159)

Taylor (162)
Washburn (162)
Yamaha (149)
Other Brands (3,366)

Amplifiers

Ampeg (141)
Crate (212)
Fender (894)
Kustom (71)

Marshall (434)
Mesa Boogie (239)
Peavey (345)
Vox (97)

Other Brands (1,986)
Parts & Accessories
(485)

Bass

Beginner Packs (48)
Fender (608)

Gibson (52)
Ibanez (128)

Other Brands (1,784)

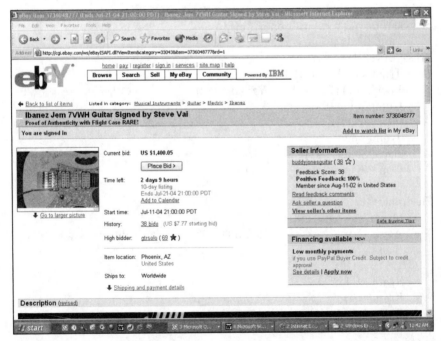

Figure 11-2 You don't have to sell Fenders and Gibsons to succeed in eBay's Electric Guitar category. Other in-demand brands are BC Rich, Gretsch, Ibanez (particularly artist-series examples), G&L, and PRS.

Electric

BC Rich (224)
Danelectro (64)
Dean (103)
Epiphone (366)
ESP (88)
Fender (3,475)
Gibson (1,642)
Gretsch (190)

Guild (72)
Hamer (88)
Ibanez (474)
Jackson (301)
Jay Turser (198)
Johnson (69)
Kramer (96)

Paul Reed Smith
  (203)
Peavey (137)
Rickenbacker (78)
Washburn (171)
Yamaha (86)
Other Electric (392)

Instruction Books, CDs, Videos

Books (1,381)

CDs (464)

Videos (1,265)

Parts, Accessories

Bodies (334)
Bridges (567)
Cables (149)
Capos (118)
Cases (697)
Effects Pedals
  (3,539)

Knobs, Jacks,
  Switches (462)
Necks (372)
Pickguards (301)
Picks (772)
Pickups (1,470)
Polishes, Cleaners (47)

Stands, Hangers (407)
Straps (735)
Strings (928)
Tuners (657)
Tuning Pegs (313)
Other Accessories
  (1,669)

Keyboard

Electronic Keyboards

Casio (279)
Ensoniq (67)
Korg (318)

Kurzweil (98)
Roland (431)

Yamaha (566)
Other Brands (725)

Organ

Hammond (166)

Leslie (88)

Other (524)

Piano

Grand, Baby Grand
  (385)

Parts, Accessories
  (130)

Upright (225)
Other Pianos (545)

Percussion

Cymbals

Crash (336)
Hi-Hat (184)

Ride (206)
Splash (87)

Sets (97)
Other (431)

<u>Drums</u>

Bass (116)	Snare (792)	World (539)
Sets, Mixed Lots (1,146)	Toms (399)	Other (1,417)

<u>Parts, Accessories</u>

Bags, Cases (211)	Hoops, Rims (48)	Stands (417)
Hardware (411)	Mounts, Assembly	Sticks, Brushes (231)
Heads (245)	Pedals (308)	

Pro Audio

<u>Cables</u>

Microphone (182)	Speaker (202)	Other (648)
Snake (276)		

<u>Computer Recording</u>

Interfaces, Hardware (672)	Loops, Samples (600)	Sound Cards (141)
	Software (510)	Other (352)

<u>DJ Equipment</u>

Amplifiers (146)	DJ Mixers (489)	Turntables (482)
Cases (318)	Headsets (236)	Other DJ Equipment (762)
CD Players (320)	Lighting (2,749)	

<u>Microphones</u>

Cables, Cords (74)	Wireless	Vintage (252)
Holders, Stands (412)	Microphones (1,214)	Other (118)
Wired Microphones (2,416)		

<u>Mixers</u>

Behringer (137)	Peavey (91)	Other Brands (895)
Mackie (202)	Yamaha (173)	

<u>Multi-Track Recorders</u>

Alesis (100)	Roland (160)	Other Brands (448)
Fostex (96)	Tascam (325)	

<u>Power Amplifiers</u>

Crown (101)	Peavey (70)	Other Brands (613)

Rack Gear

Compressors, Limiters, Gates (399)

Equalizers (336)
Racks, Cases (583)
Signal Processors (937)

Other Rack Gear (753)

Speakers

Horns, Drivers (143)
Monitors (144)
PA Speakers (557)

Woofers, Subwoofers (287)
Other (449)

eBay TIP: The hot *Musical Instruments* categories in eBay's June 2004 Hot Categories Report from hottest to less hot:

- Guitar > Amplifiers > Mesa Boogie
- Guitar > Electric > Yamaha
- Electronic > Drum Machines > Roland
- Pro Audio > DJ Equipment > CD Players
- Woodwind > Flute > Gemeinhardt
- Electronic > Drum Machines > Boss
- Guitar > Bass > Gibson
- Pro Audio > Multi-Track Recorders > Fostex
- Keyboard, Piano > Electronic Keyboards > Yamaha
- Pro Audio > Multi-Track Recorders > Alesis
- Guitar > Bass > Ibanez
- Keyboard, Piano > Electronic Keyboards > Korg
- Guitar > Electric > Epiphone

The meaning of *hot*: Conversion rates for hot categories the previous month were greater than 50 percent. Growth in bids per item (in the category) outpaced growth in listings by up to 15 percent. In other words, there's more demand than supply in these categories. For more, check out *http://pages .ebay.com/sellercentral/hotitems.pdf*.

Sheet Music, Songbooks

Sheet Music

Blues, Jazz (225)
Classical (668)
Military, Historical (399)
Movies, TV (987)

Popular, by decade (3,558)
Radio (89)
Rag (80)
Theater, Showtunes (578)

Transportation (11)
Other Sheet Music (4,501)
Other (548)

Song Books

Brass & Woodwind (191)	Piano (1,622)	Other Instruments (1,564)
Guitar (1,827)	String Instruments (258)	

String

Violin

4/4 Size (2,550)	1/2 Size (250)	Other Violins (1,848)
3/4 Size (320)	1/4 Size (190)	

Woodwind

Clarinet

Accessories & Parts (208)	Bb Clarinets (731)	Other Clarinets (778)

Flute

Accessories (462)	Pan, Wood Flutes (129)	Other Flutes (1,283)
Armstrong (75)		
Gemeinhardt (137)		

Saxophone

Alto (1,139)	Soprano (234)	Other Saxophones (196)
Baritone, Bass (93)	Tenor (469)	

Level V and Level VI *Musical Instruments* categories only appear in a few Level II categories: *Guitar, Percussion, Pro Audio, Sheet Music,* and *Woodwind.* Again, reviewing these will give you a feel for what types of items have been listed in high enough numbers to command narrow classification.

II	III	IV	V	VI
Guitar> Amp > Fender			> Guitar (804)	
			> Bass (61)	
Guitar > Bass > Fender			> Jazz (119)	
			> Precision (179)	
			> Other Fender (308)	
Guitar > Electric > Fender			> Stratocaster	> American (1,182)
				> Squier (126)
				> Other (686)
			> Telecaster (689)	
			> Other (807)	

Figure 11-3 The Selmer VI is one of the most celebrated models of saxophone. Vintage examples with good original lacquer can command $5,000 and up.

Guitar > Electric > Gibson   > ES (184)
                             > Les Paul (775)
                                                    > Custom (239)
                                                    > Standard (536)
                             > SG (130)

Guitar > Instruction > Books > Method, Instruction (339)
                             > Tab Books (414)
                             > Other Books (629)

Guitar > Parts, Accessories > Hardshell (353)
        > Cases   > Soft, Gig Bags (342)

eBay TIP: Here's a new trend in guitar effects: boutique analog pedals from the '90s are becoming as collectible and valuable as some of the earlier models from the '70s and '80s, produced by major manufacturers like Ibanez and DOD.

Guitar > Parts, Access. > Effects Pedals	> Bass (105) > Boards, Cases (84) > Chorus (154) > Compressors (101) > Delay, Echo, Reverb (257) > Distortion, Overdrive (764) > Distortion, Overdrive (760)	> Boss (156) > Boss (170) > Ibanez (75) > Other Brands (494)
	> Flangers (86) > Fuzz (81) > Multi-Effects (463) > Phasers, Shifters (137) > Processors (131) > Wah, Volume (289) > Other (878)	
Guitar > Parts, Access. > Pickups	> Dimarzio (64) > EMG (53) > Fender (293) > Gibson (112) > Seymour Duncan (153) > Other (803)	
Guitar > Parts, Access. > Tuners	> Korg (58) > Qwik Tune (22) > Other (583)	
Percussion > Cymbal > Crash	> Sabian (79) > Zildjian (176) > Other (89)	
Percussion > Drums > Snare	> DW (45) > Ludwig (161) > Pearl (83) > Slingerland (34) > Other Brands (458)	
Percussion > Drums > World	> African (179) > Indian, Middle Eastern (55) > Latin, Afro-Cuban (235) > Other (84)	

Figure 11-4 A new snare from a top maker such as Huston, Noble & Cooley, or Pork Pie can retail for $500 and up.

Percussion > Parts, Access. > Cymbal (275)
  > Stands   > Drum (145)

Pro Audio > DJ > Lighting > Controllers (271)
                                   > Effects (1,158)
                                   > Glow Sticks (141)
                                   > Stage Lighting (405)
                                   > Stands (117)
                                   > Other Lighting
                                      (640)

Pro Audio > DJ   > Numark (33)
  > Turntables   > Stanton (46)
                                > Technics (139)
                                > Other Brands (255)

Pro Audio > Mic > Wired > Drum (198)
                                 > Dynamic (493)
                                 > Recording, Condenser
                                      (677)

> Vocal (450)	> Hand, Stand (357)
	> Headset, Lavalier (36)
	> Other (57)
> Other (603)	

Sheet Music > Sheet Music > Decade
> Pre 1900 (89)
1970 to Present (1,311)

Woodwind > Saxophone > Alto
> Conn, King (76)
> Selmer (92)
> Yamaha (78)
> Other Brands (919)

MAJOR NAMES AND MAJOR SOURCES FOR INSTRUMENTS

Whether you plan to sell vintage instruments or brand new ones still in the factory box, it's critical to know the major manufacturers and makers in your industry niche. Many of the historic names in the music products industry are still in business and still producing new instruments. Instruments made by bygone companies also are often popular and collectible. Knowing that different resellers will gravitate toward different price points, we've noted manufacturers that cater to the value/student market, as well. Listings for instruments from the following manufacturers and makers all appear on eBay. (We've starred manufacturers or makers that are particularly collectible and whose instruments command higher prices. We generally don't star boutiques because their instruments are not really vintage, though often outstanding.)

Brass: Trumpet/Trombone/Tuba/French Horn

Boutique/Custom
- Calicchio *www.calicchio.com*
- Callet *www.callet.com*
- Courtois *www.courtois-paris.com*
- Edwards *www.edwardsinstruments.com*
- Egger *www.eggerinstruments.ch*
- Ewald Meinl *www.ewaldmeinl.de*
- F.E. Olds *www.feolds.com**
- Gerhard Baier *www.gerhardbaier.com*
- Kalison *www.kalison.com*
- Lawler *www.lawlertrumpets.com*
- Lawson Horns *www.lawsonhorns.com*
- Michael Rath *www.rathtrombones.com*

- Monette *www.monette.net*
- Paxman (French)
  www.paxman.co.uk
- Phaeton
- Schilke *www.schilkemusic.com**
- Schmelzer
  www.schmelzertrombone.de
- Shires Trombones
  www.seshires.com

- Smith Watkins
  www.smithwatkins.com
- Stomvi Trumpets
  www.stomvi.com
- Taylor
  www.taylortrumpets.com
- Willson
  www.swissprofi.ch/willson

Bygone
- Cerveny
- Distin

- Keefer Williams
- J.W. Yorks and Sons

eBay TIP: In *Brass, Cornet, Trumpet* is the dominant category. The Martin Committee is a sought-after model. The top end of the market on eBay appears to be around $3,500 to $5,000. The *Brass* category, according to NAMM's and *Music Trades'* 2003 Music USA report, generated $214 million in product sales in 2002.

Major
- Amati *www.amati-denak.com**
- Bach Stradivarius
  *www.selmer.com**
- B&S
  www.challengertrumpets.com
- Benge *www.unitedmusical.com*
- C.G. Conn *www.cgconn.com**
- Gebr. Alexander
  gebr-alexander.com
- Getzen *www.getzen.com**
- Hirsbrunner Tuba
  www.hirsbrunner.com
- Holton *www.gleblanc.com**

- Jupiter *www.jupitermusic.com*
- Kanstul *www.kanstul.net*
- King *www.unitedmusical.com**
- Martin *www.gleblanc.com**
- Meinl Weston
  www.meinl-weston.com
- Miraphone *www.miraphone.de*
- LeBlanc *www.gleblanc.com**
- Selmer *www.selmer.com**
- Thein *www.thein-brass.de*
- Weril *www.weril.com*
- Yamaha *www.yamaha.com*

Value/Student
- Atkinson Brass
  www.atkinsonhorns.com
- Besson
  www.musicgroup.com
- Blessing
  www.ekblessing.com

- Dynasty
  www.degmusic.com
- EM Winston
  www.emwinston.com
- Palatino

Guitar

Guitar: Acoustic
   Boutique

- Alvarez-Yairi
  www.alvarezgtr.com
- Applegate
  www.applegateguitars.com
- Avalon
  www.avalonguitars.com
- Benedetto
  www.benedetto-guitars.com
- Bourgeois
  www.bourgeoisguitars.com
- Breedlove
  www.breedloveguitars.com
- Charles Fox
  www.charlesfoxguitars.com
- Collings
  www.collingsguitars.com
- Crafter
  www.crafterguitars.com
- Crafters of Tennessee
  crafterstn.com
- Dupont (French selmer-style)
- Froggy Bottom
  froggybottomguitars.com
- Fylde *www.fyldeguitars.com*
- Gallager
  www.gallagherguitar.com

- Goodall
  www.goodallguitars.com
- Huss & Dalton
  www.hussanddalton.com
- KC Chelf
  www.kcchelfguitars.com
- Klein *www.kleinguitars.com*
- Lakewood *www.lakewood.de*
- Laskin
  www.williamlaskin.com
- Lowden
  www.lowdenguitars.com
- Maton *www.maton.com.au*
- McPherson
  www.mcphersonguitars.com
- Morgan
  www.morganguitars.com
- National Reso-Phonic
  nationalguitars.com
- Olson *www.olsonguitars.com*
- Santa Cruz
  www.santacruzguitar.com
- Shelley Park
  www.parkguitars.com
- Weissenborn
  www.weissenbornguitars.com

Bygone

- Dobro-National
  (U.S., 1933–1943)*
- Epiphone (U.S.,
  1873–1957)*
- Espana (Finland,
  1960s–1970s)
- Framus (German,
  1948–1977)*
- Gurian (U.S., 1960–1981)*
- Hagstrom (German,
  1958–1983)
- Harmony (U.S., 1897–1978)

- Kalamazoo (U.S., Gibson,
  1930s–1941, 1968)
- Kay (U.S., 1890–1979)
- Buegeleisen & Jacobson
  (B&J)
- Lyon & Healy/Washburn
  (U.S., 1876–1928)
- National (U.S., 1920s–1968)*
- Old Kraftsman (U.S., Spiegel,
  1930s–1960s)
- Regal (U.S., 1896–1954)
- R.Q. Jones (U.S., 1970s–1980s)

Figure 11-5   Chicago Music Exchange (cruzinfast1) is a top seller of world-class vintage guitars from both major and minor manufacturers.

- Silvertone (U.S., Danelectro/ MCA, 1966–1969)
- Stella/Sovereign (1920–1975)
- Stromberg (U.S., 1910–1955) *
- Vega (U.S., Odells, 1903–1970)

Mid-Size to Major
- Alhambra *www.alhambrasl.com*
- Alvarez *www.alvarezgtr.com*
- Fender *www.fender.com**
- Giannini *www.giannini.com.br*
- Gibson *www.gibson.com**
- Gretsch *www.gretschguitars.com**
- Guild (Gibson) *www.guildguitars.com*
- Hofner *www.musicgroup.com*
- Ibanez *www.ibanez.com*
- Jose Ramirez *www.guitarrasramirez.com*
- Larrivee *www.larrivee.com*
- Martin *www.martinguitars.com**
- Ovation *www.ovationguitars.com*
- Seagull *www.seagullguitars.com*
- Simon & Patrick *www.simonandpatrick.ca*
- Tacoma *www.tacomaguitars.com*
- Takamine *www.takamine.com*
- Taylor *www.taylorguitars.com**
- Washburn *www.washburn.com**
- Yamaha *www.yamaha.com*

Value

- A&L *www.artandlutherie guitars.com*
- Adamas *www.adamasguitars.com*
- Applause *www.kamanmusic.com*
- Aria/Arianna *www.ariaguitars.com*
- AR Musical (Kay) *www.armusical.com*
- Blueridge *www.blueridgeguitars.com*
- Carvin *www.carvin.com*
- Dean *www.deanguitars.com*
- Epiphone/Gibson *www.epiphone.com*

- Garrison *www.garrisonguitars.com*
- Gitane *www.gitaneguitars.com*
- Jasmine *www.jasmineguitars.com*
- Johnson *www.johnsonguitars.com*
- Kramer *www.kramerguitars.com*
- Olympia *www.olympiaguitars.com*
- Samick (Silvertone) *www.samick.com*
- Spencer *www.armusical.com*
- Wechter *www.wechterguitars.com*

Guitar: Electric/Bass

Boutique

- Alamo *www.alamoguitars.com*
- Alembic (Guitar/Bass) *www.alembic.com**
- Asbory (Bass) *www.fender.com*
- Bolin *www.bolinguitars.com*
- Brian Moore *www.bmcguitars.com*
- David McNaught *mcnaughtguitars.com*
- Eko (G/B) *www.ekoguitars.com*
- Fret King *www.fret-king.com*
- Heritage *www.heritageguitar.com*
- Jerry Jones *www.jerryjonesguitars.com*

- Parker *www.parkerguitars.com*
- Patrick Eggle *www.patrickeggle.com*
- Reverend *www.reverendguitars.com*
- Rick Turner *www.renaissanceguitars.com*
- Robin Guitars *www.robinguitars.com*
- Steinberger *www.steinberger.com*
- Valley Arts *www.valleyartsguitar.com*

Bygone

- Coral (U.S., 1954–1969, N. Daniel/Sears)
- Daion (U.S./Japanese, 1978–1983)*
- Danelectro (U.S., 1954–1969, N. Daniel/Sears)*
- Framus (German, 1948–1977)
- Hagstrom (German, 1958–1983)

- Harmony (U.S., 1897–1978)
- Kay (U.S., 1890–1979)
- Music Man (U.S., Guitar/Bass, 1970s–1984)*
- Silvertone (1954–1969, Nathan Daniel)*
- Unicord/Univox (U.S., 1960s–1978)

eBay TIP: The fretted instrument market, including acoustic and electric guitars and strings, is the largest in the music products industry. In 2002, it generated $921 million in total product sales, according to the Music USA report. Unfortunately, prices are not rising with unit sales. In fact, prices declined in 2002 due to excess global capacity, driven by increased manufacturing in China, where the cost of labor is extremely low. According to the report, this has contributed to a 20 percent decline in unit sales of guitars over $1,000. High-end acoustics sustained an 8 percent loss.

Major

- Aria *www.aria.com*
- B.C. Rich *www.bcrich.com*
- Burns *www.burnsguitars.com*
- Charvel *www.charvel.com*
- Cort *www.cort.com*
- Crafter *www.crafter.com*
- Dean *www.deanguitars.com*
- Epiphone
  www.epiphone.com
- ESP *www.espguitars.com*
- Fender *www.fender.com*
- Fernandes
  www.fernandesguitars.com
- G&L *www.glguitars.com*
- Gibson *www.gibson.com*
- Godin *www.godin.com*
- Guild *www.guild.com*
- Hamer/Slammer
  www.hamerguitars.com
- Hofner *www.hofner.com*
- Ibanez *www.ibanezguitars.com*
- Jackson
  www.jacksonguitars.com
- Modulus
  www.modulusguitars.com
- Paul Reed Smith *www.prs.com*
- Rickenbacker
  www.rickenbacker.com
- Schecter
  www.schecterguitars.com
- Warwick (Bass)
  www.warwickbass.com
- Washburn *www.washburn.com*
- Yamaha *www.yamaha.com*

Value

- Daisy Rock
  www.daisyrock.com
- De Armond *www.fender.com*
- Drive *www.switchmusic.com*
- Ernie Ball *www.ernieball.com*
- Jay Turser *www.jayturser.com*
- Johnson
- OLP *www.olpguitars.com*
- Oscar Schmidt
  www.oscarschmidt.com
- Peavey *www.peavey.com*
- Rogue
- Spector *www.spectorbass.com*
- Tokai *www.tokai-guitars.com*

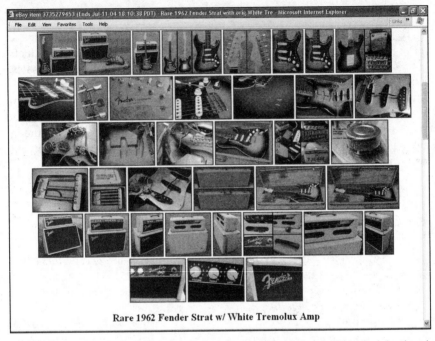

Rare 1962 Fender Strat w/ White Tremolux Amp

Figure 11-6 Now, there's how to illustrate a vintage guitar and amp. This seller's hard work paid off, too. This 1962 custom strat and white Tremolux combo amp went for more than $22,000.

Guitar: Combo Amplifiers ("But, this one goes to 11 . . .")

Boutique
- B-52 *www.b-52pro.com*
- Budda *www.budda.com*
- Carr *www.carramps.com*
- Dr. Z *www.drzamps.com*
- Garnet *www.garnetamps.com*
- Hughes & Kettner
  hughes-and-kettner.com
- Matamp *www.matamp.co.uk**
- Matchless
  www.matchlessamplifiers.com

- Randall
  www.randallamplifiers.com
- Soldano *www.soldano.com*
- Trace Elliot
  www.trace-elliot.com
- UltraSound
  www.ultrasound.com
- VHT *www.vhtamp.com*
- Zinky *www.zinky.com*

Bygone
- Alamo (U.S., 1947–1982)*
- Danelectro (see above)
- Epiphone (see above)

- Kalamazoo (U.S., 1960s)
- MusicMan (LeoFender, 1976–1984)

- National (see above)
- Supro (U.S., National Dobro/Valco, 1935)
- Traynor (Canadian, Yorkville, 1963–1976)
- Univox (U.S., 1960s–1978)
- Valco (U.S.)

Mid-Size to Major
- Ampeg *www.ampeg.com**
- Ashdown *www.ashdownmusic.com*
- Carvin *www.carvin.com*
- Crate *www.crateamps.com*
- Fender *www.fender.com**
- Fishman *www.fishman.com*
- GenzBenz *www.genzbenz.com*
- Hiwatt *www.hiwatt.com**
- Kustom *www.kustom.com*
- Laney *www.laney.co.uk**
- Line 6 *www.line6.com*
- Marshall *www.marshallamps.com**
- Orange *www.orangeusa.com**
- Pignose *www.pignoseamps.com*
- Rivera *www.rivera.com*
- Rocktron *www.rocktron.com*
- Roland *www.roland.com*
- SWR (Fender) *www.swrsound.com*
- Tech 21 *www.tech21nyc.com*
- THD *www.thdamps.com*
- Tube Works *www.genzbenz.com**
- Vox *www.vox.com**
- Washburn *www.washburn.com*
- Yorkville *www.yorkville.com**

eBay TIP: The fundamental difference between economy and new boutique amplifiers? More expensive boutique amps are often hand-wired and equipped with vacuum tubes (EL34s, 6L6, Sovtek KT88), while budget examples are typically solid-state devices with printed circuit boards and diodes. Most major amplifier companies moved to solid-state technology in the '80s, setting the stage for the boutique amp movement in the '90s, which continues today, as well as the current surge in reissues of popular amps from the '60s by the majors.

Value
- Alesis *www.alesis.com*
- Behringer *www.v-amp.com*
- Brand X (Fender) *www.brandxamps.com*
- Drive *www.switchmusic.com*
- Gorilla *www.pignoseamps.com*
- Hartke (Samson) *www.hartke.com*
- Peavey *www.peavey.com*
- Rogue
- Squire (Fender) *www.squireguitars.com*
- SwitchMusic *www.switchmusic.com*
- Zoom (Samson) *www.samsontech.com*

Boutique
- 4MS Pedals
  www.4mspedals.com
- Accutronics
  www.accutronicsreverb.com
- Addrock *www.addrock.com*
- Alfonso Hermida
  www.hermidaaudio.com
- Analog Man
  www.analogman.com
- Area 51
  www.area51tubeaudio designs.com
- Aspect Design
  aspectdesignlabs.com
- Barber
  www.barberelectronics.com
- BSM *www.europeanmusical.com*
- Budda *www.budda.com*
- Carl Martin
  www.carlmartin.com
- Core One *www.coreone.com*
- Emma *www.godlyke.com*
- Hao *www.godlyke.com*
- Jacques *www.ts808.com*
- Legendary Tones
  www.legendarytones.com
- Morley *www.morleypedals.com*
- Prescription
  www.fuzzbox.com
- Radial Engineering
  www.radialeng.com
- Roger Linn Design
  www.rlinndesign.com
- Roger Mayer
  *www.roger-mayer.co.uk**
- Soldano *www.soldano.com*
- Sub Decay *www.subdecay.com*
- SwAMP *www.swampamp.com*
- T-Rex *www.t-rex-eng.com*
- Takky *www.takkydrive.com*
- Toadworks
  www.virtualtoad.com
- Trace Elliot
  www.trace-elliot.com
- Visual Sound
  www.visualsound.net
- Whirlwind
  www.whirlwindusa.com
- Xotic
  www.prosound communications.com
- Zinky *www.zinky.com*

Guitar: Effects
Bygone
- A/DA
- Arbiter-England*
- Dallas Arbiter-England*
- Sola Sound (Tone Bender, Colorsound)
- Systech
- Tel Ray
- Thomas Organ Co. (Crybaby)*
- Tycobrahe
- Univox (U.S., 1960s–1978)
- Way Huge*
- WEM/Watkins (Copycat echo unit)*

Mid-Size to Major
- Akai *www.akai.com**
- Alesis *www.alesis.com*
- Aria *www.aria.com**
- Arion*
- ART *www.artproaudio.com*
- Behringer *www.behringer.com*
- Boss *www.boss.com**
- Digitech *www.digitech.com**

- DOD *www.dod.com**
- Jim Dunlop *www.jimdunlop.com**
- Electro-Harmonix
  www.ehx.com*
- Fulltone *www.fulltone.com*
- Furman *www.furmansound.com*
- Godlyke *www.godlyke.com*
- Guyatone *www.guyatone.com*
- Hughes & Kettner
  hughes-and-kettner.com
- Ibanez *www.ibanez.com**
- Line 6 *www.line6.com*
- Maestro *www.maestro.com**
- Maxon (Nisshin)
  www.godlyke.com
- Moog *www.moogmusic.com**

- MXR *www.mxr.com**
- Pedaltrain *www.pedaltrain.com*
- Rocktron *www.rocktron.com*
- Roland *www.roland.com**
- TC Electronics
  www.tcelectronics.com
- Tech-21 *www.tech21nyc.com*
- THD *www.thdelectronics.com*
- Tube Works
  www.genzbenz.com
- Voodoo Labs
  www.voodoolab.com
- Vox *www.voxamps.co.uk**
- Washburn *www.washburn.com* *
- Yamaha *www.yamaha.com**

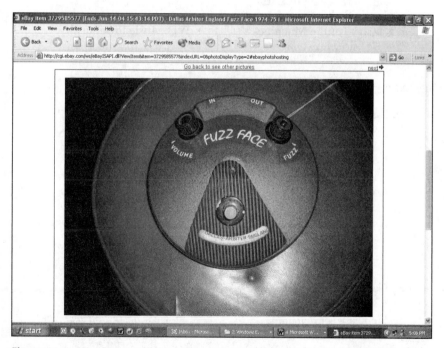

Figure 11-7 America wasn't the only country developing cool toys for guitarists in the '60s. So were the Brits, such as Jim Marshall and Clifford Cooper (Orange Amps). This classic, the Dallas-Arbiter Fuzz Face, is also English.

Value

- Alto *www.altoproaudio.com*
- Danelectro *www.danelectro.com*
- Ernie Ball *www.ernieball.com*
- Hiwatt *www.hiwatt.com*
- Korg *www.korg.com*
- Pro Co *www.procosound.com*
- Rogue
- Sabine *www.sabine.com*
- Seymour Duncan
  seymourduncan.com
- SWR *www.swrsound.com*
- VHT *www.vhtamp.com*
- Zoom *www.samsontech.com*

Guitar: Pickups

- B-Band *www.b-band.com*
- Dean Markley
  www.deanmarkley.com
- DiMarzio *www.dimarzio.com*
- Fender *www.fender.com*
- Fernandes
  www.fernandes_guitars.com
- Fishman *www.fishman.com*
- Lace *www.lace.com*
- LR Bags *www.lrbags.com*
- Performance Plus
  performanceplus.com
- Seymour Duncan
  seymourduncan.com

Guitar: Replacement Parts

- Graph Tech *www.graphtech.com*
- Kluson Tuning Machines
  www.kluson.com
- TonePros *www.tonepros.com*
- WD Music Products
  www.wdmusic.com

Keyboard, Piano

Accordions

- Accordiola
  www.accordionsusa.com
- Boorinwood
  boorinwoodmusic.co.uk
- Borsini
  www.borsiniaccordions.it
- Brandoni
  www.accordionsusa.com
- Bugari Armando
  www.bugariarmando.com
- Castagnari
  www.castagnari.com
- Delicia *www.delicia.cz*
- Dino Baffetti
  www.baffetti-accordions.com
- Excelsior
  www.accordions.com/cemex
- Fratelli
  *www.musicmagicusa
  .com/fratelli.htm*
- Gabbanelli
  www.gabbanelli.com
- Gabbanelli
  *www.gabbanelliaccordions
  .com*
- Galanti
  *www.viscount-organs
  .com*
- Giulietti
  *www.accordionsusa.com/
  giulietti.htm*
- Giustozzi
  *www.accordions.com/
  giustozzi*

- Guerrini
  www.accordions.com/
  guerrini
- Hohner *www.hohnerusa.com*
- Lo Duca Bros
  www.loducabros.com
- Monarch
  www.accordions.com/
  monarch
- Pigini
  www.pigini-accordions.com

- Saltarelle *www.saltarelle.com*
- Scandalli *www.scandalli.com*
- Sonola
  www.accordions.com/sonola
- Soprani
  www.paolosoprani.com
- Titano
  www.accordions.com/titano
- Tula
  www.accordions.com/tula

Digital Pianos/Synthesizers/Workstations
Bygone
- ARP (U.S. 1969–1981)*
- Cordovox (Italian, 1970s)
- Crumar (Italian, 1977–1987)
- Digisound (U.S., 1980s)
- Electro-Harmonix (German, 1970s–1985)*
- EMS (U.S., 1968–1984)
- Jen (Italian)
- Multivox (U.S., 1970s–1980s)
- Octave/Voyetra (U.S., 1975–1979)

- Optigan (U.S., 1970s)
- PAiA (U.S., 1960s–1970s)*
- Sequential Circuits (U.S., 1978–1987)*
- Thomas Organ Co. (1973, Moog)*
- Triadex (U.S., M.I.T., 1970s)
- Unicord/Univox (U.S., 1960s–1978)

eBay TIP: Analog synthesizers from the late '60s to early '80s are quite collectible (ARP Odyssey, PAiA Proteus, Sequential Circuits' Prophet, Moog Mini-Moog); however, that isn't as true for electronic keyboards. In brief, newer keyboards are generally better than their predecessors, offering improved sounds and functionality and encouraging players to upgrade rather than play older models. There are exceptions, such as the Yamaha DX7. Total product sales of "Portable Keyboards" and "Keyboard Synthesizers" in 2002, according to NAMM's Music USA Report, equaled $180 million and $103 million, respectively.

Mid-Size to Major
- Akai *www.akai.com*
- Alesis *www.alesis.com*
- Applied Acoustic Systems
  www.aas.com

- Arturia *www.arturia.com*
- Casio *www.casio.com**
- Clavia *www.clavia.se*
- E-mu *www.emu.com*

- Elka *www.generalmusic.com*
- EMS *www.ems-synthi
  .demon.co.uk**
- Ensoniq *www.ensoniq.com*
- Fender *www.fender.com**
- GEM *www.generalmusic.com**
- Hartmann
  www.hartmann-synth.com
- Kawai *www.kawai.com*
- Korg *www.korg.com*
- Kurzweil *www.kurzweil.com*

- Moog *www.moogmusic.com**
- Nord *www.nord.com*
- Novation *www.novation.com*
- Oberheim (Gibson)
  *www.oberheim.com**
- Open Labs *www.openlabs.com*
- Roland *www.roland.com**
- Solton *www.solton.com**
- Technics *www.technics.com*
- Wersi *www.wersi.net*
- Yamaha *www.yamaha.com**

Organs
- Hammond Suzuki
  hammondsuzuki.com (B3)*
- Leslie
  www.hammondsuzuki.com

- Lowrey *www.lowrey.com*
- Schafer & Sons
  www.coltonpiano.com
- Yamaha *www.yamaha.com*

Piano
Bygone
- Aeolian (U.S., 1887–1932)
- Aeolian-American
  (U.S., 1932–1985)
- Cable-Nelson (U.S., 1900s)
- Charles M. Steiff
  (U.S., 1850s–1900s)
- D.H. Baldwin (Baldwin,
  see below)
- Emerson, (U.S., 1850–1940s)
- Gulbransen (U.S., 1915–1969)
- Hamilton (U.S., 1900–1989)
- Hampton (Story & Clark,
  see below)
- Hardman (U.S., 1842–1982)*
- Hardman & Peck
  (U.S., 1890–1982)*
- Hobart M. Cable
  (U.S., 1900–1960s)
- Howard (U.S., 1895–1968)
- Ivers & Pond (Aeolian)
- Kimball (U.S., 1865–1996)
- Knabe (U.S., 1859–1983)

- Kohler & Campbell
  (U.S., 1900–1980s)
- Kranich & Bach (Baldwin)
- Lester (U.S., 1888–1960)
- Lindeman (U.S., 1860–1947)
- Lowrey (Story & Clark,
  see below)
- Marshall & Wendell
  (U.S., 1875–1953)
- Mason & Risch
  (Canadian, 1871–1971)
- Rönisch (German, 1845–1945,
  1990–1997)
- Schiedmayer (German,
  1853–1969)
- Sherman Clay (brand until
  1987)
- Stodart (U.S., 1870–1931)
- Vose & Sons (1851–1982)
- Wing and Son,
  (U.S., 1870–1928)

eBay TIP: The piano market (vertical, digital, electronic player, grand, and portable) was the third largest in 2002, according to the NAMM's Music USA report, enjoying total product sales of $693 million, just behind sound reinforcement and fretted instruments. It's worth noting that sales of low-cost grand pianos from China and Indonesia, retailing for under $10,000, increased more than 50 percent.

Major to High-End

- Baldwin (Gibson)
    baldwinpiano.com
- Bechstein *www.bechstein.de*
- Bluthner *www.bluthner.com*
- Bosendorfer
    www.bosendorfer.com
- Boston (Steinway)
    www.steinway.com
- Broadwood
    www.uk-piano.org/broadwood
- Cable (Story & Clark)
    www.qrsmusic.com
- Chappell *www.chappellofbond
    street.co.uk*
- Chickering *www.baldwin.com*
- Dietmann *www.bernhardsteiner
    pianos.com*
- Disklavier (Yamaha)
    www.yamaha.com
- Estonia *www.estoniapiano.com*
- Hallet Davis *www.namusic.com*
- Hamburg Steinway
    www.steinway.com
- Heintzman *www.hzmpiano.com*
- Howard (Kawai)
    www.kawai.com
- IBack *www.iback.de*
- J&C Fischer *www.baldwin.com*
- Kawai *www.kawai.com*

- Mason & Hamlin
    www.masonhamlin.com
- Petrof *www.petrof.cz*
- Pramberger
    www.youngchang.com
- Samick *www.samickpiano.com*
- Sauter *www.pianos.de/sauter*
- Schafer & Sons
    www.coltonpiano.com
- Schiedmayer *www.kawai.com*
- Schimmel
    www.schimmel-piano.de
- Schulze Pollmann
    www.schulzepollmann.com
- Seiler *www.seiler-pianos.de*
- Sohmer *www.masonhamlin.com*
- Steiner
    bernhardsteinerpianos.com
- Steinway *www.steinway.com*
- Story and Clark
    www.storyandclark.com
- Suzuki *www.suzukipiano.com*
- Williams
    www.williamspiano.com
- Wurlitzer
    www.baldwinpiano.com
- Yamaha *www.yamaha.com*
- Young Chang
    www.youngchang.com

Value

- Arcosonic (Baldwin)
  www.baldwin.com
- Astin-Weight
  www.astin-weight.com
- Conn Pianos
  www.connpianos.com
- Diapason (Kawai)
  www.kawai.com
- Everett (Wrightwood
  Enterprises)
- George Steck
  www.pianodisc.com
- Gulbransen
  www.gulbransen.com
- Hamilton (Baldwin)
  www.baldwin.com

- Hyundai (Samick)
  www.namusic.com
- Janssen (Walter)
  www.walterpiano.com
- Jasper American
  www.bosendorfer.com
- Krakauer
  www.krakauer.net
- Pearl River
  www.pearlriverpiano.com
- Rieger-Kloss
  www.weberpiano.com
- Weber (Young & Chang)
  www.weber.com

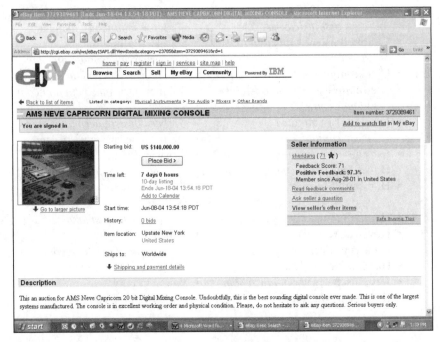

Figure 11-8 Though hard to imagine, studios frequently list 48-channel digital mixing consoles, from the likes of Neve and Otari, in eBay's Pro Audio category.

Pro Audio

Microphones/Microphone Pre-Amps
- AKG *www.akg.com*
- Aphex *www.aphex.com*
- API *www.apiaudio.com*
- ART *www.artaudio.com*
- Audio Technica
  www.audiotechnica.com
- Audix *www.audixusa.com*
- Avalon *www.avalonaudio.com*
- Behringer *www.behringer.com*
- Bellari *www.rolls.com*
- Beyer Dynamic
  www.beyerdynamic.com
- Blue Microphones
  www.bluemic.com
- CAD *www.cadmic.com*
- Coles (Ribbon)
- Crown
  www.crowninternational.com
- DBX *www.dbxpro.com*
- EAR *www.ear.net*
- Electro-Voice
  www.electrovoice.com
- Fen-Tone (Japan, 1960s)
- FMR Audio *www.fmraudio.com*
- Focusrite *www.focusrite.com*
- Gemini
- Grace Design
  www.gracedesign.com
- Great River *www.greatriver electronics.com*
- Groove Tubes
  www.groovetubes.com
- HHB *www.hhb.co.uk*

- Hisonic (Lapel, Karaoke)
- Lax-Max (wireless)
- M-Audio *www.m-audio.com*
- Marshall *www.mxlmics.com*
- Micophon (lapel)
- Nady *www.nadywireless.com*
- Neumann *www.neumann.com**
- Neve *www.ams-neve.com**
- Oktava *www.oktava.net*
- Peavey *www.peavey.com*
- Presonus *www.presonus.com*
- Pyle *www.pyleaudio.com*
- Rane *www.rane.com*
- RCA (ribbon)*
- Realistic (Radio Shack)*
- Rode *www.rodemic.com*
- Royer *www.royerlabs.com*
  (Ribbon)
- Sabine *www.sabine.com*
  (wireless)
- Samson *www.samson.com*
- Sennheiser
  www.sennheiser.com
- Shure *www.shure.com*
- Sony *www.sony.com*
- Telefunken
  www.telefunkenusa.com
- Telex *www.telex.com* (wireless)
- TL Audio *www.tlaudio.co.uk*
- Universal Audio
  www.uaudio.com
- Western Electric*
- Yamaha *www.yamaha.com*

Mixers, Analog & Digital
- Alesis *www.alesis.com*
- Allen & Heath
  www.allen-heath.com
- Alto *www.altoproaudio.com*
- ART *www.artaudio.com*

- Behringer *www.behringer.com*
- Boss *www.boss.com*
- Carvin *www.carvin.com*
- Crate *www.crate.com*
- Crest *www.crestaudio.com*

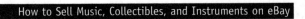
- Digidesign *www.digidesign.com*
- DOD *www.dod.com*
- EV *www.electro-voice.com*
- Fostex *www.fostex.com*
- Gemini
- Korg *www.korg.com*
- Mackie Designs
  www.mackie.com
- NADY *www.nadywireless.com*
- Neve *www.ams-neve.com*
- Peavey *www.peavey.com*
- Phonic *www.phonic.com*

- Rane *www.rane.com*
- Roland *www.roland.com*
- Samson *www.samson.com*
- Shure *www.shure.com*
- Sony *www.sony.com*
- Soundcraft
  www.soundcraft.com
- Soundtech *www.soundtech.com*
- Studiomaster
  www.studiomaster.com
- Tascam *www.tascam.com*
- Yamaha *www.yamaha.com*

Recording

Analog/Digital Recorders
Computer Soundcards, Interfaces, Software, Loops

- Akai *www.akai.com*
- Alesis *www.alesis.com*
- Boss *www.boss.com*
- Cakewalk *www.cakewalk.com*
  (Sonar)
- Digidesign *www.digidesign.com*
  (Pro Tools)
- Echo Digital
  www.echoaudio.com
- Emagic *www.emagic.de* (logic)
- E-MU *www.emu.com*
- Fostex *www.fostex.com*
- Fruity Loops
  www.fruityloops.com (loops)
- HHB *www.hhb.co.uk*
- iZ Corp *www.izcorp.com*
  (Radar)
- Korg *www.korg.com*
- M-Audio *www.m-audio.com*
- Magix *www.magix.com*

- Mackie Designs *www.makie.com*
- Marantz *www.marantz.com*
- MOTU *www.motu.com*
  (Interfaces)
- Neve *www.ams-neve.com*
- Otari *www.otari.com*
  (2-track tape)
- Panasonic *www.panasonic.com*
- Propellerhead
  www.propellerheads.se
  (Reason)
- Roland *www.roland.com*
- Sony *www.sony.com*
- Steinberg (Cubase)
- Studer* (Reel-to-Reel)
- Tascam *www.tascam.com*
- TEAC *www.teac.com*
- Technics *www.technics.com*
- Yamaha *www.yamaha.com*
- Zoom

Power Amplifiers
- Behringer *www.behringer.com*
- Carvin *www.carvin.com*
- Crest *www.crestaudio.com*
- Crown *www.crownaudio.com*
- Hafler *www.hafler.com*

- Mackie Designs *www.mackie.com*
- Peavey *www.peavey.com*
- Pyle *www.pyleaudio.com*
- Soundtech *www.soundtech.com*
- Yamaha *www.yamaha.com*

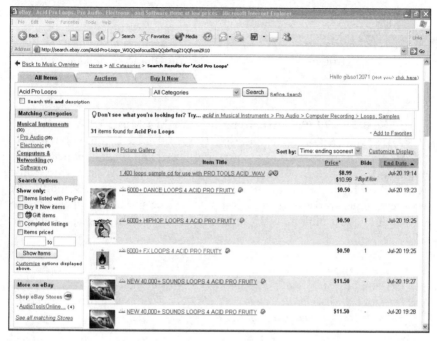

Figure 11-9   You won't find a lot of pro audio sellers selling Acid Pro 4.0 (from Sony Pictures Digital) on eBay, but you will find a lot of homemade loop compilations, which you can use in Acid.

Rack Gear
Compressors, Equalizers, Signal Processors, Other

- ADA *www.ada.com*
- Alesis *www.alesis.com*
- ART *www.artaudio.com*
- Avalon *www.avalondesign.com* (EQ)
- Behringer *www.behringer.com*
- Boss *www.boss.com*
- BSS *www.bss.co.uk*
- DBX *www.dbxpro.com*
- Digitech *www.digitech.com*
- DOD *www.dod.com*
- Furman *www.furmansound.com*
- GML *www.massenburg.com*
- Ibanez *www.ibanez.com*

- Klark Teknik *www.klarkteknik.com*
- Korg *www.korg.com*
- Lexicon *www.lexicon.com*
- Line 6 *www.line6.com*
- Manley Laboratories *www.manleylabs.com*
- Nady *www.nadywireless.com*
- Neve *www.ams-neve.com*
- Prism Sound *www.prismsound.com*
- Pultec*
- Rane *www.rane.com*
- Roland *www.roland.com*
- Sabine *www.sabine.com*

- Soundtech *www.soundtech.com*
- Symetrix
  www.symetrixaudio.com
- TC Electronics
  www.tcelectronics.com

- Urei*
- White Instruments
  www.whiteinstruments.com
- Yamaha *www.yamaha.com*
- Zoom

eBay TIP: According to NAMM's Music USA report, the sound reinforcement industry (powered mixers, nonpowered mixers, speaker enclosures, power amplifiers, and single-unit instrument amplifiers) generated $850 million in product sales in 2002, a slight decline from 2001. This number does not include sales of microphones, multitrack recorders, signal processors, and computer music products, which grossed $369 million, $76 million, $213 million, and $223 million, respectively, in 2002.

Sound Proofing
- Audimute *www.audimute.com*
- Auralex *www.auralex.com*
- HSF *www.hsfacoustics.com*

- Modular Acoustics
  www.modularacoustics.com

Speakers
Monitors, PA, Woofers
- Alesis *www.alesis.com*
- ART *www.artaudio.com*
- Audix *www.audixusa.com*
- Behringer *www.behringer.com*
- Crate *www.crate.com*
- DynAudio *www.dynaudio.com*
- EAW *www.eaw.com*
- Electro Voice
  www.electro-voice.com
- Event *www.event1.com*
- FBT
- Fender *www.fender.com*
- Fostex *www.fostex.com*
- Genelec *www.genelec.com*
- JBL *www.jbl.com*

- KRK Systems
  www.krksys.com
- M-Audio *www.m-audio.com*
- Mackie Designs
  www.mackie.com
- Peavey *www.peavey.com*
- Phonic *www.phonic.com*
- PMC *www.pmc-speakers.com*
- Pyle *www.pyleaudio.com*
- Roland *www.roland.com*
- SoundTech *www.soundtech.com*
- Tannoy Reveal
  www.tannoyna.com
- Yamaha *www.yamaha.com*
- Yorkville *www.yorkville.com*

Percussion

Drums, Snares, Heads, Accessories
Boutique

- Ayotte
  www.ayottedrums.com
- Black Swamp
  www.blackswamp.com
- C&C
  www.candccustomdrums.com
- Cadeson
  www.cadesonmusic.com
- Canopus
  www.canopusdrums.com
- Craviotto
  www.craviottodrums.com
- Drum Solo *www.drumsolo.cc*
- Dunnett *www.dunnett.com*

- King Vanguard
  www.koeniginc.com
- Noble and Cooley
  www.noblecooley.com
- Phattie *www.phattiedrums.com*
- Pork Pie
  www.porkpiedrums.com
- Precision
  www.precisiondrum.com
- RMV *www.rmvdrums.com*
- Tamburo *www.tamburo.com*
- Treeworks
  www.treeworkschimes.com
- Zickos *www.zickosdrums.com*

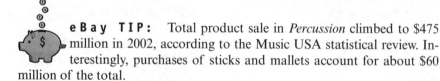

eBay TIP: Total product sale in *Percussion* climbed to $475 million in 2002, according to the Music USA statistical review. Interestingly, purchases of sticks and mallets account for about $60 million of the total.

Major

- Aquarian
  www.aquariandrumheads.com
- BAFO *www.bafo.com*
- Beato Bags *www.beatobags.com*
- Danmar
  www.danmarpercussion.com
- Drum Workshop
  www.dwdrums.com
- Evans
  www.evansdrumheads.com
- Fibes *www.fibes.com**
- GMS *www.gmsdrums.com*
- Gretsch
  *www.gretschdrums.com**
- Grover *www.groverpro.com*
- Hardcase *www.hardcase.com*
- Hart Dynamics
  www.hartdynamics.com

- Humes and Berg
  www.humes-berg.com
- Ludwig
  *www.ludwig-drums.com**
- Mapex
  www.mapexdrums.com
- Pacific
  www.pacificdrums.com
- Pearl *www.pearldrum.com**
- Pintech *www.pintech.com*
- Premier
  www.premier-percussion.com
- Protec *www.ptcases.com*
- Protechtor Cases
  www.xlspec.com
- Remo *www.remo.com**
- Rhythm Tech
  www.rhythmtech.com

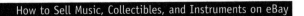

- Rogers *www.rogersdrums.com**
- Roland *www.roland.com*
- Sonor (Hohner)
  *www.hohnerusa.com**
- Stagg *www.staggmusic.com*
- Tama *www.tama.com*
- Yamaha
  www.yamahadrums.com

Value
- Arbiter
  www.arbiterdrums.com
- Attack
  www.universalpercussion.com
- Peace
  www.peacedrum.com
- Rockwood (Hohner)
  www.rockwood.com
- Slingerland (Gibson)
  *www.gibson.com**
- Sunlite *www.sunlitedrum.com*
- Taye *www.taye.com*

Cymbals
- Bosphorus
  www.bosphoruscymbals.com
- Headliner *www.headliner.de*
- Istanbul
  www.istanbulcymbals.com
- Meinl *www.meinl.de*
- Orion
  www.orioncymbals.com.br
- Paiste *www.paiste.com*
- Sabian *www.sabian.com*
- Saluda *www.saludacymbals.com*
- Stagg *www.staggmusic.com*
- Turkish
  www.turkishcymbals.com
- UFIP *www.ufip.com*
- Wuhan
  www.universalpercussion.com
- Zildjian *www.zildjian.com*

String

Banjo/Mandolin
- Applause
  www.applauseguitars.com
- Breedlove *www.breedlove.com*
- Crafter
  www.crafterguitars.com
- Dean *www.deanguitars.com*
- Gibson *www.gibson.com*
- Hohner
  www.hohnerusa.com
- Johnson
- Michael Kelly
  www.michaelkellyguitars.com
- Orpheum
- Oscar Schmidt
  www.oscarschmidt.com
- Ovation
  www.ovationguitars.com
- Tacoma
  www.tacomaguitars.com
- Washburn *www.washburn.com*

eBay TIP: Of the total school instrument market, which generated more than $570 million in sales, student stringed instruments contributed only $55 million. Conversely, the brass and woodwind market generated $214 and $302 million in sales, respectively, according to

NAMM's Music USA statistical review. Many professional grade instruments in the violin family are handcrafted by small independent makers. Visit the Violin Society of America's Web site: *www.vsa.to/violinmakers.htm*. Also visit *maestronet.com*.

Bass/Cello/Viola/Violin
- Clevinger *www.clevinger.com*
- Doreli
- Engelhardt
  www.engelhardtlink.com
- Fender *ww.fender.com*
- Glaesel *ww.glaesel.com*
- Johannes Kohr
  www.howardcore.com
- NS Design
  www.nedsteinberger.com
- Palatino
- Schiller
- Silver Creek
- Strunal
- Yamaha *www.yamaha.com*

Woodwind

Bassoon/Clarinet/Flute/Oboe/Piccolo/Saxophone

Major/Professional
- Armstrong
  www.unitedmusical.com
- Buffet Crampon
  *www.musicgroup.com**
- Chadash
  www.chadashclarinet.com
- Charles Bay
  www.baywoodwind.com
- Conn *www.cgconn.com**
- Fox *www.foxproducts.com*
- Gemeinhardt
  www.gemeinhardt.com
- Jupiter *www.jupiterflutes.com*
- Keilwerth *www.musicgroup.com*
- LeBlanc *www.gleblanc.com*
- King *www.unitedmusical.com**
- Marigaux
  *www.sml-marigaux.com**
- Martin *www.gleblanc.com*
- Morgan
  ralphmorganmusicinfo.com
- Patricola *www.patricola.it*
- Rico (Reeds)
  www.ricoreeds.com
- Rigoutat *www.rigoutat.fr*
- Selmer *www.selmer.com**
- Vandoren *www.vandoren.com*
- Vito *www.gleblanc.com**
- W. Schreiber
  www.musicgroup.com
- Winter (cases)
  www.musicgroup.com
- Yamaha *www.yamaha.com**
- Yanagisawa
  www.yanagisawasax.co.jp

Value/Student
- Amati
  www.amati-denak.com
- Artley *www.unitedmusic.com*
- Besson *www.musicgroup.com*
- EM Winston
  www.emwinston.com

- Emerson
  www.emersonflutes.com
- Hall *www.hallflutes.com*
- Howarth *www.howarth.uk.com*

- J & D Hite *www.jdhite.com*
- Palatino
- Wurlitzer
  www.wurlitzerclarinets.com

MARKET RESEARCH

You've picked a complex, fast moving, yet fascinating industry in which to build your eBay business. Keeping up with changes and trends even in a single music-products industry niche can be challenging. We're sure you can see that after reviewing the hundreds of makers and manufacturers servicing this massive industry, which generates billions of dollars in sales every year. Fortunately, the Internet, and eBay for that matter, has made developing a real expertise in a niche you are interested in much easier. Here are some key Internet resources to bookmark for your business, some of which we noted in Chapter 4.

First, it's definitely in your interests to become a member of NAMM, though this can be difficult because you need referrals, and to subscribe to *Music Trades*, both of which provide useful statistical information on gross

Figure 11-10 NAMM and Music USA's essential annual statistical review of sales in the music products industry.

merchandise sales in the various music products categories. NAMM's annual statistical review of the industry, MusicUSA, from which we pulled the preceding data in our Major Names section, is just one resource NAMM offers (see Figure 11-10). Harmony Central is vital as well, because you can gauge opinion not only on current products in all the categories, but also, as a vintage dealer, learn about classic gear, which is often rated by users, and read up on bygone manufacturers. Another interesting site is Prepal, which aggregates realized prices for vintage instruments and equipment off the Internet, including eBay. It even provides an up-and-down pricing-trend indicator. Prepal.com also is an excellent industry overview. Turn to these resources for your music–products research.

- Harmony Central *www.harmonycentral.com*
- International Music Products Association *www.namm.com*
- MusicToyz *www.musictoyz.com*
- The Music Trades *www.musictrades.com*
- Prepal *www.prepal.com*
- Sonic State *www.sonicstate.com*
- Usenet *rec.music.makers*
- Yahoo Groups, Music, Instruments *http://launch.dir.groups.yahoo .com/dir/Music/Instruments*

Here are some Internet destinations and portals for each of our *Musical Instruments* categories. Try searching for more on your favorite Web Directories, like Yahoo and Google. Because there are countless sites, we can only cover the major ones here.

Brass

- Hornplayer.net
  www.hornplayer.net
- International Trombone
  Association *www.ita-web.org*
- International Trumpet Guild
  www.trumpetguild.org
- Trombone Page of the World
  www.trombone-usa.com
- Tuba Central
  www.tubacentral.com
- Windplayer Online
  www.windplayer.com

Guitar

- Acoustic Guitar Central
  www.acguitar.com
- Bass Player
  www.bassplayer.com
- Gruhn Guitars
  www.gruhnguitar.com
- Guild of American Luthiers
  www.luth.org
- Guitar Notes
  www.guitarnotes.com
- Guitar Pedal.com
  www.guitar-pedal.com

- Guitar Player
  www.guitarplayer.com
- Guitar World
  www.guitarworld.com
- Guitarist *www.guitarist.com*
- MusicToyz *www.musictoyz.com*

- ToneFrenzy
  www.tonefrenzy.com
- Ultimate Tone
  www.ultimatetone.com
- VintageGuitar.com
  www.vintageguitar.com

Harmonica

- Harmonica Links.com
  www.harmonicalinks.com

Keyboard, Piano

- Accordions.com
  www.accordions.com
- Electronic Musician
  electronicmusician.com
- The Gas Station
  www.gasstation.com
- Old Pianos
  www.oldpiano.com
- Piano.com *www.piano.com*
- The Piano Page
  www.ptg.org

- Piano World
  www.pianoworld.com
- Synthesizer Playground
  keyboardmuseum.org
- Synthmuseum.com
  www.synthmuseum.com
- Synthzone.com
  www.synthzone.com
- Virtual Piano Shop
  www.pianouk.com

Percussion

- Drum!
  www.drumlink.com
- Drum.com
  www.drum.com
- DrummerWorld
  www.drummerworld.com
- Latin Percussionist
  www.latinpercussion.com

- Modern Drummer
  moderndrummer.com
- Not So Modern Drummer *www*
  .notsomoderndrummer.com
- The Percussive Arts Society
  www.pas.org
- PMC *www.playdrums.com*

Pro Audio

- Digital Pro Sound
  digitalprosound.com
- EQ
  www.eqmag.com
- Home Studio Review
  homestudioreview.com

- HRC
  homerecordingconnection.com
- Mix Online
  www.mixonline.com
- ProRec.com
  www.prorec.com

- Recording Magazine
  www.recordingmag.com
- Sonic State *www.sonicstate.com*
- Sound On Sound
  www.sospubs.co.uk
- The Tapeless Studio
  www.tapeless.com
- TapeOp *www.tapeop.com*

String

- British Violin Makers
  Association
  www.bvma.org.uk/index.htm
- Cello Heaven
  www.celloheaven.com
- Four String Banjo Links
  www.4shelties.com/banjos
- Mandolin Café
  www.mandolincafe.com
- Maestronet
  www.maestronet.com
- The Violin Society of America
  www.vas.to

Woodwind

- British Double Reed Society
  www.bdrs.org.uk
- Flute.com *www.flute.com*
- Flutes Are Fun!
  www.harpsong.org
- International Clarinet
  Association *www.clarinet.org*
- International Double Reed
  Society *www.idrs.org*
- The International Saxophone
  Home Page
  www.saxophone.org
- National Flute Association
  www.nfaonline.org
- SaxKing
  www.saxking.com
- Sax on the Web
  www.saxontheweb.net

eBay TIP: As you develop a customer base and list, ask your customers what brands they are most interested in. Their answers will probably surprise you. Include fun trivia questions and polls in your product newsletters and bulletins to garner opinions and insights from existing customers. Offer repeat buyers a couple free CDs to participate in a survey that features questions regarding which instruments you should carry more of and which ones you could drop.

The other good thing about exploring these smaller informational sites is that many accept advertising via which you can promote your Web site, eBay Store, or eBay listings. Moreover, if customers end up buying in your eBay Store because of that advertising, then eBay will credit you 50 percent of that item's final value fees through its Store Referral program.

TOP BUYER SEARCHES

Let's talk about buyer keywords for instruments. Knowing how instrument buyers search on eBay is critical because the search terms tell you what your potential customers are looking for, and that provides you valuable insight into what brands, products, and models you should be sourcing. As we mentioned in Chapter 10, eBay offers two extremely valuable tools for identifying the search terms buyers are using most in every category:

- Common Keywords: *http://keyword-index.ebay.com/A-1.html*
- eBay Keyword: *http://buy.ebay.com*

As previously mentioned, Common Keywords provide sellers an immediate way to evaluate if they are actually selling the specific products that their buyers are searching for. This is invaluable. Common Keywords not only enables sellers to write more targeted listing titles that appear in buyer search results more often, but also enables them to give themselves a bit of a reality check. A quick spin through Common Keywords and sellers will see what their buyers really want and if their business is actually meeting demand. If not, it might be time for sellers to augment or upgrade their product lineup, replacing some of their slow movers for the items reflected in the search terms. Moreover, as we mentioned before, Common Keywords raises awareness for items that sellers didn't realize were as relevant as they are and helps point their business in lucrative new directions.

Let's illustrate this: Look up "Fender" and you'll see buyers aren't just searching for Strats and Teles, but also Bandmasters, Customs, Broncos, Jaguars, Jazzmasters, Musicmasters, Mustangs, P-Basses, and Precisions, not to mention an array of Fender amps, from Bassmans, Blackfaces, Champs, and Deluxes to Princetons and Pro Reverbs, and every Fender part under the sun—even Fender decals, logos, and emblems, a hot little niche. In short, you'll get a glimpse at a significant piece of the Fender market on eBay by looking at one page.

Common Keywords "Fender Mexican" and "Fender Japan" also indicate there's a market for budget brands. Another interesting takeaway is that Common Keywords such as "Fender blue" and "Fender red" reveal that colors really do matter. It appears not everyone wants that classic sunburst look. Finally, Fender's Common Keywords provide a revealing look at what Fender manufacturing years are likely hot on eBay: '57, '59, '62, '65, '68, '69, and '72. Look up "Gibson" and you'll find '57 is the year for Les Pauls. No surprise, really; that's the year this famous model was introduced. That's good to confirm, however, because it suggests how up-market the eBay guitar market has become.

And what about Gibson? There are scores of electric and acoustic models to choose from, whether you're a vintage dealer or a B-stock reseller. Before you buy that next J200, J45, Hummingbird, Dove, Les Paul, Epiphone, SG, or ES (Electro Spanish) model, it would be good to review which of these models are being searched for most regularly, because that indicates where the buying is happening. Well, here's the answer:

Gibson 335	Gibson J (as in 45, 200, etc.)
Gibson banjo	Gibson LG (unexpected . . .)
Gibson black (interesting . . .)	Gibson LP
Gibson Epiphone	Gibson mandolin
Gibson ES	Gibson SG
Gibson Explorer	Gibson signed
Gibson historic	Gibson USA
Gibson Hummingbird	Gibson vintage

Want to know what's cool (as in desirable) in Yamaha Keyboards? eBay's keyword database gives you a good hint: the DX7, DGX, and budget DJX. Let's do a few more. How about violins? Here are some revealing terms: violin 4/4, violin bow, violin case, violin German, violin Italian, violin new, violin strings, and violin viola cello. If you deal in violins, that probably confirms some of your suspicions. Now, let's do a woodwind comparison: Selmer vs. Conn. Five keywords for Selmer (Selmer Bundy, Selmer C, Selmer clarinet, Selmer Paris, and Selmer saxophone) and four for Conn (Conn 8D, Conn Connstellation, Conn Director, Conn trumpet). Surprisingly, no Selmer "Mark," as in the popular Mark VI. You can do this exercise for every instrument category and learn a lot about your buyers' interests and tastes.

Now onto eBay Keyword pages, which can be used in conjunction with Common Keywords. As previously noted, these pages aggregate all of the listings on eBay that relate to a single search term. Like Common Keywords, as a result, they underscore demand for particular brands and products. Here's a list of musical instrument terms with eBay Keyword pages. When reviewing pages, be sure to look at the "Popular Searches" at the bottom (see Figure 11-11). One final bit of advice: use these keywords as a starting point, not an ending point. There's obviously more to know, more to sell. However, these terms do help you form an initial outlook, if you are considering cross-selling in a category outside you main area. (To bring up a page, just place one of the keywords after the above URL, like this: *http://buy.ebay.com/**acoustic**.*)

acoustic	amp	body
adapter	amplifier	bose
alpine	audio	boutique (guitar)
(manufacturer)	banjo	bridge

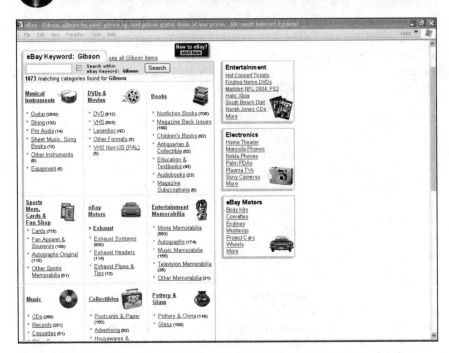

Figure 11-11   Don't forget to look at the "Popular Searches" at the bottom of each page.

cabinet	firebird	marshall
cable	gibson	martin
cartridge	guitar	mixer
case	guitars	monitor
casio	hawaiian	music
challenger	heritage	musical
clamps	ibanez	national
compressor	jackson	neck
console	jaguar	pa
control	japan	pacific
custom	jbl	panasonic
decal	kenwood	parts
decals	les paul	paul smith
deck	lighting	pedal
dj	logo	piano
drums	long (cord, strap)	pickups
effects	magazine	pioneer (pro audio)
electric guitar	marantz	player
fender	mark (selmer)	pro audio

rack	speakers	traps
recorder	stand	turntable
recording	sticker	usb
roland	string	vintage
sheet	subwoofer	violin
software	supreme	wood
sonic	system (P.A.)	yamaha
speaker	tacoma	

TRACKING THE MARKET

All right, enough about buyer search terms, let's talk about keeping current on your market: music products and musical instruments. As we discussed in Chapter 10, you'll use eBay's Completed Item search in conjunction with your My eBay page to save searches for the last two weeks of closed listings. This will allow you to track realized prices for up to 100 products, brands, and models that you sell, and also attach e-mail notification to 30 of your favorite completed item searches. (To learn more, visit *http://pages.ebay.com/ myebay/favoritesearch.html.*) Just as important, you'll recognize what opening bids and Buy It Now prices for the kinds of items you sell were ineffective and garnered no bids, which will help you find the current sweet spot.

eBay TIP: Another good way to track what categories and brands are hot is eBay Seller Central's "In Demand" item under "Sell By Category," featuring brand picks and top buyer searches: *http://pages.ebay.com/sellercentral/sbc/musicinst/whatshot.html*
Stay tuned to eBay's monthly Hot Items by Category report, which reveals what internal eBay categories are hot, very hot, and super hot and where buyer demand is greater than supply. Check it out now: *http://pages.ebay.com/sellercentral/hotitems.pdf*
Finally, keep an eye on eBay's Solutions Directory (under Services) for third-party applications that enable you to collect historical pricing data for your music products.

So what kinds of Completed Item searches should musical instrument sellers be creating? Try this strategy. First, create searches for the popular makers, manufacturers, and brands you carry so that you can get a bird's eye view of the market in your area and gauge the competition (and the penetration of specific companies on the site). One step down, try running searches for specific models that you sell, being careful to include their exact model signatures—DX7, ES 335, Neumann U87—in your search terms. The goal here is to see if the market is reaching saturation in any of your products and to follow how their prices are trending. This is critical because musical instrument buyers are savvy and price sensitive. Since the burst of the stock market bubble, many musicians don't have as much disposable income for their musical adventures and toys. They're going to shop around, hit the search engines, head to Musician's Friend, and maybe even walk in the door at Guitar Center or Sam Ash. In other words, these searches aren't just a diversion, something to do once you're done listing your items. They're important. In order to be competitive in a fast-moving market, you need to know where you should be setting your Store and Buy It Now prices. Your completed-item price guides help you gauge that. Current values also inform how to set your opening prices on no-reserve auctions. You can't reduce the opening of an item a set percentage, say 15 to 25 percent, to attract bids if you're not up-to-date on the item's current value.

Try creating some searches for the new items that you are reading about in major magazines and on gear Web sites, in order to gauge if the eBay market is embracing them. This will help you determine not only if you should try to sell them on eBay, as an authorized dealer or a B-stock reseller, but also if you should carry them on your Web site and in your shop. If something is hot on eBay, it's reasonable to assume it will also sell well elsewhere. If it's getting a lukewarm reception, you know to source fewer or none at all. Finally, every month or every other week (depending on how hardcore you are), track a new batch of very up-market items or more esoteric brands and models, both boutique and vintage (leveraging some of the excellent guides that are available in print) to evaluate if the market in your niche is expanding, contracting, or staying about the same—a reflection of the prevailing interests at large.

eBay TIP: If you have a staff, you might want to have each member of your team create his or her own eBay ID, something you'll do anyway as you grow, so they all can have their own My eBay page. Then, assign each of them one of these search groups. Managing more than 50 searches on your My eBay page can become daunting.

BOOSTING SALES WITH STELLAR LISTINGS

Because each category in *Musical Instruments* is fairly distinct, we'll give some general listing content and design tips for musical instrument and product sellers and then try to give a few more specific ones for each of the main categories.

Create Trust with Your Buyers

In the *Musical Instruments* and *Music Products* category, having a well-formatted, well-conceived HTML template is fairly critical, probably more so than in *Music* and *Music Memorabilia*. There are a couple of reasons for this. Even in the budget instrument range, buyers are going to spend at least a few hundred dollars. That means there is greater risk on their end and they'll be shopping with a critical eye. If your listing doesn't have some polish, effectively communicating who you are and why you are a safe bet, some buyers might hesitate in buying from you. Additionally, many musical instruments have complex feature sets and specs. HTML templates enable you to table and present this material effectively, and even link to it from a tool or navigation bar at the top of your listings. If you have an existing business, graphical templates also enable you to showcase your logo and brand.

Unless you sell authorized product, which enables you to use manufacturer stock photos, you'll want to offer several views of the item. To do this without turning your listing into a scrolling mess, you'll want an HTML template with clickable "thumbnail" images, which provide buyers immediate access to all of your glamour shots and close-ups. Perception is important, too. Besides getting a good deal, musicians want to buy from kindred spirits, other musicians and gear heads. Graphical templates, featuring creative headers, backgrounds, and text treatments, enable you to set the right tone and vibe and to make that connection.

Have a Site That's Easy to Navigate

Sellers who offer a variety of instruments and products across several categories, from student orchestra instruments to pro audio to more mass-market guitars, drums, and keyboards, should consider designing some left-hand navigation into their template which references all of their lines and links to their categories in their Store (see Figure 11-12). Additionally, as previously mentioned, sellers should include a Store search box in their listings. eBay has made this easier than ever via a new eBay Store feature. You might also want to provide buttons or links to other listings by brand.

Let Buyers Know Who You Are

If you are an authorized dealer, make this known in your listings. You can develop a graphic that highlights this fact and design this into your template header or near the top of your listings (see Figure 11-13). This way, your guarantee will always be right up front in the same place, reinforcing the fact that you sell authorized products. Also, in bold, emphasize strongly that you are offering your items with a warranty. This is particularly important for sellers offering expensive pro audio. This should probably come right after

Figure 11-12 Here's a nice example of a seller placing Store category links in his template's left margin.

your header or listing headline. If you are a member of any important association, such as NAMM, emphasize this as well.

Describe Condition and History

Vintage dealers, B-stock resellers, or authorized sellers, offering their clearance items or returns, should take special care to describe the condition and the history of the item. Many buyers are knowledgeable about the items themselves, their specs and functionality. What buyers want to know is the item's past, how much it's been played, how long it's been used, if it's been gigged, if it sat in a box, if it's had repairs, and other historical information. Describe this carefully and concisely. Don't just say, "Sounds Great!" This is much better: "Display Model, Never Used."

Special Considerations for Different Instrument Categories

If you're selling brass and woodwind instruments, take special care to identify their key, model number, plating, and audience (student, intermediate, professional). Emphasize if they have parts, such as a "mod" or "bell," from an-

Figure 11-13 Pro Gear Warehouse effectively promotes the fact that it is an authorized dealer of its products.

other maker, particularly if this enhances their value. Highlight special engravings and marks. Provide provenance, if a notable regional jazz or orchestra player owned the instrument.

> *Guitars, Amps, Effects:* Give some historical context for historically significant models. Explain why the item is important. If vintage, provide the year, serial number, and numbers in production for that year or overall. Provide particulars about the item's dimensions, construction, materials, and features (flame top, pickups, tailpiece, bridge, tubes, speakers, cones, circuits, wattage, covering, etc.), particularly if they are out of the norm or increase value. Explain marks and notations that demonstrate the item's authenticity. Offer the history of ownership, if notable, especially if a notable musician owned it. If selling a custom, limited-edition artist-series guitar, for example, a PRS Santana or Clapton Strat, state its production number. Add some comments about the artist and the artist's impact on that make, too.
>
> *Digital Keyboards, Pianos, Workstations, and Vintage Synthesizers:* State the number of keys. Emphasize the size of the ROM cartridge. Bullet

out the item's feature set. Give the critical numbers: voices, samples, drum sounds, effects, user programs, patches, presets, and others. List some primary, cool effects, particularly simulations of old analog sounds. Note if a CD-R is included in the unit. If used, note if it comes with a stand, bench, foot pedal, gig bag, and all manuals and discs. If vintage, give some history and explanation. As for fine pianos and vintage organs, particularly Hammond B3s, detail all exterior and internal restoring and refurbishing to improve look and operation. Provide serial numbers. Emphasize woods and materials. Take pains to describe freighting and shipping processes to reassure buyers.

Strings: Highlight the make, size, and dimensions of the instrument. Note if it is for collectors, professionals, students, or beginners. If it is antique or vintage and handmade, emphasize the instrument's date, country of origin (Italy, Germany), and maker. Give some background on the maker or luthier and why it is notable. Specify if the luthier himself (whose name is on the label) made the instrument. Provide provenance, if it adds to the allure of the item. Emphasize the materials, construction, and finishing of both high-end and budget instruments. Market why your budget lines are a good value, emphasizing the playability and workmanship. Provide serial numbers for banjos and mandolins. Give history for bygone makers. Describe interesting inlays.

THE RIGHT PHOTOS

As a musical instrument seller, dealing in antique, vintage, or B-stock, take the time to shoot professional photos and bring out the drama in your items. If you don't, you will do your sales a tremendous disservice.

1. Musical instruments and amps should be shot from several angles, front, back, and the side, to give customers the opportunity to properly vet the piece. Don't just provide a single shot or two taken from a distance. This will severely hurt your credibility, unless you provide an e-mail address and phone number for inquiries. Many instruments have the same tried and true designs. They need to be illustrated up close at the component level.
2. Provide a full-length glamour shot of the item as well as close-ups of each section of the instrument, from the F-holes to the scroll, the mouthpiece to the bell, the tailpiece to the headstock. Also provide close views of any checking or chips to the instrument finish, wood, or covering that you highlight in your description.
3. Take special care to photograph the item's label inside the body or cabinet of the instrument or device as well as the logo, inlay, or de-

cal on a headstock or the face or front of the item. Many people won't bid on an item if you don't provide a readable shot of the logo or label. This is particularly true with guitars, amplifiers, effects pedals, banjos, mandolins, pianos, and organs. Antique violins are an exception, because they are often faked.

4. If you can take your item apart without damaging it, as is the case with solid body guitars, combo amplifiers, analog effects pedals, and other analog equipment, do so and shoot the internal components. For example, many vintage amp sellers will remove tubes and shoot them separately up close as a way to authenticate the item. Vintage electric guitar sellers will often remove telecaster necks to shoot the serial number on the bolt-end side of the neck. They also remove and photograph pickups separately and take off tone and volume knobs to shoot the guitar's "pots."

5. Before shooting your instrument or piece of equipment, wipe it down with a nonabrasive cloth to remove smudges and glare. Polish up plated metal. Shoot the instrument against a classy background, such as the felt interior of its case (see Figure 11-14). This is often a nice effect. If that's not an option, then photograph the item against a felt background of your own device. Of course, this wouldn't be as appropriate for old-timey stringed instruments. For these, try an American flag as a background. Photographing fretted instruments outside against a natural background in natural light is often dramatic. If possible, shoot them in their stand. Avoid shooting against dark or busy fabrics, rugs, or household objects. They're distracting.

6. Digital workstations and Pro Audio equipment don't usually require excessive shots. If you don't have access to stock manufacturer photos, then take one or two dramatic shots. These are tools, not really pieces of visual art. However, it is often effective to position and photograph keyboard and Pro Audio devices (that are small enough to manipulate) at an angle, instead of directly from the front. This highlights the item's true dimensions. Experiment and see what looks good.

CUSTOMER INCENTIVES THAT WORK

Margins are tight on most musical instruments and products, but there are still some incentives that you should consider. Give these some thought.

1. Combine shipping on the purchase of multiple accessories, such as cases, cords, straps, adaptors, cleaning supplies, and the like. If you net a big sale, give the buyer a few freebies, such as a complimen-

Figure 11-14   Nice presentation. Love that classy background.

tary mouthpiece or horn oil or some patch chords for the studio
monitors they just bought.

2. Regardless if you're selling new or secondhand instruments, providing the buyer a trial period will make a good impression. After
all, buyers are purchasing sight unseen and will only hear the instrument or device for the first time after they open the box. A
couple of days is usually good enough. You might also consider
having a no-questions-asked return policy. This typically increases
sales more than it spikes returns.

3. List your authorized products as auctions with an attractive opening, but a higher Buy It Now price at the manufacturer's minimum
advertised price. That way, you still comply with MAP, but you are
also able to give Internet buyers the opportunity to get a better
deal, possibly even better than they could at one of the major
chain retailers or Musician's Friend.

4. If you are remarketing off-price refurbished or end-of-life inventory (that B-stock we've been talking about so much), consider offering a warranty with it via a third-party warranty provider. If the
product malfunctions, the buyer has the service fix it for them.

eBay has partnered with N.E.W. to offer various consumer electronics and equipment remarketers this option. Explore it here: *http://pages.ebay.com/help/warranty/buyer_overview.html*

5. Add some "bells and whistles" to your listing to increase buyer confidence. A prime example is to embed sound files in the listing that give buyers an approximate feel for how the instrument or device sounds.

6. Sell internationally. It's likely that some items in your inventory won't be available overseas. Before going ahead with this, though, make sure this is allowed in your dealer agreement and that your products are compatible abroad.

7. During the holidays, offer special offers, such as gift-wrapping, gift cards, and gift-recipient shipping. During the holiday season, keep an eye out for eBay promotions and merchandising events, which can drive traffic to your listings. Here's the music-merchandising calendar: *http://pages.ebay.com/sellercentral/calendar.html*. During busy buying periods, consider using some eBay listing upgrades to garner more visibility for your listings and eBay Store.

8. For more general thoughts on this subject, review Chapter 9.

We're making some headway. Now it's on to music memorabilia.

12

Becoming a Music Memorabilia Specialist

Ahh, the rush of outbidding the competition for a first pressing of "The Beatles vs. The Four Seasons"; snatching away a Gibson Super Jumbo, signed by the whole crew at the Grand Ole Opry; scoring an early Nirvana demo tape and signed publicity shot—torn jeans and all. These are the experiences your memorabilia customers live for. Are you ready to provide them? All right, then—let's get deeper into the mechanics of running a music memorabilia business on eBay. As in our early industry chapters, we'll dissect the category itself to give you a feel for what types of items are in greatest supply in the category. Remember, eBay's category architecture reflects what is being listed by sellers, and what sellers are listing reflects what customers are buying. In other words, eBay's buyers and businesses are constantly playing an important part in defining eBay's category structure. As the buyers and businesses define the broad trends in each major category, eBay carefully redraws the category map.

After breaking down the music memorabilia category, we will examine a number of other major topics: how to source music memorabilia more specifically, where to go on the Internet to do your own market research, what market forces are driving the music memorabilia market, what search terms buyers are using, where you should advertise your business off eBay, and finally, what elements go into successful memorabilia listings.

ANATOMY OF A CATEGORY

This overview will give you a better grasp of what categories in *Music Memorabilia* are really hopping and which ones are doing a slow waltz. As previously mentioned elsewhere in this book, *Music Memorabilia* is a bit different from *Music* and *Musical Instruments* in that it is not a Level I category in eBay parlance. It's actually a Level II within *Entertainment Memorabilia,* which also features the important related Level II category *Autographs.* That in mind, let's jump right to *Entertainment Memorabilia*'s important music-related subcategories.

Entertainment Memorabilia > Music Memorabilia (Level II)
Entertainment Memorabilia > Autographs > Music (Level III)
Music Memorabilia (Level II)

Big Band, Swing	Jazz	Rap, Hip-Hop
(Level III)	Opera	Reggae
Blues	Pop	Rock-n-Roll
Classical	Punk	Other
Country	R&B, Soul	

Autographs (Level II)

Movies	Television	Other
<u>Music</u> (Level III)	Theater	

eBay's Level III *Music Memorabilia* subcategories are organized by musical genre, of which *Rock-n-Roll* is the largest. Further category divisions in *Music Memorabilia* are by artist (Level IV) and then type of memorabilia (Level V), such as apparel, handbills, posters, and the like. The Level IV subcategories in Autographs > Music also are organized by genre—the same ones, in fact, used in *Music Memorabilia.* As in our other intensive chapter category overviews, we've left in some actual listing numbers from a recent search on eBay, to give you a general feel for supply and demand in *Music Memorabilia.*

eBay TIP: A quick review of *Music Memorabilia*'s Level IV artist/group categories reveals which musical acts' memorabilia is being most actively traded on eBay. Sell only certain groups: track them on your "My eBay" page with the Favorite Categories feature.

Music Memorabilia (Level II)
<u>Country</u> (Level III)

Dixie Chicks (39)	George Strait (51)	Tim McGraw (142)
(Level IV)	Hank Williams (82)	Willie Nelson (92)
Faith Hill (42)	Johnny Cash (121)	Other Artists (3,974)
Garth Brooks (94)	Shania Twain (145)	

Pop

Abba (86)	Cher (138)	Mariah Carey (131)
Backstreet Boys (123)	Christina Aguilera	Michael Jackson (708)
Britney Spears (558)	(253)	'N Sync (257)
Celine Dion (47)	Madonna (1,291)	Other Artists (16,548)

Punk

Clash (88)	Sex Pistols (259)
Ramones (135)	Other Artists (2,900)

R&B, Soul

Apparel (76)	Novelties (61)	Other (592)
Concert Memorabilia	Photos (293)	
(97)	Posters (275)	

Rap, Hip-Hop

Apparel (1,092)	Novelties (227)	Other (1,404)
Concert Memorabilia	Photos (244)	
(117)	Posters (771)	

Figure 12-1 According to a recent search on eBay's Hot Category Report, Abba items were in demand.

Rock-n-Roll

AC/DC (417)
Aerosmith (547)
Avril Lavigne (63)
Beach Boys (148)
Beatles (5,872)
Bob Dylan (434)
Bon Jovi (448)
Bruce Springsteen (359)
Dave Matthews Band (261)
David Bowie (513)
Def Leppard (157)
Doors (375)
Eagles (96)
Elton John (190)
Elvis (5,815)
Fleetwood Mac (243)
Foo Fighters (61)
Grateful Dead (1,897)

Guns N' Roses (247)
Hard Rock Café (4,466)
Iron Maiden (623)
Janis Joplin (156)
Jimi Hendrix (438)
KISS (2,536)
Korn (315)
Led Zeppelin (645)
Linkin Park (207)
Lynyrd Skynyrd (195)
Metallica (749)
Moody Blues (41)
Nirvana (392)
Ozzy Osbourne (612)
Pearl Jam (280)
Phish (172)
Pink Floyd (812)
Prince (233)
Queen (504)

Radiohead (169)
Red Hot Chili Peppers (99)
Rolling Stones (1,432)
Rush (189)
Santana (86)
Smashing Pumpkins (97)
Stevie Ray Vaughan (141)
Sublime (68)
System of a Down (82)
The Who (298)
Tool (218)
U2 (556)
Van Halen (203)
ZZ Top (52)
Other Artists (38,954)

Finally, let's take a close look at the Level V subcategories in *Music Memorabilia*. What does this reveal? Currently, there are only seven artist categories that generate enough listings to require additional category division into types of memorabilia. Interestingly enough, these are all in *Pop* and *Rock-n-Roll*. These artists are:

- Music Memorabilia > Pop > **Madonna**
- Music Memorabilia > Pop > **Other Artists**
- Music Memorabilia > Rock-n-Roll > **Beatles**
- Music Memorabilia > Rock-n-Roll > **Elvis**
- Music Memorabilia > Rock-n-Roll > **Grateful Dead**
- Music Memorabilia > Rock-n-Roll > **Hard Rock Café**
- Music Memorabilia > Rock-n-Roll > **KISS**
- Music Memorabilia > Rock-n-Roll > **Pink Floyd**
- Music Memorabilia > Rock-n-Roll > **Rolling Stones**

While memorabilia from artists in other genres, particularly blues and country, can be very valuable, most of the action is in rock-n-roll. The above majors all have some variation of the following subcategories:

Music Memorabilia > Pop/Rock-n-Roll > (Level V)

Apparel	Glassware (Hard	Photos
Cards (KISS)	Rock)	Pins, Buttons
Concert Memorabilia	Guitar Picks	Posters
Concert & Movie	Handbills	Record Awards
(Elvis)	Music Instruments	Stickers
Figurines (Beatles,	Novelties	Trading Cards (Elvis)
KISS)	Patches	Other Items

MAJOR NAMES AND MAJOR SOURCES FOR MUSIC MEMORABILIA

Of course, if you sell music memorabilia, you can't just two-step your way down to Target and pick up what you need. There are no wholesalers minting classic boxing-style posters and handbills, RIAA record awards, and the like. (Licensed T-shirts would be the only exception.) So how, really, do you get your hands on this stuff? Here are a few thoughts on that subject, some tried and true, others a bit more novel.

One point before we get too far into this: Sourcing memorabilia is a networking game. Above all else, it requires building mutually beneficial relationships with other sellers, from dealers like yourself to broker middlemen for the music and concert promotion business to estate-sale specialists and regional auctioneers to major collectors and maybe, if you're fortunate, a few stars themselves—after all, they're just people, too. In essence, you have to network with people, whether they are in your town or on the other side of the world, and develop a true rapport with them. At the end of the day, there's really no magic formula. This society is loose and fragmented. Getting involved requires persistence, smarts, a bit of personality and charm, and a willingness to work with people. Above all else, you have to come through in the clutch and do exactly what you say you will when an opportunity presents itself. As in anything, if you fool with someone, they'll cross you off their list and so will the person who might have referred you. There's always another person to deal with.

eBay TIP: Get to know the other dealers on eBay who aren't in direct competition with you. Buy from them and sell them things they might need in order to initiate a relationship with them. You need friends in this business.

Fortunately, the Internet and e-mail have made this networking process much easier. They provide us an unparalleled way to advertise ourselves to potential sources. They enable us to search out individuals who are selling material and to quickly contact them electronically in order to set up face-to-face meetings, where we can vet material, ask questions, and gain their confidence for an additional transaction. However, the Internet is only a start. You won't be a success in the memorabilia business (or any business with restricted supply, for that matter) sitting at your desk in front of the computer. It's crucial to set up shop on the Web, build awareness for yourself on eBay, and advertise in publications like *Goldmine* that you have ready cash for good collections. You also have to hit the road and travel to the supply, at collector shows, outdoor markets, local estate sales, or a company's warehouse. You have to make yourself real for people. Otherwise, they will suspect you are not. Now let's talk sources.

Estate Sales and Garage and Moving Sales

These types of sales are certainly not a new concept, but they are and will always be sources where supply that you might want will surface. We don't have to spend too much time here, but estate sales, garage sales, and moving sales are worth noting and a good way to find inexpensive items. These sales are a local phenomenon, so the best way to find them is to turn to your local newspapers. If you live in a large city, you can also try to search the Web for local companies and brokers who handle estate sales or estate liquidations in your city or region and get on their contact lists. Hit the popular community site *craigslist.com* too.

eBay TIP: When searching the Web for estate sale companies, specify that you don't want the word "Real," as in Real Estate, to be included in your search.

If you build a rapport with some reps and educate them about what you need and what it is generally worth, they might consign or sell you material in advance of public sales, particularly if you demonstrate a willingness to pay them a reasonable amount. They're not looking to make a killing, just a reasonable amount quickly.

Regional and National Dealers and Auction Houses

Another traditional outlet for your kind of supply is dealers and auction houses that specialize in music memorabilia. There are more than you might think, especially when you add historic autograph and antique toy specialists to the mix. (The latter have less of this material than, say, a Lelands or Mastro, but they do carry it from time to time.) We have listed some of the major ones here. Consider watching regional auction houses that specialize in antiques and collectibles. Occasionally, someone will consign them something you'd like to have. Introduce yourself to the companies in your area so that if something good walks in their door, they know to notify you.

Also, keep an eye on their sales in order to compete for items that fit your needs. This isn't a waste of time. When something does turn up, there will be far less competition for it. Remember, the specialists in this niche aggressively advertise their sales to collectors and other dealers. A good source for local auction companies is the National Auctioneers Association (*auctions .auctioneers.org*). Online bidding/catalog services Live Auctioneers (*www.live auctioneers.com*) and icollector (*www.icollector.com*) also are great resources. From the following list, use the majors for networking and the more regional auctioneers for buying.

- Alexander Autographs *www.alexautographs.com*
- American Memorabilia *www.americanmemorabilia.com*
- Bonhams & Butterfields *www.butterfields.com*
- Cooper Owen *www.cooperowen.com*
- Christie's *www.christies.com*
- Cohasco (autographs) *www.cohascodpc.com*
- Dallas Auction Gallery (instruments) *www.dallasauctiongallery.com*
- Early American (autographs) *www.earlyamerican.com*
- Edison Gallery (phonographs) *www.edisongallery.com*
- Eldreds (instruments) *www.eldreds.com*
- Guernsey's (various, unique) *www.guernseys.com*
- Hakes Americana & Collectibles *www.hakes.com*
- Julien Entertainment *www.julienentertainment.com*
- Kruk Cards *www.krukcards.com*
- Lelands *www.lelands.com*
- Mastro *www.mastronet.com*
- Morphy Auctions (toys) *www.morphyauctions.com*
- Philip Weiss Auctions *www.philipweissauctions.com*
- Phillips *www.phillips.com*
- Poster Auctions International *www.postersplease.com*
- Poster Connections *www.posterconnection.com*
- Profiles in History *www.profilesinhistory.com*
- Randy Inman Auctions *www.inmanauctions.com*
- RM Auctions *www.rmauctions.com*
- Santoro & Shienbaum Auctioneers *www.santoroandshienbaum.com*
- Signature House *www.signaturehouse.net*
- Skinner (instruments) *www.skinner.com*
- Sotheby's *www.sothebys.com*
- Starwares.com *www.starwares.com*
- Waddingtons (instruments) *www.waddingtonsauctions.com*
- Wolfgang's Vault *www.wolfgangsvault.com*

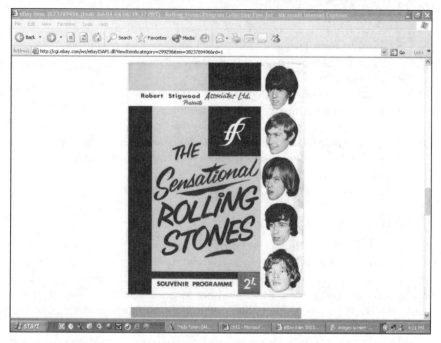

Figure 12-2 Nice hair, guys.

Event Management and Concert Promoters

Moving up the chain, some dealers are able to go straight to the source and buy from event management and concert promotion companies, such as Bill Graham Presents, the most famous of these. Here is an example of how this arrangement works. San Francisco dealer Wolfgang's Vault currently manages Bill Graham's current collection of concert promotions. Every major city has its own Bill Graham, who bills and promotes live music acts. These companies own the copyrights to the promotional materials they produce; however, they're in the business of putting on music, not selling memorabilia. Many of these companies have inventories of posters, handbills, promo cards, and T-shirts stashed in storage facilities or warehouses. That's the stuff you want, either to resell right off the bat or to vault away to sell later. Dealers we talked with said they did not work directly with concert promotion companies, but with middlemen who brokered deals between them. We'll leave that up to you, but here are some major names to familiarize yourself with in the industry.

- Arden Barnett *www.bandradio.com*
- Barry Clayman Corporation *www.barry-clayman.co.uk*

- Bill Graham Presents *www.musicfeatures.com/bgp*
- Clear Channel *www.clearchannel.com*
- Concert Southern Promotion *www.atlantaconcerts.com*
- Electric Factory Concerts *www.electricfactory.com*
- Festival Productions *www.festivalproductions.net*
- Goldenvoice *www.goldenvoice.com*
- JL Entertainment Agency *www.jlentertainment.com*
- Nitelite Concert Promotion *www.nitelite.com*
- Other Voice Productions *www.theothervoiceproductions.com*
- Smiling Dog Productions *www.lovelandnet.com/smilingdog*
- T&K Productions *www.tandkproductions.com*
- Walther Productions *www.walther-productions.com*

Manufacturers and Wholesalers

A source of supply for sellers specializing in rock T-shirts and new music collectibles are manufacturers of licensed apparel. A few major manufacturers have licensing agreements with various copyright owners, allowing them to legally produce T-shirts and other clothing with popular band logos and artwork. A variety of wholesalers then distribute these items to offline and online resellers. As in other industries, sellers have to meet certain requirements in order to become wholesale buyers, namely, acquire a resale license, pass a credit check (if not buying C.O.D.), and provide a tax ID. Resellers also have to meet modest initial minimum orders (150 shirts, usually). These wholesalers often sell a wide variety of novelty items too, from stickers and hats to pins and flags. This material can bulk up your inventory and presence on eBay, but it can also give your brand the wrong image.

- American Tee Shirt *www.americanteeshirt.com*
- Backstage Fashion *www.backstage-fashion.com*
- Giant Merchandising (manufacturer) *www.giantmerchandising.com*
- JSR Direct *www.jsrdirect.com*
- Liquid Blue (manufacturer) *www.liquidblue.com*
- Rock Merch Universe *www.rockmerchuniverse.com*

 eBay TIP: Selling both true memorabilia and new collectibles can be confusing for your buyers. You may want to specialize.

MARKET RESEARCH

The Internet is an invaluable market research tool. It provides a wealth of sources with which you can start to cultivate an expertise in music memorabilia, whatever the genre you're interested in. That in mind, here are some first-rate destinations for music memorabilia dealers and enthusiasts, where they can round out their knowledge, learn more about key niches, and also get insights into what's heating up and what's cooling off.

- *www.collect.com* (Krause)
- *http://launch.dir.groups.yahoo.com/dir/Music/Genres*
- *http://launch.dir.groups.yahoo.com/dir/Music/History*
- *rec.music.collecting*
- *rec.music.collecting.vinyl*
- *rec.music.collecting.misc*
- *rec.music.marketplace*
- *rec.music.marketplace.vinyl*
- *rec.music.marketplace.misc*

ADVERTISING OPPORTUNITIES FOR MEMORABILIA

Frankly, eBay has become the place to not only sell but also advertise, because it exposes so many people to your memorabilia. Just the same, there are some other specialty record and memorabilia trades you should probably utilize as your sales increase. There is an offline market in collectibles. This includes an older generation of record collectors, who are interested in collectibles, and buyers concerned about fraud on eBay who would rather buy from established dealers offline. Additionally, advertising online (off eBay) and in print will help you expose your Web site to premium collectors and sell your higher-end material that does not always do as well on eBay.

- Autograph Collector *www.autographcollector.com*
- Discoveries *www.collect.com/records*
- Goldmine *www.collect.com/records*
- Planet Collector *www.planetcollector.com*
- Record Collector *www.recordcollectormag.com*

You might want to advertise in some specialty music magazines and fanzines, if you specialize in one artist or group, such as Elvis, The Beatles, The Rolling Stones, The Monkees, and U2, or any of the other truly established acts of rock, country, and popular music (see Figure 12-3).

Figure 12-3 Not everything has to be ultra-vintage to be collectible. This guide from Rush's 1980 Permanent Waves tour is a great example.

MARKET DRIVERS AND IMPLICATIONS

As we've suggested in our two earlier industry-intensive chapters, this book is more about how to sell music-related goods on eBay than what to sell, but we do want to provide you some useful analysis of the direction and shape of our three markets. Let's do that now, based on our discussions with a variety of memorabilia PowerSellers. Before we get started, though, consider this: the *Music Memorabilia* category is like a grid of objects and interests. Some people collect large sections of that grid, others smaller areas. Some collectors focus on a single square or two, while a select few try to collect as much as they can.

Memorabilia Is Valuable Because It's Rare

What's considered valuable in music memorabilia today, particularly the ephemera (paper stuff), is only so because it was once thought to be disposable. As mentioned in Chapter 2, that fact has limited supply and increased prices as interest in and demand for music nostalgia have risen. This applies to low- and mid-range items, such as ticket stubs, as well as some of the more investor-quality pieces, for example, those mass-merchandised Beatles lunchboxes and Monkees dolls.

Implications: As a dealer, you should try to sell ephemeral objects that you know were produced in reasonable numbers (by record labels and event companies). They don't have to be one particular type, but you should have some confidence that they were seen by a fair amount of people. In the grand scheme, the hope is that people had them, lost them, or threw them away and now want them back. Once you can start providing these objects, transition to related items the average person didn't know he or she could get. Examples are concert crew and staff shirts or, more commonly, laminated backstage passes.

Fans Want Memorabilia

The music memorabilia market on eBay is generally more fan-focused than investor-driven. Essentially, this is because music collectibles don't have as much intrinsic value as some other types of antiques, such as coins, pottery and glass, furniture, and musical instruments, things that were made to stand the test of time.

While the first printing of "A Day on the Green, #1" two-color poster is totally cool (see Figure 12-4), it's never going to fetch as much as, say, an exceptional gold coin. (It's not gold, after all.) The value of a lot of music memorabilia is equal to people's sentimental value for it, and that can increase and decrease with each generation. (There are exceptions, of course, which we will discuss below.) Our guess is that 80 percent of the music memorabilia on eBay and the Internet is worth less than $1,500, with a high percentage of that in the $100 to $500 range.

Why is this important to know? Because collectors and investors collect for different reasons and thus buy in different ways. Both certainly appreciate what they acquire; however, investors are interested in ROI (return on investment) and resale. That's less the case with enthusiasts who collect for personal reasons.

Implications: Collectors buying for investment will pony up cash for the same item multiple times, if they think it's in their interests, just like a trader who buys multiple shares of stock. Fans, in contrast, generally want diversity, not multiples. They'd rather spend money on what they don't have, fill in the gaps, so to speak, than stockpile established items in the hopes of making money (though making money can be the happy result of any collection). These different goals have a bearing on what dealers should buy and how they should buy. For one, dealers targeting fans might want to carry a more diverse catalog than a seller catering to investors with narrow tastes. The dealers probably should carry a spectrum of things that represent an artist or group's entire career in favor of duplicates of just vintage items.

Figure 12-4 Where have all the good times gone?

Here's an illustration why. It's quite likely that a seasoned enthusiast might have older pieces but perhaps not a newer item from, say, a reunion tour or good comeback album. (This is not to say you shouldn't buy something important if you can get it for a good price.) Just consider bands like Fleetwood Mac or The Eagles. A passionate fan might have the "Hotel California" paraphernalia, but not the "Hell Freezes Over" stuff.

Another implication to consider is that when buying for fans you have to be careful not to buy too much of the same thing in bulk, even though this is the most economical way to source. Why? You can't sit on most of this merchandise forever like a very established antique and think it will always net you a profit. With everything you buy, it's important to know what it is worth, how much you can sell it for, and how much your market can absorb. That's one reason to specialize in just a few types of items but for a large number of different musicians or groups. Since there's less room for error when buying, it's best to be more conservative and just try to master the vetting of a few kinds of memorabilia.

People Want Their Favorite Artists

There are all manner of collectors in the music memorabilia game (specializing in a real variety of particular types of things), but many focus on one or two artists or bands or a genre of music, important and relevant when they came of age. That genre might be the hopeful Motown sound of the '50s, the psychedelic, antiestablishment rock of the late '60s, the "song-power" arena rock of the '70s, the big-hair heavy metal and early rap of the '80s (Remember the Fat Boys? They were "fresh."), the Subpop-indie rock of the mid-'90s, or the eclectic jam-band stuff around today (Dave Matthews, Phish, String Cheese Incident). Why is this? Memorabilia collectors tend to have an intense connection to particular groups and artists because they associate them with the fun times in their lives when they were free and young. That's really it. They want things not because they think it will be worth money some day, like a genuine Honus Wagner, but because it connects them to those green pastures of yesteryear, when they were goofing with buddies up on the rooftop over a few brews. Anyway, 30- and 40-something nostalgia always propels the lower half of the market (under a few hundred dollars).

Implications: A fair amount of collectors will buy a wide variety of items that relate to a specific artist or genre with which they feel a real affinity. One collector might buy everything from tickets, laminates, and boxing-style posters to autographed press kits, promo photos, and recording contracts to mass-merchandised lunchboxes and figurines. The artist, not the thing, motivates many collectors, particularly at the low end of the market. (Of course, the reverse can be true, too. We're not giving hard and fast rules here.)

Mass-Produced Collectibles

You might be tempted to buy new mass-marketed items, such as Elvis collector plates from The Bradford Exchange or the New Ozzy Osbourne and Jimi Hendrix figures from McFarlane, to name just a few examples. Keep this in mind, however: generally, it takes quite a while for these items to significantly increase in value (see Figure 12-5). The same was true of the original mass-marketed rock toys and housewares. The new figures are made to be collectible, making them, in fact, less valuable in some people's books. The reason the old mass-merchandised items are valuable now is because they were not intended to be so. These objects are true cultural artifacts that serve to document a certain time and place. Thus, they have true meaning.

Implications: To make a good return on this material, you might have to wait a long time. Much of this stuff is mass-produced, but it doesn't necessarily have mass appeal. If you can sell it at a decent margin, though, go for it.

Timeless Artists and Objects

There are some timeless, rather than temporal, artists and objects, which the music memorabilia community looks at as investments. These include first pressings of rare vinyl records; notable, authentic autographs; certain culturally important music posters and artifacts; and artist-owned objects, such as their instruments (Eric Clapton's "Blackie"), original costumes (Gene Sim-

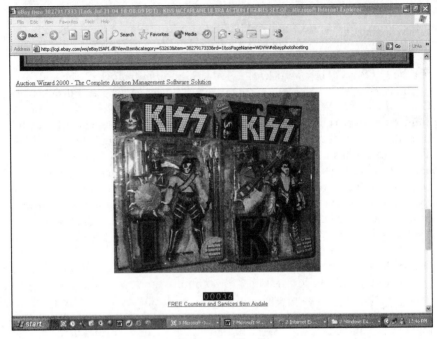

Figure 12-5 Cool, yes. Collectible? Only time will tell.

mons' high-heeled boots), and personal effects (one of the King's letters). Unfortunately, this material is generally the bailiwick of major auction houses, particularly Bonhams & Butterfields and Christie's, and some important specialists (Cooper-Owens, Lelands, Mastro, Stacks). Misrepresentation and fraud on the Internet have made it harder to sell this material on eBay, unless you are a well-known dealer.

Implications: The above points don't preclude you from trying to source and sell investment-quality memorabilia on eBay and, more realistically, your Web site. Just be prepared to provide a rock-solid appraisal of the item from a recognized specialist and a lifetime guarantee of authenticity to your buyers.

Current Events

What's going on in the world around us has a real effect on what people, including casual buyers, serious collectors, and investors, end up buying. Major music and film releases, for example, which receive mass-market distribution and promotion, can create a buzz that influences what people want. Consider the Austin Powers movies, which revived interest in '60s mod fashion and music. *Almost Famous* got people thinking about the '70s. *Swingers* took us back to the '50s and helped spark interest in the swing thing. Ironically, the tastemakers that choose to fund and produce these mainstream releases are really just picking up on trends that are already in play and then making them more accessible to the public at large.

eBay TIP: The mass media seem to recycle and update whatever was hot with youth culture 20 years ago. Hence, the cultural critics, from VH1 to *Cosmopolitan*, are now telling twenty-somethings to get preppy with those Izods and turned up collars. What does that mean for you? Selling memorabilia for bands from their eras that defined the looks.

Implications: The achievements, scandals, and, sadly, deaths of culturally significant people also have a profound effect on what's being bought and sold. The passing of Brother Ray no doubt increased interest in this legend's catalog and memorabilia. And, yes, the Super Bowl shenanigans of Janet Jackson might have temporarily excited interest in her music.

TOP BUYER SEARCHES

There are important eBay Keyword pages that music memorabilia collectors should know. As previously noted, eBay creates these pages to highlight popular searches that relate to a great variety of different eBay categories. That means demand for items related to these words is significant.

There are some good reasons to review these pages. As mentioned before, they allow you to compare your theories and assumptions about your market to reality—what people are actually buying or trying to find. For example, you might choose not to sell "8×10 photos" because there's a glut of them on eBay, but as eBay's Keyword pages suggest, people want them (both originals and reprints). eBay's Keyword pages also often reveal collectible opportunities you might not have considered. Take the term "sheet," which is used by music stamp collectors searching for music stamps and music memorabilia enthusiasts who collect rare and different sheet music. Then, there is the term "plate," used in listings for rock-related collector plates. Or, how about "framed"? It looks like eBay buyers do like framed memorabilia. These pages also show what supergroups are truly popular with eBay buyers. Some might surprise you: Limp Bizkit, Sound Garden.

While a keyword page might have category links to music memorabilia, the keyword might be more applicable to other categories. Take terms like "Celine Dion" and "Jennifer Lopez," which are more relevant to the *Music* category. Sure, there is memorabilia for these stars, but you have to wonder if their stuff will have long-term value. For a complete list of eBay Keywords, go to *http://buy.ebay.com.* Now, here are some of the major keywords with pages for music memorabilia. To bring up a page, just place one of the keywords after the above URL, like this: *http://buy.ebay.com/***acdc**.

acdc
aerosmith
album
aretha franklin
autograph
autographed
band
bb king
beach boys
beatles
billy joel
blues
bob dylan
bon jovi
bobblehead
britney spears
broadway
bruce springsteen
cd sealed
cd single
celine dion
cher
christina aguilera
clapton
concert
dave matthews
david bowie
dixie chicks
duran duran
eagles
elvis
figure
fleetwood mac
foil (foil stock
    posters)

framed
frank sinatra
goth
grateful dead
hendrix
hits
import
jackson
james taylor
jennifer lopez
jersey
jimi hendrix
jimmy buffett
joplin
kiss
led zeppelin
limp bizkit
louis armstrong
lp
lyle lovett
metallica
oop
parker
pearl jam
phat farm
phish
pictures
pin
pink floyd
plaque (awards)
plastic (busts)
plate (collector plates)
platinum (records)
playing (playing
    cards)

playing cards
plush (plush KISS
    dolls)
police
pop
postcard
poster
posters
press (press kit,
    photo)
prince
promo
proof (CD cover)
quicksilver
    (messenger service)
ray charles
rem
rockabilly
rolling stones
rush
shania twain
sheet
signed
signed photo
signed 8×10
signed 8×10 photo
simon garfunkel
sound garden
streisand
the doors
the rolling stones
tom petty
van morrison
vintage

Let's also discuss that other indispensable tool, Common Keywords, which allows you to review thousands of common search terms related to your merchandise (see Figure 12-6).

Go to *http://keyword-index.ebay.com* to see how eBay buyers are searching for all kinds of items related to your merchandise. It's essential. A link to Common Keywords is available in the "Popular Search Terms" box on most category index or search results page. To pick out all the relevant terms from this source for music memorabilia sellers would be impossible. There are just too many. One approach is to use the eBay Keyword pages as a starting point to see what general topics are hot. Follow these pages' links into the general-listing area and then go into the Common Keywords tool from there.

TRACKING THE MARKET

Now, let's talk about using eBay's completed item search and My eBay tool to track the music memorabilia market. Because music memorabilia collectors generally collect a few individual artists or genres of music, you should probably follow their lead and set up your searches the same way. In short, design them after the musical acts that you sell. To make it easier, instead of setting up 100 searches, just track the truly hot bands in which you specialize, as well as a few you feel are starting to surge. If you get too crazy, you'll spend an in-

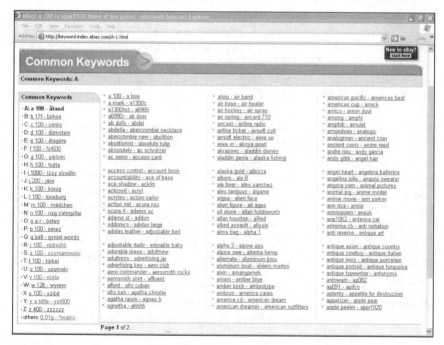

Figure 12-6 Here's a listing for serious collectors.

ordinate amount of time reviewing e-mails and realized prices. (Some sellers spend hours a day tracking their market.)

If you specialize in few very specific types of memorabilia, such as recording contracts, tour books, programs, and record awards, then create searches for those, too. Depending on how large these categories are, get more specific in the wording of your term. For example, if your focus is boxing-style posters, setting up a generic "Poster" search might not help you. The trick here is to identify search terms that people really use and to model your pricing searches after those. If you have some major collectors with special tastes and interests, such as antique phonographs or vintage music advertisements featuring country stars or jazz musicians, then you might want to design searches for those, as well. There are two reasons for this: you can see if other sellers are targeting this niche (and targeting your buyers) and, if so, you can see how they're pricing their property. Finally, create some Favorite Categories so you can get an overview of the market. Select Level II categories so that there is some action to review when you look.

BOOSTING SALES WITH STELLAR LISTINGS

As discussed in Chapter 9, designing a professional HTML listing template for your listings is fundamental. It doesn't have to be boring, but it does have to effectively display your images, organize your information logically (with the most important information at the top), and feature fonts that are easy to read. Avoid information overload. Provide the targeted information your collectors need to be confident enough to bid or buy. You know all this, though—let's talk specifics.

- Give all of your auction descriptions a good headline in a large bold font. In the headline, abbreviate the most pertinent details. For example, name the artist or group and what type of object you're selling. Then include one other key selling point or detail. For instance, if it is a numbered edition of something, include its number: 56/150. If it's an original (or reprint, RP), feature that in the headline.
- Under your header, state the condition of the piece clearly and give it a grade. Note, in bold, if it is an original or a reprint of some kind. If it is a reprint, give its printing number, as in 2nd or 3rd.

Write out the exact title or text that is on the object and place it in quotation marks. If it's a poster or ticket, reference the show name, date or day, venue or arena, and artist or band. Repeat the edition number. Try to research the show and give some color about what happened.

- Regardless of what kind of object or ephemera you're selling, be sure to give its exact dimensions. Sometimes auction photos can make buyers believe an item is bigger than it is. Protect yourself from complaints.
- Dedicate a space in your item description to item provenance—that is, history of ownership. How did you get your hands on that Beatles autograph, and who owned it before you? (Be general in your listing. You don't want to invite competition.)
- If you personally grade your material, include a grading table which defines your grades. If you have fixed shipping prices for different types of items, table that information also.
- Make sure your template is consistent in every listing. This reinforces your branding and helps buyers better assess what you're selling, and they'll like you for that.
- Put your best foot forward. Include some feedback comments in your listings that are particularly creative and label them as testimonials. Reference your company mission statement. For more thoughts on this, see Chapter 9.

THE RIGHT PHOTOS

Music memorabilia is easier to shoot than some types of merchandise, but your shots still have to be great. After all, you have to prove that your items are authentic. Since a lot of memorabilia is flat and two-dimensional, there's less need to shoot such items from multiple angles or photograph internal components. That said, there are some special considerations for shooting ephemera, autographs, original objects, and brightly colored posters and handbills.

- Most important, if your object or piece of ephemera is autographed, include multiple images of the object and of the actual autograph. If a piece has several autographs—John, Paul, George, and Ringo—provide a photo of each. Also, autograph images have to be sharp. If autograph images are fuzzy, collectors won't bite. Finally, letters and certificates of authenticity on letterhead should be photographed. Make sure letterhead can be clearly read. Try to size your images as uniformly as possible and use a template with thumbnails so that they can be noted at a glance.
- If you're selling colorful vintage posters, provide a full shot and a few close-ups of details, so that buyers can appreciate the finer graphics and images. After all, this is half of the posters' appeal. If you are selling psychedelic or alternative rock posters, which use vi-

brant inks, practice your Photoshop so that you can properly present their colors. If posters have tape marks or pin holes, shoot them, so that customers are aware of the extent of damage.

- Three-dimensional objects need to be shot multiple times and shown from the front, back, and sides. As with any piece of memorabilia, include close-ups of wear and damage. You might even Photoshop in an arrow that calls out the damage. If you are selling a set, such as a foursome of Beatles Nodders, then shoot them individually. Classic '70s and '80s rock T-shirts should be shot back and front. Shoot them on a white background, slightly ruffled, to give them some dimension. Avoid the common mistake of shooting your items on a bedspread; pastel flowers and stripes don't jive with music memorabilia.

- Showcase your objects. Shoot them against a properly colored backdrop, which highlights their natural colors. One idea is to have both a light and dark cloth background. Shoot all of your objects from the same distance so that they look consistent (see Figure 12-7).

- Retake shots that feature your flash's reflection, which looks unprofessional.

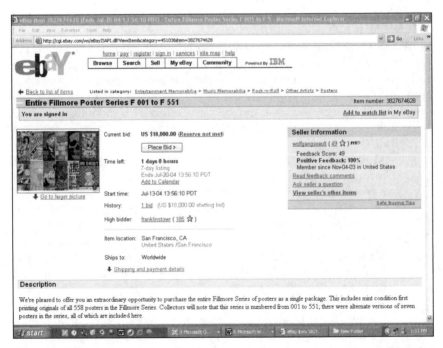

Figure 12-7 Try not to shoot quality memorabilia from a distance against a distracting backdrop.

CUSTOMER INCENTIVES THAT WORK

In the memorabilia trade, buyers are worried most about fraud. Ease their fears by providing customer incentives that say you care about them and your items.

- Most important, provide your buyers a money-back lifetime guarantee. The few headaches it causes will be well worth the increased sales it generates. Merchandise this incentive on all of your eBay pages, from your listings to your About Me page to your eBay Co-Op advertisements.
- If you are selling items that are often faked, include a letter of authenticity from a recognized appraiser on letterhead with your item, showing you've done your due diligence. If it's a Beatles autograph, Frank Caiazzio is your man.
- Provide provenance or history of ownership, including the name of the current owner and the opportunity to speak with him or her.
- Donate some of the proceeds of the sale to a worthy charity and promote this in your listings with the charity's logo and contact information.
- If you're selling something truly rare and expensive, offer a piece of related memorabilia with it as a bonus. A seller recently offering the suede jacket Bob Dylan wore on the cover of "Blonde on Blonde" threw in an autographed copy of Dylan's "Greatest Hits" album.
- Offer to make customers special packing, shipping, and insurance arrangements to ensure their investment is protected. Tell them you pack to withstand the package's being dropped. Consider offering buyers PayPal financing, if you're selling items in the thousands of dollars.
- For more general thoughts on this subject, refer to Chapter 9.

This is all really just the beginning, as any long-term eBay music memorabilia seller will tell you. You have an exciting future ahead of you selling in this category. Speaking of the future, let's go to the next chapter: the future of music selling on eBay. Some very interesting developments lie ahead.

13

The Future of Selling Music on eBay

Now that we've looked at the eBay music opportunity from top to bottom, let's take a moment to recall something we mentioned at the very beginning of this book. Music inspires. It fuels the soul. It keeps us reaching, striving . . . believing. Keep that in mind when your eBay climb gets tough. Throw on your favorite fight song, whether it's Survivor's "Eye of the Tiger" or Sinatra's "I Did It My Way," and don't look back.

What lies ahead for eBayers of the musical persuasion? There's not just one answer to that question, as you might guess from reading this book. Each of the three main types of music sellers we have profiled will be affected by different trends.

Volume CD sellers will continue to be a force on the site, aggregating a wide array of value-priced items. After all, who doesn't like a CD for $3, even if it is Vanilla Ice or Night Ranger? If retail music sales remain flat or trend downward, the best of these businesses with purchasing power will continue to grow, as more product becomes available to them through various product disposition channels.

You can also expect many of these sellers to diversify their inventories with new formats and entertainment experiences, from DVD movies to reissue Super Audio CDs, and evolve into more general entertainment resellers. Their goal is to reduce their inventory costs by buying in greater volume, broaden their appeal with eBay buyers, and increase the visibility of their brand on eBay. Look around and you'll see that conversion already taking place.

Finally, technologically, these companies will also be on the leading edge, as they seek to further automate product fulfillment, customer service, and inventory management. To help sellers facilitate group purchases, expect eBay to roll out a robust shopping cart–style checkout service.

Niche music tastemakers also should become a more important segment in the category, who specialize in hip genres and educate customers about particular trends and related lifestyle products such as apparel. The upside here: higher product margins, increased customer loyalty and repeat business, and the opportunity for diversification into additional products for eBay cross-selling. It's quite likely that some of these tastemakers will begin to introduce artists and acts on eBay that have limited distribution either in the United States or internationally. As a result, eBay might become a form of distribution for independent acts that are unsigned or underserved by a small label. In this situation, local artists would seek to be carried by notable independent record shops and distributed via their Web and eBay catalogs.

In the music products business, eBay will continue to be an important sales channel for off-price, off-warranty resellers as well as authorized dealers, specializing in discount or boutique instruments, both of which have profited tremendously from the global reach of the Internet. As small authorized dealers with physical storefronts struggle to compete with large chain retailers, greater numbers of surplus instruments and accessories will end up in the hands of secondary-market resellers, who will offer them on eBay and their Web sites "new in box" without a warranty. That means better prices, but also greater risk for consumers.

Surplus resellers can expect competition from authorized dealers selling their own B-stock on eBay. Major manufacturers that continue to push restrictive Internet policies will run the risk of losing dealers or alienating new ones. We suspect some music businesses will opt against entering into dealerships with some majors in favor of selling other existing dealerships' unwarranted surplus on the Internet, including eBay. Others will determine it's more prudent to sell high-end boutique products from makers that are Internet friendly and do not have unreasonable minimum advertised price policies.

Sales of value-priced and high-end boutique instruments will continue to surge both on eBay and the Internet because traditional retail is still dominated by the major brand names. This fact forces budget manufacturers and boutique makers to authorize their dealers to sell online, where they can reach qualified customers and promote their brands. As a result, more of these companies' instruments will end up on dealer Web sites and eBay, the most significant online marketplaces.

Expect value-instrument sellers to not only carry other manufacturers' lines but also develop their own brands of instruments, produced by overseas manufacturers. For example, MusicLandCentral now offers its own Sanatoga line of electric guitars, produced by one of Jay Turser's overseas manufacturers. Also expect an increase in the sale of imported generic instruments. These are marketed as exactly the same instruments that brand name manufacturers are selling for a higher price, just without the label. What's the budget downside? While not all value instruments are bad, not all examples are good, either. Unfortunately, an increase in value instruments on eBay most likely means an increase in instruments of lesser quality, which aren't worth buying, on the site. If customers get burned buying budget items, there could be a backlash against value lines on the site. This places the burden of proof on value sellers, who must devise merchandising techniques that demonstrate why their competitively priced instruments are of a higher caliber than others.

If eBay's *Musical Instruments* category continues to grow, you can expect some of the major names to become less resistant to Internet sales. In fact, that's happening already. Many major makers in band instruments already sanction Internet sales. Both Martin and Taylor have created MAP policies in the last year or two, according to sellers with whom we spoke. That suggests that they are preparing to allow their dealers to sell new online. One other possibility is the emergence of authorized Internet dealers. These would be Internet-only dealers, authorized to sell a manufacturer's products on their own Web sites, eBay, and other online marketplaces.

In regard to vintage equipment, expect Internet sales of established names and models to remain strong but prices to remain somewhat flat, unlike during the late 1990s. (We're still recovering from 9/11.) As the boutique market grows in size and legitimacy, the low- to mid-range vintage market will lose some of its momentum. In essence, some portion of amateur musicians will buy new boutique instead of vintage. In our opinion, the most successful vintage sellers will be able to effectively market their gear for specific applications and educate customers about their use.

What about music memorabilia? Fraud in autographs will continue to be a concern and limit the high-end market on eBay. To address this, more dealers will offer lifetime warranties of authenticity with their items, enabling buyers to obtain a full refund if they find an item isn't authentic at a later date. Also, current trends in pop culture, as they always have, will continue to have a bearing on what is bought and sold on eBay. Some dealers will continue to make markets in new types of music collectibles, which are available in greater supply or can even be manufactured. One current example is inexpensive instruments autographed "in person" by today's popular musicians. As noted in Chapter 2, greater mass interest in collecting also could have a bearing on the profitability of entertainment memorabilia in the future. If fewer music-related objects and pieces of ephemera are seen as disposable, then more of this material will be around, reducing its rarity and subsequently its value. As for what to buy and sell, gain an appreciation for which artists are truly timeless and which ones are temporary. Separate the trendsetters from the copycats, then study their careers and various periods so that you can make an educated case for why their artifacts and objects are worth collecting. Buyers have big ears. Tell them why something has meaning, and they'll be more inclined to buy it.

Well, it's been a great journey. Thanks for coming along. We hope you learned a lot. Now, get out there—and good luck to you! Perhaps we'll meet again someday on eBay when you're selling that Goodall concert-size guitar, that Rudy Van Gelder reissue, that Dylan Rolling Thunder Revue tour poster, that Speedy West box set, those infield seats for the Boss at Pac Bell, that Way Huge guitar pedal, that Petty-autographed "Damn the Torpedoes" album, that pair of M-Audio studio monitors, that . . .

Index

About the Authors

William M. Meyer is a corporate communications specialist and technology writer, as well as a performing musician and occasional music critic, whose reviews and profiles have appeared in *Acoustic Guitar*, *Acoustic Guitar World*, *All Music Guide*, *Dirty Linen*, and *Harp Magazine*. For the last five years, he has worked professionally in the online auction industry, first as the Director of Content for top seller-services company AuctionWatch (now Vendio) and more recently as a consultant and contract writer for eBay and other related Internet companies. He also spent several years as a senior-level editor at the influential media company CNET, where he covered the retail games industry. Bill also finds time to contribute regularly to the *San Francisco Chronicle's* Home and Garden section. He lives in San Francisco, California, a walk away from the Pacific Ocean, with his wife, Tricia, and dog, Miles.

Dennis L. Prince is a well-recognized and long-trusted advocate for online auctiongoers who continues in his tireless efforts to instruct, enlighten, and enable auction enthusiasts and business owners and assure his readers' success every step of the way. By continually mining and monitoring the trends and opportunities within the online auction business realm, he has maintained a vantage point for presenting fresh and immediately applicable methods to help online buyers and sellers get the most from their auction efforts. His advocacy of online auctioning and good business practices has earned him recognition as one of the *Top Ten Online Auction Movers and Shakers* by Vendio (formerly AuctionWatch). His insight and perspectives are regularly sought out by others covering the online-auction industry. He has been featured in the nationally distributed *Entrepreneur* magazine (2003) and *Access* magazine (2000) and has been a guest of highly rated television and radio programs, such as TechTV, BBC-Radio, and CNET Radio.

Prince has regularly been commended for his unique insight, personable, style, and fearness observations that have been celebrated as timely, truthful, and often gutsy in his readers' estimation. Besides his previous books about eBay and Internet commerce, his vast editorial contributions to industry stalwarts like Vendio, Krause Publications, Collector Online, and Auctiva have earned him a great regard in his ongoing analysis of the online-auction industry. He likewise maintains active interaction with his personal network of auction enthusiasts, Power Sellers, and passionate collectors, online and off-line.